Entwined with V

To Nat Sobel — Thanks for your support and your valuable feedback on my manuscript.

Entwined with Vietnam

A Reluctant Marine's Tour and Return

THEODORE M. HAMMETT

Foreword by W.D. Ehrhart

[signature]

August 8, 2022

McFarland & Company, Inc., Publishers

Jefferson, North Carolina

Unless otherwise noted, all photographs are from the author's collection.

LIBRARY OF CONGRESS CATALOGUING-IN-PUBLICATION DATA

Names: Hammett, Theodore M., author.
Title: Entwined with Vietnam : a reluctant Marine's
tour and return / Theodore M. Hammett.
Description: Jefferson, North Carolina : McFarland & Company, Inc., Publishers, 2022 |
Includes bibliographical references and index.
Identifiers: LCCN 2022026677 | ISBN 9781476686011 (paperback : acid free paper) ∞
ISBN 9781476646152 (ebook)
Subjects: LCSH: Hammett, Theodore M. | Vietnam War, 1961-1975—
Personal narratives, American. | United States. Marine Corps.
Medical Battalion, 3rd. | United States. Marine Corps—
History—Vietnam War, 1961-1975. | United States. Marine Corps—
—Military life. | Hammett, Theodore M., 1945—Travel—Vietnam. |
Vietnam—Description and travel. | BISAC: HISTORY /
Wars & Conflicts / Vietnam War
Classification: LCC DS559.5 .H356 2022 | DDC 959.704/3092—dc23/eng/20220609
LC record available at https://lccn.loc.gov/2022026677

BRITISH LIBRARY CATALOGUING DATA ARE AVAILABLE

ISBN (print) 978-1-4766-8601-1
ISBN (ebook) 978-1-4766-4615-2

On the cover: *inset*: the author in Quang Tri, 1968
(author's collection); Hanoi, old and new: Hoan Kiem
Lake with Turtle Tower and Vietcombank Building
(photograph by Sơn Đặng, used by permission)

Printed in the United States of America

*McFarland & Company, Inc., Publishers
Box 611, Jefferson, North Carolina 28640
www.mcfarlandpub.com*

To Nancy, for obvious reasons

Table of Contents

This is the past,
an intimate diamond,
reappearing....
—Gerald Costanzo,
"Report from the Past"

Vietnam. Not a day goes by
without that word on my lips.
—W.D. Ehrhart,
"For a Coming Extinction"

Acknowledgments

I have many people to thank for many things that led to this book being completed. Thanks to my Harvard classmate, poet, and dear friend Jerry Costanzo, who directs the Carnegie-Mellon University Press, for reading several drafts of my manuscript and offering many helpful suggestions as to content and language and strategies for publication. Thanks also to Jerry for allowing me to use part of his poem "Report from the Past" as an epigraph for this book. When Jerry first published this poem in 1973 and dedicated it to me, I was still an aspiring academic historian. Jerry probably didn't foresee that I would use these lines of his to introduce a very different kind of history almost half a century later.

I am grateful to Ray Arsenault, my Brandeis graduate school compatriot and great historian of the Civil Rights movement and race relations in the U.S., as well as to Nat Sobel, Masie Cochran, Win McCormack (another Harvard classmate), and Khanh-Van Hoang-Isabel Ngo for reading my manuscript and providing extremely valuable suggestions and guidance. Greg Nobles, an old friend from my history days, also gave me helpful advice.

Thanks to my Harvard roommate Steve Saltonstall for reading the manuscript and allowing me to use his essay on the 1966 confrontation with Robert McNamara, in which Steve was a major player. I am grateful to my other Harvard roommates John Ballard and Warren Bowes for their friendship over the years.

Several members of my family—including my sisters Peggy and Janet, half-sister Nan, step-sister Jill, and stepbrother Jiggs—read the manuscript and provided useful suggestions. My wife Nancy's brother Steve Haaga made a number of valuable suggestions regarding tone and accuracy. I very much enjoyed my discussions with Steve on these points.

My daughter Abigail also read the manuscript and offered invaluable suggestions, which saved me from some serious errors of tone and presentation. Our talks about these issues were intense and heartfelt. Abigail's passionate commitment to justice and her sharp but nuanced eye for harmful distortions and generalizations have been a revelation for me. She was the first member of my immediate family to travel with me to Vietnam and visited Nancy and me numerous times when we lived there, the last time with her husband Theo Offei. Abigail also came to love Vietnam. Having Abigail and Theo and their little daughters (Nancy's and my granddaughters) Ignazia ("Iggy") and Alessia ("Sisi") living together with us in Watertown helped me complete the manuscript and provided many lovely moments of joy and hilarity along the way.

Thanks to my Marine compatriots for good times, good work, and good talks. Beirne Lovely, Drew Ley, and Bern Bradstreet, members of our little Boston area Marine reunion group in recent years, died in the last few months of my work on this book. I miss them and treasure their memories. Jon Feltner and Al Kyle remain. Bob Koury recollected for me several important episodes of his Vietnam combat experience.

I feel great affection and gratefulness for my Vietnamese colleagues and friends. I remember with special fondness my friend Đoàn Ngữ. As civil society leaders, Khuất Thị Hải Oanh and Khuất Thu Hồng have done remarkable work for the Vietnamese people on many dimensions, and I thank them for allowing me to describe some of that work and the collaborations we enjoyed. Thanks also to Nghiêm Thị Hà Vân for reviewing the manuscript and inserting the Vietnamese tone marks, to Nguyễn Dịu for reminding me what Hương typically cooked for us for our office lunches, and to Kiều Thanh Binh for always great bia hơi sessions.

I am grateful to W.D. "Bill" Ehrhart, whose Vietnam War poetry and memoirs I greatly admire and have used extensively in these pages, for agreeing to write a foreword. I also had several extremely rewarding conversations with Bill about aspects of the manuscript.

Thanks to Clay Risen and Nick Fox of the *New York Times* op-ed page staff for helping me sharpen the story of my relationship with my father over the Vietnam War for a piece in the *Times*' "Vietnam '67" series. Thanks to my fellow editors of and contributors to *The Choices We Made*, the Harvard Class of 1967's e-book on the War, now deposited in the Harvard University Archives.

I have benefited greatly from my reading in the vast literature of the Vietnam War in all its forms, including history, journalism, memoir, fiction, and poetry. I acknowledge especially the work of Frances Fitzgerald, Mary McCarthy, Bernard Fall, Gloria Emerson, Martha Gellhorn, Noam Chomsky, Neil Sheehan, David Halberstam, J. William Fulbright, Christopher Goscha, Max Hastings, the U.S. Marine Corps History and Museums Division (Charles R. Smith, Jack Shulimson, Leonard A. Blasiol, and David A. Dawson), Christian Appy, Arnold Isaacs, Howard Jones, Max Boot, Mark Bowden, Don Oberdorfer, Ronald Spector, George Packer,

C.D.B. Bryan, Nick Turse, Gerald Nicosia, Fredrik Logevall, William Duiker, Doug Bradley and Craig Werner, Philip Beidler, John Balaban, Myra MacPherson, Sarah E. Wagner, Michael J. Allen, Kristin Hass, Michael Herr, Jonathan Schell, Seymour Hersh, David Lamb, John Laurence, Tim O'Brien, Philip Caputo, William Broyles, Jr., Tracy Kidder, John Parrish, Anthony D'Aries, James Carroll, Wayne Karlin, Ron Kovic, Lewis B. Puller, Jr., Bruce Weigl, Larry Gwin, Larry Heinemann, W.D. Ehrhart, Jack McLean, Doug Anderson, Rodger Jacobs, Allen Glick, Phil Ball, Mai Elliott, Le Ly Hayslip, Robert Stone, Tobias Wolff, Bảo Ninh, Bobbie Ann Mason, Karl Marlantes, Viet Thanh Nguyen, Andrew X. Pham, Robert Olen Butler, Lady Borton, Lê Minh Khuê, Nguyễn Phan Quế Mai, Nguyễn Ngọc Tư, Tạ Duy Anh, Michael Casey, and Ocean Vuong. *The Vietnam War*, a documentary film by Ken Burns and Lynn Novick, is also extremely valuable.

Of course, I must also express my gratitude to the composers and performers of the music that is such an important part of my story.

I am grateful to Dylan Lightfoot, the editor at McFarland & Co. who accepted my manuscript and to the rest of the staff there who helped see the book through to publication.

Many of the "obvious reasons" for my dedication of this book to Nancy should be clear from the story I tell. Among other not necessarily obvious reasons is that Nancy carefully read and painstakingly commented on several versions of the manuscript. Her suggestions contributed significantly to the improvements I was able to make. I thank Nancy for her love and her continuing support and encouragement; and also for agreeing to move to Vietnam with me in 2008.

Vietnam (CIA World Factbook).

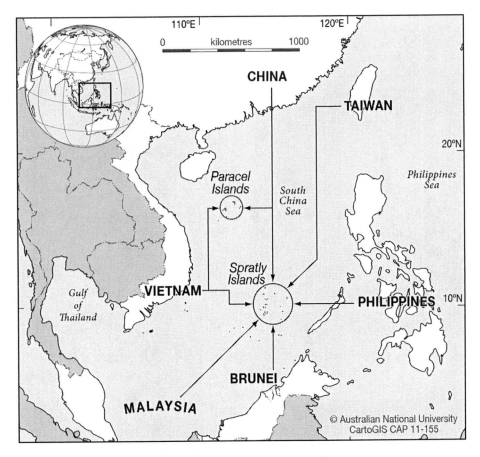

The disputed islands in the East Sea, AKA "South China Sea." (Map reproduced with permission for CartoGIS Services, Scholarly Information Services, the Australian National University, CC-BY-SA 4.0).

Foreword

by W.D. Ehrhart

Theodore Hammett's *Entwined with Vietnam: A Reluctant Marine's Tour and Return* is the most unusual war memoir I've ever read. And I've read a whole lot of them over the years, from Joseph Plumb Martin's Revolutionary War memoir *Private Yankee Doodle: Being a Narrative of Some of the Adventures, Dangers and Sufferings of a Revolutionary War Soldier* to Clint Van Winkle's Iraq War memoir *Soft Spots: A Marine's Memoir of Combat and Post-Traumatic Stress Disorder*. But I've never read one like this.

For starters, it is really two memoirs in one, the "two tours" Hammett writes about being separated by many decades and about as different as—well—night and day. Hammett's "first tour" is as a Marine lieutenant during the American War in Vietnam, an experience he was largely browbeaten into by a domineering father against his own wishes and feelings about the war.

Of this tour, Hammett writes with painful honesty and disarming humility. Assigned as the supply officer for a medical battalion, he is, as he readily admits on more than one occasion, "stuck in the rear with the gear." He sees no combat, drinks heavily, conducts himself with marginal military discipline, and is contemptuous of the Vietnamese, the Marine Corps, military hierarchy, and the war itself.

Apparently, he manages to qualify for the Combat Action Ribbon, a decoration awarded to personnel who have come under enemy fire, but I'll be darned if I can figure out what happened to allow him to qualify for that one. The saving grace is that he seems to be as puzzled by it as I am.

Hammett also listens to a lot of music. The whole first half of this memoir is like strolling through the Rock & Roll Hall of Fame Museum in Cleveland. Like a lot of Vietnam War veterans and many others of our generation, music was the constant background, the yardstick, a mnemonic device through which we measured and remember our coming

1

of age. Elvis Presley, Bob Dylan, Barry McGuire, Jefferson Airplane, the Beatles, the Rolling Stones, Buffy St. Marie, Cream, Judy Collins, Simon & Garfunkel, the Zombies, the Fifth Dimension: the list goes on and on. (Indeed, lyrics would make up a large part of this book if the music publishers didn't make it impossibly difficult and expensive to quote more than a few words of any song.)

Being reminded of all those artists and songs is a stimulating and enjoyable experience in and of itself, and Hammett writes about himself and his life with such lack of pretension that one cannot help but admire him even as he presents himself as a less-than-admirable Marine. Not a disgrace, to be sure, but not very admirable either. Just a young man who went to war because he could not stand up to his father, and who got through the war as best he could manage with the situation he found himself in, grateful and relieved that he did not find himself in combat.

And then comes Part II of this memoir. A Harvard graduate of 1967, after his discharge from the Marines, he hoped to become a historian, and to that end earned a doctorate from Brandeis. But by 1976, ironically due to the glut of PhDs earned by men staying in school in order to avoid being drafted for Vietnam, there were few good jobs available for academic historians.

Instead, Hammett took a job with Abt Associates, a worldwide research and consulting company dealing with issues of public health, social and economic policy, housing, education, criminal justice, and the environment. In 1985, he began working on projects involving HIV/AIDS policies and prevention, first domestically and then internationally. In 1997, at the end of a stay in China working with the Chinese government on HIV prevention among drug users, Hammett took his first postwar trip back to Vietnam.

A few years later, his interest in Vietnam whetted by that visit, he became involved in a cross-border project involving both China and Vietnam, and he found himself frequently visiting Vietnam between 2002 and 2008. And then in 2008, Hammett got the opportunity to live and work in Vietnam on a long-term basis. Eventually joined by his wife, he lived in Hanoi for almost four years, and traveled often around the rest of the country.

This he considers his "second tour." This also involved HIV/AIDS issues, especially how to avoid its spread among people who inject drugs and those involved in what is politely referred to as the sex trade, how best to treat those with HIV/AIDS, and how to destigmatize and treat drug users and sex workers rather than simply ostracizing them as morally weak misfits.

During this tour, he came to realize—with no little chagrin—how badly he had misunderstood and misread the Vietnamese people and their culture during his first tour. He came to love Vietnam and the Vietnamese people, and he writes about both with enthusiasm and warmth and admiration.

Indeed, this second half of the book reads almost like a travel guide. There are chapters on living in Vietnam as an "ex-pat," on the birds and animals of Vietnam, on Vietnamese culture, on Vietnamese food and the best restaurants and noodle shops in which to eat it, and on how to successfully cross the motorbike-filled chaos of Vietnamese streets without becoming roadkill.

Hammett also details the successes and frustrations of working with the Vietnamese government and the communist party (overlapping, but not synonymous), the joys of working with his many wonderful colleagues and friends, and an assortment of observations on postwar and contemporary Vietnam. His departure from Vietnam this time around was bittersweet. Vietnam had come to be a part of him.

Nor had it seen the last of him. In 2015, he decided to attend a reunion of his Marine Corps Basic School class at Quantico, Virginia. And in 2016, he returned to Vietnam once again, this time in the company of members of that group. By the end of Hammett's memoir, he has circled back to both his domineering father and the Marine Corps his father pressured him into joining. But I'm not one to spoil an ending, so if you want to learn how it all turns out, you'll just have to read it for yourself.

W.D. Ehrhart, memoirist, poet and editor, was a major presence in the Ken Burns and Lynn Novick documentary *The Vietnam War*, and is the author of *Thank You for Your Service: Collected Poems*, among many other books.

Key Dates

1954
May—Fall of Dien Bien Phu
July—Geneva Accords, French
   War ended
1955
October—Ngo Dinh Diem
   installed as President of the
   Republic of Vietnam (South
   Vietnam)
1963: 16,300 U.S. advisors in
   South Vietnam
November—Diem ousted by
   coup and assassinated in
   Saigon
November 22—President John
   F. Kennedy assassinated in
   Dallas
1964: 23,300 U.S. advisors in
   South Vietnam
June–July—Hammett attended
   first PLC summer camp
August—Gulf of Tonkin
   "incident"; first U.S.
   bombing of North
   Vietnam; Congressional
   passage of Tonkin Gulf
   Resolution
1965: 184,300 U.S. troops in
   South Vietnam
February—VC attack on base at
   Pleiku
March—First American combat
   units (U.S. Marines) landed
   at Danang
November—U.S. Army Battle

of Ia Drang Valley: first U.S.
   encounter with NVA
1966: 385,300 U.S. troops in
   South Vietnam
February—J. William
   Fulbright's Senate Foreign
   Relations Committee
   hearings on Vietnam War
June–July—Hammett attended
   second PLC summer camp
July–August—Operation
   Hastings, first USMC
   operations in Northern I–
   Corps near and into DMZ
August—Operation Prairie,
   continued USMC operations
   in Northern I–Corps
September–October—USMC
   battles for Mutter's Ridge
1967: 485,600 U.S. troops in
   South Vietnam
June—USMC "Hill Fights" for
   Hills 861, 881 North, and 881
   South, near Khe Sanh
June—Hammett graduated
   from Harvard and began
   USMC active duty
Summer—Establishment of
   "McNamara Line" sensors
   and USMC strong points,
   including Con Thien, Gio
   Linh, and Khe Sanh, just
   below DMZ to prevent
   NVA penetration of South
   Vietnam; Marines in

5

heavy fighting with NVA in "Leatherneck Square" bounded by Con Thien, Gio Linh, Dong Ha and Cam Lo.

November—NVA bombardment of Con Thien

November—U.S. Army and NVA Battle of Dak To

1968: 536,100 U.S. troops in South Vietnam

January–Apri—Bombardment of Khe Sanh

January–March—Tet Offensive: VC and NVA attacked 36 provincial capitals and 5 autonomous cities, including Saigon, Hue, and Danang

January 30–March 3—Battle of Hue

February 7—NVA overran U.S. Army Special Forces camp at Lang Vei, west of Khe Sanh; first NVA use of tanks

March 16—My Lai massacre

March 26—2nd Lt. Hammett arrived in Vietnam

March 31—LBJ announced that he would not seek re-election as President and halted bombing over Northern North Vietnam

April—Khe Sanh relieved by U.S. Army 1st Air Cavalry Division; Vandegrift Combat Base established

April 4—Martin Luther King assassinated in Memphis

May—Gen. Raymond Davis succeeded Gen. Rathvon Tompkins as Commanding General, 3rd Marine Division

May—First meetings of Paris peace talks resulted in 5-month deadlock over shape of negotiating table

May—"Mini-Tet" including USMC battles with NVA around Dai Do, near Dong Ha

June 6—Robert F. Kennedy assassinated in Los Angeles

June—Khe Sanh Combat Base abandoned and destroyed

June—Gen. Creighton Abrams succeeded Gen. William Westmoreland as commander of U.S. forces in Vietnam

August—3rd Medical Battalion moved from Phu Bai to Quang Tri

August 26–29—Democratic National Convention, Chicago; "police riot" against antiwar demonstrators

October—LBJ announced halt to bombing over all of North Vietnam; Paris peace talks resume

November 5—Richard Nixon elected President

1969: 475,200 U.S. troops in South Vietnam

January–March—USMC Operation Dewey Canyon, Ashau Valley

February 25—NVA attacks on USMC Fire Support Bases Russell and Neville

April 6—1st Lt. Hammett left Vietnam

May 10–20—U.S. Army 101st Airborne Division and NVA Battle of "Hamburger Hill," Ashau Valley

June 28–July 1—Stonewall Riots, New York

July 20—Moon landing

August 6–7—Manson murders, Los Angeles

August 15–18—Woodstock Music and Arts Fair, Bethel, New York

November 15—Largest march against the Vietnam War (500,000 people), Washington

December 6—Altamont Speedway Free Festival

1970: 334,600 U.S. troops in South Vietnam

May—Cambodia invasion; Killings at Kent State and Jackson State

June—1st Lt. Hammett released from active duty

1971: 156,800 U.S. troops in South Vietnam

February–March—Operation Lam Son 719, ARVN invasion of Laos, failed

1972: 24,200 U.S. troops in South Vietnam

March–October—NVA "Easter Offensive"

July—Watergate break-in

October—Henry Kissinger asserted that "peace is at hand"

November—Nixon re-elected President

December—"Christmas Bombing" of North Vietnam, including Hanoi

1973: 50 U.S. troops in South Vietnam

January 27—Paris Peace Accords signed

February—U.S. POWs released by North Vietnam

May–November—Senate Watergate hearings

1974

August 8—Nixon resigns Presidency

1975

April 30—Vietnam War ended; Vietnam unified

1975–1985: "Subsidy Period" in Vietnam

1978–1989: Vietnam's invasion of and war with Cambodia

1979

February–March: Vietnam's brief Border War with China

1982

November: Vietnam Veterans Memorial opened in Washington, D.C.

1986—*Doi Moi,* or "renovation" of Vietnam's economic system began

1995

July 11—U.S. and Vietnam re-established diplomatic relations

1997

September—Hammett visited Vietnam for the first time since the War

2001

October—Cross-Border HIV Prevention project began

2008–2012: Hammett lived and worked in Hanoi

2017–2018: Hammett lived and worked in Hanoi

Acronyms

31 BVP: 31 Buena Vista Park, Cambridge

AFVN: Armed Forces Vietnam Radio

ARVN: Army of the Republic of Vietnam (South Vietnam)

ATS: Amphetamine-type stimulants

CBO: Community-based organization

CDC: U.S. Centers for Disease Control and Prevention

CHA: Chestnut Hill Academy, Philadelphia

CSO: Civil society organization

DMZ: Demilitarized Zone

FSB: Fire support base

GDP: Gross domestic product

GFATM: Global Fund for AIDS, Tuberculosis, and Malaria

HFG: Health Finance and Governance project

HIV/AIDS: Human immunodeficiency virus/ Acquired immune deficiency syndrome

HPI: Health Policy Initiative project

LAX: Los Angeles International Airport

LBJ: Lyndon Baines Johnson

LGBTQ+: Lesbian gay bisexual transgender queer (or questioning)

LRP: Long-range patrol

MACV: Military Assistance Command Vietnam

MIT: Massachusetts Institute of Technology

MOH: Ministry of Health

MOLISA: Ministry of Labor, Invalids and Social Affairs

MOS: Military occupational specialty

MPH: Master of public health

MP: Military police

MSM: Men who have sex with men

MTA: Metropolitan Transit Authority (now MBTA, Massachusetts Bay Transportation Authority)

MUST: Medical unit, self-contained, transportable

NCO: Non-commissioned officer

NGO: Non-governmental organization

NIH: U.S. National Institutes of Health

NROTC: Naval Reserve Officer Training Corps

NVA: North Vietnamese Army

PEPFAR: U.S. President's Emergency Plan for AIDS Relief

PLC: Platoon Leaders Class

PLHIV: Person/People living with HIV

POW: Prisoner of war
PTSD: Post-traumatic stress
   disorder
PWID: Person/People who
   inject drugs
PX: Post Exchange
RAF: Royal Air Force
R&R: Rest and recuperation
REMF: "Rear-echelon
   motherfucker"
RPG: Rocket-propelled grenade
RVN: Republic of Vietnam
   (South Vietnam)
SAM: Surface-to-air missile
"Seabees": the U.S. Navy's
   Mobile Construction
   Battalions
SDS: Students for a Democratic
   Society

SPNs ("Spins"): Separation
   Program Numbers
USAID: U.S. Agency for
   International Development
USMC: U.S. Marine Corps
USO: United Service
   Organizations
VA: Veterans Administration
VAAC: Vietnam
   Administration for HIV/
   AIDS Control
VC: Viet Cong
VUSTA: Vietnam Union of
   Science and Technology
   Associations
VVAW: Vietnam Veterans
   Against the War

A Note on the Music, Vietnamese Tone Marks, and Names

The music of the Vietnam War era is an integral part of my story. I wanted to include portions of the lyrics of many of the songs that were most important to me. Like many authors, I found that gaining permission to use song lyrics is difficult and expensive. As a result, I had to limit my quotation of lyrics to brief excerpts from a small number of songs. However, I have included, in footnotes for specific songs, links to URLs at which full lyrics may be found. In addition, I have created a public playlist: (*https://open.spotify.com/playlist/0zV3cTdhV7oLZDgLAQqAH2*), which includes all the songs and other pieces of music mentioned in the book, in the order of their appearance. I hope these measures will help readers appreciate, or re-acquaint themselves with, the greatness of the music and its crucial relationship to the stories of so many Vietnam veterans and others who took diverse paths during this turbulent era.

I have given diacritical (tone) marks for Vietnamese words and most proper names of Vietnamese people, with the exception of Vietnamese-American people. I have omitted tone marks for place names and some commonly Anglicized terms such as Viet Cong, a convention frequently used in books about Vietnam for English-speaking audiences.

With their permission, I have used the real names of many living individuals. I have also used the real names of people who have died. Some names, primarily those of living people whose military rank was below full colonel, have been changed.

Introduction

Three months into my Marine Corps tour of duty in Vietnam in 1968, my girlfriend Nancy wrote me with what must have seemed at the time like prescience:

> Don't be unhappy. When we've been married 50 years and we're old and doddering, think how short these lousy 13 months will seem. And think how glad we'll be when you get back and never have to think a single thought about Vietnam again.

Well, think again. My entwinement with Vietnam, the first strands of which began to pull at my consciousness in the early days of the war, has lasted almost all my subsequent days. Vietnam has been, and remains, inextricably woven into who I am: with my doubts about myself, my opinions, and my ultimate worth; my relationship with my father; my love for Nancy; and the quality of my memories. The overriding strand is that my feelings for Vietnam and the Vietnamese people changed dramatically since I first landed there in March 1968.

I caved in to my father's pressure to become a Marine officer and go to a war I had come to believe was wrong. I couldn't be certain enough of my opposition to the war to take any direct action against it. Or maybe I was just a coward. Nancy's constant emotional presence and support, and my hope of returning home to marry her, as well as a lot of booze and great music, got me through my tour. But I hated Vietnam and the Vietnamese people, even though I didn't know any of them. Later, I came to feel guilty for my country's devastation of Vietnam in an unjust cause and my own role in mistreating the Vietnamese people. I began to hope for a chance to return to Vietnam to do something positive. Almost by chance, that opportunity arose to atone for my sins. When I did return for a second "tour," to live and work in Vietnam in a new role, I came to know, respect, and like many Vietnamese people and to love the country, its scenic beauty, its food, and many aspects of its culture.

Many veterans and others, including my Harvard classmate, dear friend, and poet Jerry Costanzo, have said that Vietnam is the one war that

Americans, or at least our Baby Boomer generation, never seem able to get over. Maybe this is why the volume of autobiographical novels, memoirs, historical analyses, and films about Vietnam is larger than for any other American war and continues to grow. After Marine veteran W.D. Ehrhart enrolled in Swarthmore College and an article about him appeared in the college newspaper, he was besieged by the same questions from his fellow students. Many of them demanded to know "did you kill anyone?" and "how did it feel?" Ultimately, Ehrhart experienced a series of explosive epiphanies about the war and his actions in it.[1]

I was quite different, probably because my experience in the war was so different. I really didn't think or talk much about the war for some years. When I got to graduate school, I don't remember anyone asking me about it. Few of my colleagues even knew I had been there. I tended to "sand the edges" of my feelings deliberately to avoid horror and outrage, which might have demanded action, in favor of an almost purely intellectual opposition to the war.

The large number of accounts by Vietnam veterans may stem from a desire to protest their pervasive experience that, as Jamie Bryant put it, "In over ten years, there has really never been anybody who has asked me: 'What happened to you over there? What was it like?'"[2] In 1982, another veteran said "Nobody's really told the story of Vietnam yet."[3] The obsessive effort to find, identify, and return home the remains of every one of the approximately 2,500 American missing in Vietnam was no doubt fueled by resentment of an apparent national amnesia in the years immediately after the war, when the lost and missing, as well as returned veterans, were essentially forgotten or wished out of sight—or worse—by the U.S. government and most of the American people.[4] The disproportionate intensity of the drive to recover remains and the sometimes conflicting and largely irrational and misguided crusade to rescue POWs still allegedly alive in Southeast Asia many years after the war ended, vastly exceeded any such efforts in previous wars that left far more Americans missing. These decades-long movements were also driven by the fact that we lost the war.[5]

One Vietnam veteran who never did get over the war was Lewis B. Puller, Jr., the son of "Chesty" Puller, perhaps the most famous U.S. Marine hero. He followed in his father's footsteps and became a Marine infantry platoon commander in Vietnam. In October 1968, Puller lost both his legs and parts of both his hands to a booby-trapped howitzer shell in the deadly "Riviera" region south of Danang. Miraculously, he survived, but deep ambivalence, turning to fury, about the war, the Marine Corps, and his country ultimately drowned him in drink and depression. Fully 26 years after being wounded and five years after the final scene in his memoir, by which time he had been sober for eight years and seemed to have substantially healed, Puller took by gunshot what remained of his own life.[6]

My story pales by comparison with Puller's and those depicted in many harrowing Vietnam combat memoirs. Thus, it may be at least partly out of guilt that I spent my wartime in a relatively safe rear-echelon position, and persistent doubt about the intrinsic interest of my own experience, that I present a good deal of my view of the war through the eyes and words of others. Somehow, I felt that I had to enrich my own weak broth of experience with some powerful shots of the lives of people who may have been braver, more decisive, and much more wounded and tormented than me.

However, my choice to refer so much to the accounts of others also stems from the power and richness of that combat literature. Indeed, I have long been obsessed with all dimensions of the culture of and about the war and America in the 1960s.

In about 1978, I tried for the first time to write something coherent about my relatively prosaic experience of the war. I didn't get very far but here is how it started:

> Sitting in the stifling tin-roofed Marine Air Terminal in Danang at 6 a.m. with sweat dripping off my nose, I tried to reconstruct what had brought me to this pass. It was late March 1968. The Tet Offensive was winding down, although a reinforced Marine regiment was still hemmed in at Khe Sanh. Hue had been re-won from the North Vietnamese and reduced to rubble in the process. Robert Kennedy and Martin Luther King were still alive, but not for long. It was three months into the most turbulent year of recent American history, and I sat in Danang with what seemed like a lead weight in my stomach. I was a Marine second lieutenant with shiny gold bars [derisively, "brown bars" to many hardened NCOs] to advertise my rookie status. I was not pleased to be a Marine second lieutenant. I aspired to a career as a historian. I did not relish the thought of participating in this particularly gruesome and futile slice of history. I would rather write about it. But maybe I would have the chance to do both. Not for a long time, as it turned out.

I have been unlike most of the approximately 3.5 million Vietnam veterans, "each in his or her own personal way, going there, coming back, and then learning to live with it forever after, mainly alone."[7] I did not have to deal with my war experiences, such as they were, alone or at home. And my story does not lead to the "moral and emotional dead-end" found by Arnold Isaacs in most novels and memoirs by Vietnam veterans.[8]

After my release from the Marine Corps, I had what proved to be a very short career as an academic historian and ended up with a long career in research and consulting, primarily in public health and development of HIV/AIDS programs and policies. This second career provided a surprising opportunity to renew my involvement with Vietnam, this time in a very different way. So, I had "two tours" in Vietnam, the first during the war from March 1968 to April 1969 and the second, living in Hanoi, as director of an HIV/AIDS policy project from October 2008 to May 2012. Even then, my Vietnam story didn't quite end. I attended a reunion of my Marine comrades in 2015 and toured sites of our Vietnam service with some of them in 2016. Finally, I had the chance to return for a final, briefer work assignment in Vietnam from June 2017 to September 2018.

In telling my story, I have indulged my historian's natural love of, maybe even obsession with, particularity and sense of place, time, sound, and description; and my fascination with coincidences. I also wanted to preserve the detail of my memories as aging inevitably eats away at them. Hence the specification of locations, names, dates, songs, and other details, all of which I realize may represent poor literary form. However, F. Scott and Zelda Fitzgerald did feel it was important to recall and recount all of the hotels they had ever stayed in.[9] In any case, I ask the reader's indulgence, for I hope that recalling and recounting these details have helped enrich the story and, if it's of any interest, conveyed who I really was, what I came to be, and how all this happened.

Nancy has been my partner—sometimes physically present and sometimes not, but always emotionally with me—in these two tours and all of my Vietnam journeys, as well as in my whole life for now even more than the fifty years she referred to in her 1968 letter.

The history of relationships as, indeed, any history is very difficult even to remember, let alone write, without documentary evidence. I feel immensely grateful that somehow, through all of the subsequent moves in our lives, Nancy and I were able to preserve the letters we wrote to each other before and during my first tour in Vietnam, as well as the audiotapes we recorded for each other during that tour.[10] The tapes we later had transferred from the original five-inch reel-to-reel format (I doubt that you can even find a machine to play these anymore) to compact discs. These letters and tapes capture, like nothing else could, our experiences and attitudes. Jack McLean's powerful Vietnam combat memoir *Loon* is also based primarily on the letters the author wrote to his parents and others while in the Marine Corps.[11] Likewise, the bulk of Rodger Jacobs' book consists of almost 150 verbatim letters he wrote to his parents from Marine Corps boot camp at Parris Island through his hospitalization in Japan after being seriously wounded in Vietnam. In his letters, however, Jacobs sanitized his combat experience for his parents. The full horror only begins to emerge in the italicized commentary he placed between the letters.[12]

While Nancy's and my letters and tapes by no means reveal as much physical danger, death, and suffering as McLean's or Jacobs's, they do tell a story of two people caught up in war and baring their feelings, fears, and hopes about it and about each other. Still, it is very hard at the age of 75 to put myself back into the shoes, thoughts, and emotions of a 22-year-old going off to a war I had come to think was wrong, with no idea what might befall me there, and leaving behind a girlfriend for whom my love had only recently become clear.

I wonder what veterans of our recent wars in Afghanistan and Iraq and their loved ones at home will use to recover and weigh their experiences and feelings. No one writes letters anymore or presumably records their telephone or social media conversations or systematically archives their emails or text messages. This seems like it will be a great loss.[13]

In Penelope Fitzgerald's lovely collective biography of her father and his three brothers, she quotes from her uncle Ronald Knox's diary: "The longer one lives, the more one's pleasures are conditioned by memories."[14] Perhaps it is also true that, as Elizabeth Bowen wrote, "memory is to love what the saucer is to the cup";[15] or that memory may become, in John Cheever's words, "a sentimental faculty."[16] Those other Fitzgeralds seem to have agreed: "it is sadder to find the past again and find it inadequate to the present than it is to have it elude you and remain forever a harmonious conception of memory."[17] I guess, to some extent, I have begun to live more and more in the past, which, as John Banville's protagonist Max Morden strikingly claims, "beats inside me like a second heart."[18] In my mental and dream life, I seem always to be returning—to Vietnam, to my father, to Nancy.

But how important and how accurate are one's personal memories? Viet Thanh Nguyen argues that personal memories of the war are only part of a much more complex and very political "industry of memory" that he hopes will give way to a more just and collective "ethics of memory."[19] While I find Nguyen's argument insightful, I also maintain that personal memory (and observation) have important roles to play in telling the full story.

As to the accuracy of memories, there are many opinions. Since memoirs are, almost by definition, based on memories, Robert Atwan asserted that in considering memoirs, readers should "learn more about the operation of memory."[20] For example, Freud's concept of "screen memories" posits that memories of childhood are, in fact, "formed" by a person's later experiences and circumstances so that "what is important is suppressed and what is indifferent is retained." It is a psychical "compromise" in which the most important or perhaps disagreeable aspect of a real event is displaced by a related but seemingly trivial image.[21]

At a 2019 reading by "Warrior Writers" from various American wars, one Vietnam veteran referred to memories as "just the most recent re-scriptings of things that are lost." Lenny Snyder, the Abby Hoffman-based character in Joshua Furst's novel *Revolutionaries*, refers to "the act of remembering [as] crying over the never-was."[22] Paul Fussell, in *The

Great War and Modern Memory, asserts that it is difficult to distinguish
between an ostensibly factual memoir and a first autobiographical novel,
but he does allow for "recognition scenes" that can capture with accuracy
our "buried lives."[23] Christian Appy interviewed 300 people on all sides
of the Vietnam War for his oral history and "often felt that their histories
were just outside, pounding on the door, pouring through every crack, as
vivid and present as ever."[24] A Vietnamese girl, whose mother had suffered
terribly on the battlefield, "wished I could hug her so hard, to squeeze out
all the terrible memories."[25]

Luckily for me, the preserved letters and tapes clarify and fortify the
stuff (and, I hope, the truth) of my memories and provide some valuable
clues, at least, as to what it was like back then and how we really felt. To be
sure, we were young and, in many ways, immature, spoiled, and snobbish
children of the Sixties, and some of the things we said and wrote and did
may embarrass us now.

Beyond what is documented in the letters and tapes, might my memory have taken liberty with the facts? Might I have even inadvertently
made some things up, imagined some events that never happened, or
quoted some words that were never spoken?[26] Might these indulgences
cause me to "lose authority as a storyteller?"[27] I'm afraid so, but I must
acknowledge and take responsibility for that. I can only say that, like my
performance of duty as a Marine officer in Vietnam, I did the best I could
under the circumstances.

Nostalgia may make for "gilding the lily" of real life. Memoirist Jeannie Vanasco reminds us that "nostalgia, for hundreds of years was considered a chronic mental illness."[28] According to Sarah Churchwell, F.
Scott Fitzgerald "became America's poet laureate of nostalgia because he
understood its perils as well as its allure: nostalgia wants to falsify the past,
whereas history tries to clarify it."[29]

In what may be a fool's errand, I have tried to be both nostalgic and
historian. Nancy sometimes suggests that my memories are making her
out to be someone different from and better than who she really was. I
disagree. She has also alleged that I have romanticized our relationship.
Nancy actually wanted me to shrink her role in the story but, in the interest of truth and my own feelings, I could bring myself to take out only a
few details. I may be guilty of some embellishments of the facts or of my
feelings—but, I hope, not too many. I am convinced that my memory is
better and stronger than hers. And my memories convince me of how fortunate I have been, despite the inevitable ups and downs and some rough
patches over the years, and how blessed I continue to be, to have Nancy as
my life's companion. Without her, my story would be greatly diminished.

Part I: My First Tour

1

Going to a War I'd Come
to Think Was Wrong

It was early May 1966, my junior year at Harvard. I had decided that I did not want to be in the Marine Corps or go to Vietnam. I was going to withdraw from the Marines' Platoon Leaders Class (PLC), to which I was scheduled to report for my second summer camp in June. I told my father this in the course of a long argument on the telephone, which actually began over my confession that I had overspent my allowance and needed more money to pay my tuition bill. Already angry about this, my father became more enraged when I went on to announce my intention to quit the Marine Corps program because I opposed the war. "You're spitting on everything I believe in!," he shouted. The next morning, he summoned me home to explain why he shouldn't take me out of school and effectively disown me. This would likely have meant my being drafted almost immediately.

I asked my history tutor if I could get a scholarship to stay at Harvard. He said that it might be possible. But I faced the prospect of severing ties with my father if I stood up for my opposition to the war. My parents were divorced, and my mother and stepfather were active opponents of the war. She marched and picketed repeatedly and displayed an "Another Mother for Peace" bumper sticker on her car; he also marched, wrote countless letters to the editor, and later successfully defended William Stringfellow and Anthony Towne who were indicted for harboring the antiwar activist priest Daniel Berrigan at their house on Block Island. They surely would have supported me if I had chosen active resistance. It seems incredible and inexplicable to me now, but I never even talked to my mother and stepfather about my decision. Neither did they ever reach out to me about it. I guess I felt overpowered by my father and maybe my mother still did as well. In the end, I wasn't able to make the break with him.

James Carroll did split with his father, an Air Force general working for Defense Secretary Robert McNamara, who likened his son's antiwar

21

activities to those of "kooks" who burned the flag and accused the U.S. of deliberately bombing hospitals and civilians in North Vietnam.[1] In any case, with neither the pride of my father's "Greatest Generation" nor the commitment of the bravest opponents of the Vietnam War, I capitulated to my father. I would stay in the Marine Corps, despite my feelings about the war.

I am a member of the Harvard Class of 1967. In Henry Adams's autobiographic *Education,* he averred that "no one took Harvard College seriously."[2] However, our class seemed to be the bridge from a carefree—from today's perspective, perhaps benighted—undergraduate culture of "spring riots" and "panty raids" to serious confrontation of government officials, student strikes, and occupation of university buildings. My time at Harvard was similar to John Buchan's at Oxford at the turn of the 20th century, "one of those boundary periods the meaning of which is missed at the time, but is plain in the retrospect."[3]

Actually, our freshman spring riot in 1964 was itself a transitional one, as it had the somewhat higher than usual purpose of saving the sycamore trees along Memorial Drive from removal to make way for a proposed inner-belt highway. The Metropolitan District Commission police were not as savage as Bull Connor's forces in Birmingham the previous spring, but they did use dogs to break up the crowd and I saw them beat a few students with billy clubs on DeWolfe Street. In response to the canine deployment, the crowd chanted "Dogs need trees!"[4] That inner-belt highway was never built, and the sycamores still stand.

Harvard's Memorial Hall commemorates the 246 Harvard men killed in the Civil War and Memorial Church in Harvard Yard displays plaques listing the 373 killed in World War I and 697 in World War II. Vietnam was different, with only 22 Harvard deaths over one of the nation's longest wars, even fewer than the 35 from Yale noted by alumnus Karl Marlantes, a decorated Marine Vietnam veteran and author of an acclaimed autobiographical novel and a powerful memoir.[5]

In the class of 1967, we all had to face and make dire choices about military service and the war in Vietnam. The war was an existential fact of life every day and every hour. In a 2017 speech at the Ho Chi Minh City University of Social Sciences and Humanities, Harvard President Drew Faust recalled the "terrible demands" of war like those that faced Harvard students and indeed all American young men of draft age fifty years earlier. "War [Faust said] often proves to be a quintessential 'moment of truth' both for individuals and their societies." She had written eloquently of the unprecedented and variegated burden of death in the American Civil War.[6]

The Vietnamese people faced even more daunting choices—which side to take in what was emerging as a bitter and relentless civil war. As

Mai Elliott relates in her memoir *The Sacred Willow,* virtually every Vietnamese family had members on both sides: "With the end of the war, the tangled web of relationships between the communist and noncommunist sides was revealed to its full complexity."[7]

The (overwhelmingly white) privilege of attending Harvard brought my classmates and me many opportunities, unavailable to those poorer and less well-placed, to avoid going to an inconvenient or immoral war on the other side of the world. Among other things, exempt occupations, phony doctors' letters, influence on draft boards, and six-month reserve stints—as well as principled resistance, registering as conscientious objectors, going to jail, and moving to Canada—meant that only about 40 (or 3 percent) of my classmates served in Vietnam and only two were killed there. Naval aviator John Martin died when his fighter crashed attempting to land on the carrier *Oriskany* in the South China Sea; Marine lieutenant Charles Ryberg was killed while serving as an artillery forward observer in Quang Tri Province.

No one from the Harvard classes of 1969 to 1972 died in the war. Twenty-seven percent of the class of 1970 responding to a 25th reunion survey reported that they had failed the draft physical, while only one percent of these said they were in poor health 25 years later.[8] James Fallows, of that class, avoided the draft by causing his weight to fall to 120 pounds, below the minimum for his height, and telling the examining physician at Boston Navy Yard that he had contemplated suicide. Six years later, in a famous essay, Fallows lamented that "so many of the bright young college men opposed the war [but] so few were willing to resist the draft, rather than simply evade it." He admitted to feeling shame that he had been among the evaders who "so willingly took advantage of this most brutal form of class discrimination ... that ... let the [poor] boys from Chelsea[9] be sent off to die."[10]

My story represents one example of "The Choices We Made"—the title of a powerful panel discussion at our Harvard 25th reunion and an e-book with entries from almost 200 classmates and a three-hour open-microphone discussion at our 50th. These testimonies make it clear, decades on, how unsettled we still feel about our choices and the elusive lessons of Vietnam. Like James Fallows, who graduated three years after us, we admitted the privilege that enabled so many of us to evade service no matter the depth of our feelings about the war and acknowledged that so many of those who fought the war had no "choice" whatsoever in the matter. In these sessions and their essays 25 and 50 years after the fact, my classmates expressed so much sadness, doubt, guilt, anguish—name the emotion and it was present. This is what seemed to make the Vietnam War so different and so much more troubling than earlier wars.

My father enlisted in the Marine Corps soon after he graduated from Harvard in 1942—like Nick Carraway and his father at "New Haven," we were exactly a quarter century apart.[11] My father led an infantry platoon in the South Pacific, including in the first assault wave on Bougainville in the Solomon Islands in 1943. Several of his close friends, including two Harvard roommates, were killed in the war. He must have seen and done terrible things, but he rarely spoke about his experience. I do remember one story he told of how he and some fellow Marines urinated on the site of the death of Japanese Admiral Yamamoto after his bomber had been shot down and crashed there. I recall looking repeatedly at some books my father had on the exploits of his (and later to be my) 3rd Marine Division. The photographs showed dead and disfigured Marines and Japanese soldiers; jungles torn to shreds by gunfire; and Marines using flamethrowers to incinerate or flush out Japanese troops in caves. Despite my father's reluctance to talk about the war, it appeared always to have been his peak experience, after which the rest of his life, most of it spent in a successful career as a Philadelphia lawyer, seemed anti-climactic and vaguely disappointing. For him, the war was like the "dramatic turbulence" of Tom Buchanan's "irrecoverable" football game.[12]

During parties at our house when I was a young boy, my father, after a few pitchers of milk punch had been consumed, "drilled the troops," with the guests using broomsticks for rifles and marching to his commands through the house and out into the yard—"hup, tup, thrip, fuh, to the reah mahch," etc. He also used his best drill instructor's voice to call my Cub Scout troop to attention for the Pledge of Allegiance.

1st Lt. Philip Hammett, USMC, and Suzanne (Suzie) Saul, Radcliffe '44, were married from my mother's house in Germantown, Philadelphia just after D-Day and only a week after my father returned from the war in the Pacific. They had not seen each other in almost two years. After the wedding, they moved to Klamath Falls, Oregon, a climate conducive to my father's recovery from the filariasis he acquired in the Solomon Islands. Presumably, I was conceived in Klamath Falls. After his release from Marine Corps active duty in 1945, my father completed law school at the University of Pennsylvania and then joined his father-in-law's Philadelphia firm. He and my mother and, by 1951, my two sisters Peggy and Janet, and I lived in half of a double house in Chestnut Hill owned by his parents-in-law.

My father didn't pay much attention to me in my boyhood. I remember much later his marveling at how much time his children spent with their kids and remarking frankly and without apparent regret that he had spent as little time as possible with his. There are a few snapshots of my father holding a football for me to place kick. He did give me a nice baseball glove and take me to a few Philadelphia A's games at Shibe Park. The A's were my first favorite team and I got to see my first sports hero, the pint-sized lefty pitcher Bobby Shantz. He may be the reason I became a lefty myself.

My father revealed some troubling attitudes in those early days. I always rooted for the underdog Brooklyn Dodgers against the New York Yankees in their perennial World Series matchups. But my father was for the Yankees because, he told me, the Dodgers had too many "colored" players. He recalled how, when he was on the Horace Mann School basketball team in New York, he had disliked playing against Black people because they "smelled bad." My mother and her family had all attended Germantown Friends School and I started there in kindergarten. But GFS was Quaker, co-ed, and had, particularly for those days, a substantial number of Black students. I formed friendships with several of them and went to their homes to play. My father wasn't happy about this and so, after third grade, he transferred me to the all-male and all-white Chestnut Hill Academy.

Perhaps tired of being overborne by his wife's family and feeling stifled in her father's law firm, Dad left and formed his own small firm with a colleague in 1954. In the summer of 1955, while my mother, my sisters, and I were—pursuant to family custom—at the Saul's "camp" in the Adirondacks, my father took up with Ann, the proverbial lady down the street. She would be only the first of many—in fact, maybe she wasn't even the first.

My parents' breakup came that fall. I heard one big argument. Soon, I noticed my father wasn't living with us anymore. He would come to see us one evening a week while my mother was at choir practice at St. Paul's Church. Sometimes he was late, and there would be more yelling and slamming of doors. My mother told me that I would have to become "the man of the house." We all watched Elvis, discreetly televised only from the waist up, singing "Don't Be Cruel" on *The Ed Sullivan Show.*

I knew my father had met someone else. Based on some soap-opera cliché, I thought it was probably his secretary. He invited me to dinner at the Racquet Club downtown, where he was living at the time. I took the Chestnut Hill Local in to meet him. He told me that it wasn't his secretary, but Ann, whose son Jiggs was a playmate right there on Evergreen Place.

In the summer of 1956, I was sent to visit an aunt and uncle and cousins in Atlanta. I took the Crescent Limited by myself and had my own roomette. Sophisticatedly, I sipped Coke and played solitaire in the club car while other passengers drank whiskies or gin-and-tonics and complained about jobs and families. Arriving in Atlanta on this trip and the following summer when I spent a week at a YMCA camp in the Great

Smokies of South Carolina with a cousin, I noticed with surprise the signs designating water fountains, toilets, and waiting rooms as for "White" and "Colored." My cousins took me to visit the Confederate Memorial at Stone Mountain. I still have a souvenir piece of granite from Stone Mountain, which I have looked at amid the recent justifiable calls for the monument to be dismantled. Otherwise, I enjoyed the thick chocolate milk shakes at Zesto's and attended an Atlanta Crackers minor league game at Ponce de Leon Park.

That same summer, while I was in Atlanta, my mother was meeting Ned Hastings, a lawyer in Providence, Rhode Island, who became her second husband. A year later, after I had served as Uncle Ned's best man in his marriage to my mother (I would also be best man for my father's subsequent three marriages), my sisters and I moved to Rhode Island. We gained two new stepsisters in Jill and Judy. I started seventh grade at Gorton Junior High. The Russians launched Sputnik and President Eisenhower federalized the Arkansas National Guard to protect Black students integrating Little Rock High School. I loved Buddy Holly's "That'll Be the Day" and "Peggy Sue." The Yankees were finally beaten in the World Series, but by the Milwaukee Braves rather than the Dodgers.

I didn't get along with Uncle Ned, whom I compared unfavorably to my father. It infuriated me when Uncle Ned complained that my father was not making his child support payments. Dad's new law firm was failing, and he and Ann were drinking heavily. Nevertheless—and, in retrospect, incredibly—my mother asked my father if I could return to Philadelphia and live with him. My father had sought custody of me in the divorce settlement, but his father-in-law had threatened to "ruin him" if he pursued this. My Hammett grandparents remained extremely fond of my mother. After she decided to send me back to Philadelphia, my grandfather Louis Hammett wrote to tell her "how much I admire the courage and wisdom you have shown in reaching an extremely difficult decision.... We must hope and trust that Ted can be brought out of his present difficulties, no matter how much it hurts to do the things that seem most promising."

When I had my own child, the enormity of what my mother had been willing to do became very clear. Sending my daughter away, under any circumstances, would have been inconceivable.

I did return to Philadelphia and rejoined seventh grade at CHA. At my first boy-girl party, I drifted around the floor nervously with my first hoped-for girlfriend, whom I had met at the dancing class I otherwise hated, to the sentimental strains of the Everly Brothers' "All I Have to Do Is Dream" and Johnny Mathis' "The Twelfth of Never."

My father's and Ann's drinking got even worse. I often accompanied Dad to the state liquor store where he would buy two fifths of cheap

Colonel Lee Bourbon. Ann's mental illness, for which we never knew the diagnosis, also worsened, requiring several periods of hospitalization. During one of these, I was sent to live with my maternal grandparents, ostensibly so Mama Saul could help care for a skin condition that was probably associated with the unhappiness and stress of my home life. One Friday evening, I came home to find Ann passed out on the kitchen floor. Another time, when my Hammett grandparents were visiting us in Philadelphia, Ann went into the kitchen and began screaming uncontrollably. We sat at the table continuing our dinner and pretended it wasn't happening.

I bonded with my stepbrother Jiggs. We loved watching the old horror movies on TV, introduced by "Roland" on "Shock Theatre." One late night, perhaps after watching "Dracula" or "The Invisible Man," we were asleep, and my father and Ann began a loud, drunken argument. Ann crashed into Jiggs' room and took hold of the upright of his bunk bed as my father tried to drag her away by her hair. The next morning, this event was not mentioned.

Of course, Jiggs and I fought some, too. Once I got mad at him when we were playing basketball and I threw the ball at his head. He flew into a rage and attacked me with his fists. I ran away. My father angrily called me a "quitter."

My half-sister Nan was born in 1962. Soon after the birth, Ann had to go into the hospital again. For most of that spring, Dad and Jiggs and I cared for infant Nan. After Ann came home from the hospital, she and Dad stopped drinking for some time. But it did not last. Ultimately, drink and drugs claimed Ann in 1972, after my father had left her to live in New York with his new woman friend who would become his third wife. Shockingly, he also left Nan in the care of her mother.

After I moved back to Philadelphia, I was sent off to spend most summers at the Sauls' Forked Pine Camp on Long Lake in the Adirondacks. I loved this place and those idyllic summers with my cousins, especially Jeff Van Denbergh. Jeff's older brother Rose taught me to smoke cigarettes. We went to the Cobblestone Inn in the village, where at least for a while it was possible to get served underage. I drank Carling Black Label at the Saturday dances until the Cobblestone cracked down. Then, I had to drink my rum and cokes outside and dance around the parking lot to the overheard music of "The Corvettes" until I puked in the bushes. We often got lost in the fog on the lake on our way back to Forked Pine; sometimes we had to sleep in the boat until the fog lifted.

I developed a crush on Rose's pretty girlfriend Ellen, who was almost two years older than me. Sometimes, we would dance at the Cobblestone. One night, after visiting Ellen at her camp at the end of the lake,

I accidentally set the outboard motor afire while refueling it. The whole stern end of the boat was charred. False but enduring family lore has had it that I was smoking a cigarette while pouring in the gas. To be honest, I was in some respects a spoiled and entitled, but also somewhat troubled, teenager already beginning to indulge fantasies of myself as the doomed romantic.

My father, who sometimes jokingly referred to our family as part of the "impoverished aristocracy," seemed to want me to do everything he had done. He wanted me to go to Phillips Exeter Academy for my last year of high school, which I successfully resisted. I was enjoying my high school years in Chestnut Hill—especially the wild parties at homes where the parents were absent, inattentive, or themselves too drunk to notice.

In my yearbook biography at Chestnut Hill Academy, my friend Jim Whitaker wrote that I, along with friends "Gatesie" [Bill Gates] and "Logue" [Logie Bullitt], "improvised many ribald verses to an ever-popular Ray Charles song" ("What'd I Say?"). We sang along with Bo Diddley albums in our Senior Common Room and I loved Phil Spector's and the other "Girl Groups"—the Crystals ("He's Sure the Boy I Love"), Bob B. Soxx and the Blue Jeans ("Why Do Lovers Break Each Other's Hearts?")[13], and the Shirelles ("Will You Still Love Me Tomorrow?")—and the early Motown sounds of Smokey Robinson and the Miracles ("You've Really Got a Hold on Me") and the Marvelettes ("Please Mr. Postman"). This music provided the soundtrack for my continuing series of unrequited crushes on girls, which I considered tragic at the time.

In fact, what was truly tragic—albeit, no doubt, typical of my race and social class—was my blindness to the exploding struggle for racial justice in America in the 1960s. My friends and I were happy to listen and dance almost exclusively to African American music, but we had little or no knowledge of or interest in lunch counter sit-ins, Freedom Rides, attacks by police and dogs on Black children demonstrating for civil rights, or George Wallace attempting to "block the schoolhouse door." Bruce Springsteen tells Barack Obama in their 2021 podcast that in his high school years in Freehold, New Jersey, and to this day in white America, "we have loved Black people and brown people when they're entertaining us but when they want to live next door, we remain a tribal society."[14]

Dan Charles, my beloved history teacher at CHA, took me on a tour of the Gettysburg battlefield and I was fascinated by the military history, but he never taught me what the Civil War was really about. My CHA commencement took place June 12, 1963, the very day the civil rights leader Medgar Evers was murdered in Jackson, Mississippi. I never even heard about this event, much less thought of it as I recited my hackneyed valedictory about our graduation being "not only an end but a beginning."

When we drove drunk in Chestnut Hill, which we often did, and were stopped by the police, they would just drive us home and tell us not to do it again. Later, during college, as I wandered (staggered?) along Kirkland Street in Cambridge after a hard night of partying, an officer approached me, and I had the presence of mind to conceal my can of beer under my heavy Navy pea-jacket. "What's that under your coat?" he asked. "What coat?" I replied, and he just laughed and told me to go home. Now, I see these benign and permissive encounters with police as evidence of my white privilege, in stark contrast to what might have happened on these occasions had I been born Black.

I played varsity football at Chestnut Hill Academy, which was a social necessity, but I hated it and I wasn't any good. I also played varsity basketball and wasn't much good at that either. I was a starting guard my senior year and we won one game the whole season. Even after I avoided going to Exeter for the end of high school, my father thought I was emotionally unready for college so I should do a post-graduate year there. I successfully resisted that as well.

In any case, my father wanted me to go to Harvard, which I did after briefly considering Yale. The headmaster at CHA assured me that I had no need to apply anywhere but Harvard. My Harvard interview occurred at the height of the Cuban Missile Crisis. When the interviewer asked me what I thought of the crisis, I simply told him "what my father thinks." Afterwards, I worried that the interviewer would wonder why I didn't have any ideas of my own. Despite the poor interview performance and mediocre SATs,[15] my fourth-generation "legacy" status no doubt secured my admission.

I arrived at Harvard for my freshman year in September 1963. My father had played freshman football at Harvard and wanted me to go out for an intercollegiate sport. I lied to him, saying that I had tried out for freshman basketball but had been cut after a week.

President Kennedy was assassinated on November 22. I saw a young man, in his grief, beating his head against a tree in Harvard Yard. People were crying everywhere, including me. At the age of 15, I had made phone calls for Kennedy's 1960 campaign and attended two of his big rallies in Philadelphia. I loved him without reservation. Some came to believe that J.F.K. would have ended the nascent war in Vietnam had he lived. For many, the assassination seemed to usher in a downturn in American fortunes. Fifty-seven years later, Bob Dylan reported in his magisterial "Murder Most Foul," that on the day of the assassination "the age of the anti–Christ has only just begun."[16] The arrival of the Beatles during Christmas vacation offered only temporary comfort.

My father remained in the Marine Corps Reserve after World War II and retired as a lieutenant colonel in 1960. His ashes were later inurned at Arlington National Cemetery with full honors. My generation's more complicated war lay beyond the horizon when I joined the Harvard Class of 1967. My father felt military service was a duty that all young men should fulfill and wanted me to follow in his footsteps as a Marine officer. I agreed to this and, a month after JFK's death, presented myself at the Philadelphia Navy Yard for my physical to join Platoon Leaders' Class (PLC). This program required two six-week summer camps and, upon college graduation, commissioning as a second lieutenant and three years of active duty.

I attended my first PLC summer camp in 1964. At this time, the war in Vietnam seemed to many but a minor irritant on the other side of the world. The U.S. had some "advisors" there assisting the government of South Vietnam to ward off the Viet Cong guerrillas. It wasn't going very well but few people seemed to care. It didn't have even the urgency of Thomas Jefferson's "fire bell in the night"—his term for the foreboding issue of slavery at the time of the Missouri Compromise in 1820.

My father, as I recall, gave me no hint of what to expect in that first PLC summer at Quantico's Camp Upshur. It was mainly a blur of drill instructors screaming wake-ups with GI cans crashing down the middle of the squad bay, screw-ups on the drill field ("Hammett, you look like a monkey trying to fuck a football!"), and forced marches in full pack in the Virginia heat and humidity as punishment for failed "junk on the bunk" inspections ("Sergeant, they had to pack candidate McDonald in ice"; Drill Instructor: "They should have packed him in shit!"). Our senior drill instructor was removed after this episode. It was unclear who we were being prepared to kill. Little was said about Vietnam during those six weeks.

Of course, all of that was about to change. The Gulf of Tonkin "incident" came in early August 1964, a week after my first PLC session ended. We bombed North Vietnam for the first time. *The Pentagon Papers*[17] later revealed that the U.S. government lied to the American people not only about the immediate cause, but also about the overall objectives, of our war in Vietnam. The Gulf of Tonkin incident, presented as justifying our first direct military action, did not occur as described to the public. Moreover, the U.S. and South Vietnam had for months before the incident been engaging in provocative actions against the coastline of North Vietnam. The Johnson administration had also been preparing detailed plans for a wider war involving U.S. forces and had already drafted the resolution, which was then submitted to Congress, ostensibly in response to the events in the Gulf of Tonkin.

Nevertheless, after the Tonkin Gulf Resolution things quieted down, at least as far as most Americans knew. This was the result of a deliberate policy of the Johnson administration to keep Vietnam out of sight and off the public mind until after LBJ won the 1964 election.[18] In February 1965, a Viet Cong attack on an outpost at Pleiku killed six Americans and wounded more than one hundred. This prompted the implementation of already planned escalation moves: regular bombing of North Vietnam and increasingly open combat roles for American troops. In March, the first Marine units landed at Danang and the "American War," as the Vietnamese call it, began in earnest.[19]

At first, I bought the administration's line that we had to stop the advance of communism in Southeast Asia. I was generally too busy partying and continuing to have my heart superficially broken by a succession of young women. I drove to New York City on a Saturday evening with a classmate, and we went to the Peppermint Lounge near Times Square, where I think Joey Dee and the Starliters (of "Peppermint Twist" fame) were still playing. I slept in my friend's car while he was with his girlfriend in her apartment. My roommate Steve Saltonstall and I gave a keg party in Adams House. WMEX's famous deejay Arnie "Woo-Woo" Ginsburg also made an appearance—he of the famous variety of car honks and ads for the "clam bucket" at the "Adventure Car Hop, Route 1 in Saugus."

I was also coming increasingly to love the study of history, but I failed at first to see and learn the lessons of history for our Vietnam policy. My views of the war were beginning to change in 1965, however. The summer of 1965 was the off-summer between my two PLC camps. I had a menial job at a Weyerhaeuser paper plant outside of Philadelphia, but I quit in mid–August and spent the end of the summer at my grandparents' camp in the Adirondacks. Watts was in flames that August and Black people were dying there, but I wasn't paying much attention to that.

The music was everywhere—I think 1965 was one of the greatest years in music history: Bob Dylan "going electric" at the Newport Folk Festival and producing arguably his greatest work, especially "Bringing It All Back Home" and "Highway 61 Revisited"; the Byrds' first album, released with the recent landing of the first Marine units in Danang in the deep background, including "Mr. Tambourine Man," "Chimes of Freedom," and "Spanish Harlem Incident," all written by Dylan and featuring Jim (later Roger) McGuinn's jangly, ringing Rickenbacker 12-string[20]; the Beatles break-out albums (especially *Rubber Soul*, with my favorite "I'm Looking Through You"); and the Stones in full voice ("[I Can't Get No] Satisfaction" and other great songs in *Out of Our Heads*, no doubt one of the greatest ever partying and dancing records).

Maybe because of their grittier sound and more rebellious personae, I preferred the Stones to the Beatles for a time. I saw them at the Worcester Memorial Auditorium in one of their early U.S. tours in April 1965, and later that year at the old Boston Garden. I loved how Bill Wyman stood and played stoically with his electric bass held almost straight up; on my album cover of *December's Children.... And Everybody's* (including "The Singer Not the Song"), I drew an arrow to Wyman's photo with the caption "Hammett."

The 2019 film *Echo in the Canyon* chronicles the birth and explosion of folk rock in Laurel Canyon and greater L.A. in the period 1965–1967. Graham Nash hyperbolically asserts that this represented one of the most creative bursts in the history of artistic endeavor.[21] However, the film does not portray the time and place with a monochromatic "those were the days" nostalgia. While the war in Vietnam is not explicitly mentioned, a vague undercurrent of trouble simmers beneath the joyful zaniness of the scene. Barry McGuire's "Eve of Destruction"[22] was also a hit in the summer-fall of 1965,[23] but Marine veteran and poet W.D. Ehrhart recalled that

> The Eve of Destruction was just a song.
> Surf was up at Pendleton. The War in Vietnam
> was still a sideshow half a world away,[24]

I must have listened to all the iconic songs a million times. The Lovin' Spoonful's hit debut "Do You Believe in Magic?"[25] was released in the summer of 1965. This song happily proclaimed that the magic of the music lives in all of us. However, in retrospect at least, Dylan's "Like a Rolling Stone," another anthem of that summer, with its almost screamed refrain question "How does it feel?!" accompanied by Al Kooper's lilting organ,[26] captured my inchoate questioning of the war.

As the reality of the war came increasingly into focus and the decisions we all had to make about it came to dominate our lives, the music was a ubiquitous part of that experience. "Chimes of Freedom"[27] was particularly resonant for me: "Flashing for the warriors whose strength is not to fight." I could see myself in these words, much more than I could envision being a Marine in Vietnam. It began to dawn on me that if this and the other songs I was listening to were right, then the war must be wrong.

It wasn't only about my emerging opposition to the war. Dylan's additional call for freedom for "every hung-up person in the whole wide universe" also spoke to my recurrent periods of doubtless overblown misery fueled by excessive drinking and continued unhappy experiences with girls. In November 1965, at the seeming nadir of one of these spells, I wrote (in a letter never sent) to Jackie Hunsicker, an old friend from Chestnut Hill, who I had invited to the Harvard-Princeton football weekend my freshman year, that I was "self-consciously fucked up—but I love to be fucked up.... Who's going to feel sorry for me now?"

I was never a big dope smoker in college—it tended to make me paranoid. But I was pretty heavily into speed, which I used extensively for studying and paper writing. Some of my best work, including my undergraduate honors thesis, was done under the influence of Dexamyl. However, it also caused me some predictable problems. In my American literature course in the spring of junior year, F. Scott Fitzgerald's *Tender Is the Night* was the reading period assignment. Fortified with my pills, I spent all night before the final exam reading the book and, of course, loved it. It was the subject of the exam's first question, scheduled for 30 minutes of the three hours. Unfortunately, I spent 2½ hours on that first question, leaving only 30 minutes for the rest of the exam. Somehow, miraculously, I escaped with a C. My essay on *Tender Is the Night* must have been truly brilliant.

I had gotten a good start drinking in high school. During stretches of my college life, I was a big drinker, sometimes to the point of blackout. My drunken behavior was not always harmless to others. About 3 a.m. one Sunday, several friends and I drove into Boston and deliberately sought out a store window on a deserted street. I may have been the one to throw the bottle that shattered the plate glass and triggered the alarm as we raced away. Another late night, I was drinking mint juleps and smoking cigarettes with a friend on the sofa in his Quincy House suite. After I left, a fire started, burning several rooms and blackening the side of the building. My friend was awakened by the firefighters and was lucky to escape. The *Harvard Crimson* reported that the fire could have been caused by a cigarette and the history page on Quincy House's website states that this was the cause.[28] Nevertheless, Harvard officially termed the fire "electrical" in origin and asked us no questions.[29]

Yet another long day and night, I consumed 30 beers and made a total fool of myself. I was at a party at the Pi Eta Club, another legacy of my father's, an organization much closer to the brawling jock fraternities of the South than to the patrician Final Clubs to which many of my preppie Harvard friends belonged. The Pi Eta even had toga parties. I attended one but eschewed the toga. On my 30-beer day, however, I was very drunk as the Pi Eta party drew to a close around midnight. I wasn't ready to end my epic day and night, however, so I got the bright idea to invite everyone from the Pi Eta over to the Putnam Avenue apartment of some guys I only barely knew. I did not call them beforehand to see if this would be OK. About 50 people showed up at that apartment unannounced and clearly unwanted. The inhabitants outwardly made the best of the situation but afterwards we were no longer even vaguely friends.

In drunken and often illegible poems, I reveled in my miserable sensitivity or my sensitive misery, as the case may be. I thought I was going to

With Warren Bowes (right): Early in my 30-beer day.

be the latter-day Thomas Wolfe or Edmund Tyrone in O'Neill's *Long Day's Journey into Night*. During college, I had begun writing an autobiographical novel about a boy who had a series of sad failures with girls that ended in his suicide. However, I only wrote a few pages of it. Sometimes, I was almost sorry I hadn't drunk myself to death. It would have made for a better sad story.

I cannot pinpoint a specific event that turned me against the Vietnam War. Maybe it was the bloody battle of the Ia Drang Valley the same month of November 1965 I had written my "fucked-up" letter to Jackie and been at least partly responsible for the Quincy House fire. It was the first time that American troops had met the North Vietnamese Army in a major battle. Or maybe it was just the relentless escalation with no apparent result and the increasing death and destruction on all sides with no clear object. I was also influenced by the 1966 hearings of J. William Fulbright's Senate Foreign Relations Committee and his book *The Arrogance of Power*.[30]

The Pentagon Papers[31] revealed that, once the U.S. active engagement in hostilities became known, our government falsely stated that the primary objective was to defend South Vietnam. In fact, our main, but unstated, aim was to avoid a humiliating defeat that would undermine the credibility of our commitments.

No more accurate was our government's claim that we were fighting to halt aggression by North Vietnam against the South. The CIA strongly argued that the Viet Cong insurgency in the South was, at that stage, largely indigenous and little dependent on support from the North, so our bombing the North would likely have no effect on it. Equally questionable, according to the CIA, was our claim that we had to prop up a critical Southeast Asian "domino" lest it, and subsequently its neighbors, fall to a Communist Chinese onslaught.[32]

One of Vietnam veteran W.D. Ehrhart's furious epiphanies on the war came from reading *The Pentagon Papers*: "Vietnam a mistake? My God, it had been a calculated, deliberate attempt to hammer the world by brute force into the shape perceived by vain, duplicitous power brokers.... Oh, it was all here.... Never once had they told the truth—to me, or to anyone."[33]

This seems a correct assessment, particularly regarding the government's constant lying to the public. Fifty years later, *The Afghanistan Papers* disclosed a similar pattern of false and misleading statements among U.S. military and civilian decision-makers and between a series of administrations and the public.[34] In Afghanistan, an American military leader told a colleague that our primary mission there was to "avoid another Vietnam"—the first lost war in our nation's history. Indeed, there is a haunting sameness between the U.S. wars in Vietnam and Afghanistan on many dimensions: both asymmetrical wars with unclear or shifting objectives; costly battles to occupy ground that was almost immediately abandoned; inability to distinguish enemies from friends; local people playing both sides in order to survive; cover-up or excusing of atrocities; lying about progress; abandoning allies; wholesale violations of rules of engagement; and troops' taking and displaying enemy body parts as souvenirs.[35]

Both "Papers" also reveal the extent to which our policies were, in fact, the result of tragic and unintentional mistakes. David Halberstam brilliantly details how a group of non-ideological realists, ostensibly devoted to evidence-driven decision-making, became trapped in a disastrous policy of military intervention and relentless escalation in Vietnam. This resulted from some combination of their accepting false evidence reported by military leaders, their simultaneous desire to avoid nuclear confrontation but still prevent Communist expansion by means of limited warfare, and their willful or unwitting blindness to reality. Of course, throughout this decision-making, a critical piece was entirely missing: what would be best for the Vietnamese people.[36]

The U.S. bombed Hanoi for the first time in late June 1966. Some families evacuated their children from the city to keep them safe. My future Vietnamese colleague and friend Đoàn Ngữ, six years old at the time, was sent to live with relatives in Lang Son Province on the border with China.

Even as my opposition to the war emerged, I didn't become an activist against it. Nor had I been active in the civil rights movement. In 1965, to my later shame and regret, I had declined the invitation of my roommate Steve Saltonstall and my later roommate John Ballard to go with them to Selma, Alabama, and join the march to Montgomery in support of Black voting rights. Neither did I join Steve at the November 1966 confrontation of Robert McNamara outside Quincy House. Steve had helped plan this action, during which he asked McNamara how many civilian deaths had occurred in Vietnam "at our hands"—McNamara dishonestly replied, "I don't know."[37] I did attend Cambridge's first "Human Be-In," hardly real activism, in the spring of 1967 and participated in just one antiwar demonstration, the largest of them all in November 1969 in Washington, while I was still in the Marine Corps after returning from Vietnam.

By the spring of 1966, I had decided that I was against the war. And I had met Nancy. She was the pretty, bright, and funny Wellesley roommate of John Ballard's girlfriend, who had repeatedly urged us to meet. Our first meeting occurred in the late winter of 1966 when Nancy came to visit Tigger, the cat that she and her roommates had had in their rooms in Claflin Hall but had been caught with and decided to pass on to John, Warren Bowes, and me in Adams House. Harvard also prohibited pets, but we weren't discovered. Tigger lived to be 19. He went to live with my father and Ann in Philadelphia after that year and came back to us in Cambridge after Ann died in 1972.

When Nancy came to visit Tigger, I had to go downstairs to inform her that it was after "parietal hours," which limited when women could be in male students' rooms. (These rules were abolished in one fell swoop the year after I graduated.) A few weeks later we had another, slightly awkward arranged meeting—call it a preliminary, not a date—at the Friendly's Ice Cream shop in Wellesley and then, on April Fool's Day—which we later took to be our anniversary—we had our first real date. We went to see Eugene O'Neill's *Long Day's Journey Into Night* at the Loeb Drama Center and afterward for Chinese food at the Hong Kong in Harvard Square, where we saw a guy passed out with his face in a plate of fried rice. It was unclear which was more depressing, the play or that guy.

I have always loved *Long Day's Journey* and indeed all of O'Neill's work. Late at night in Adams House, my roommate John used to recite dramatically Jamie Tyrone's soliloquy to his brother Edmund ("Listen, kid you'll be going away") and, from *A Moon for the Misbegotten*, the older Jim

Tyrone character's drunken lament to his farm tenant Josie Hogan about the train trip that he spent with a cheap prostitute as his dead mother's body rode "in the baggage coach ahead." Nancy ever after resisted going to depressing plays about Irish people: "Is there any other kind?" she asked. Perhaps this was because of her own three-quarters' Irish heritage.

I was young and confused—maybe "clueless," as Nancy now terms both of us at that time. I gave in to doubt and fear. If I had it to do over again, I hope I would have been truer to my principles, such as they were, and refused to serve in Vietnam. John Balaban, for example, was granted conscientious objector status, but then demanded to do his alternative service in Vietnam, where he worked for the Committee of Responsibility to identify children with grievous war wounds and evacuate them to the U.S. for surgery and care.[38]

I also wish that I had joined more actively in the antiwar movement during and after my time in the Marine Corps. Recently, I met a former Navy officer and a Quaker, who, with a group of like-minded active-duty officers, filed as conscientious objectors and protested the deployment of Navy vessels to the war zone. The extensive resistance to the war among active-duty service members, through demonstrations, newspapers, and off-base coffee houses, is the subject of an exhibit called "Waging Peace" and an accompanying book.[39] I saw the exhibit at the War Remnants Museum in Ho Chi Minh City in 2018.

I still fear that my actions or lack of them were driven by a dual cowardice—that I was both afraid to fight in the war and afraid to stand up against it. Tim O'Brien said that his decision was driven by only the second of these: "I was a coward. I went to war."[40] I admitted to something like this at the session on Vietnam at my 25th Harvard reunion.

Marine veteran William Broyles came to the very edge of a principled refusal to go to the war. In 1969, he left Norton Air Force Base shortly before his flight to Okinawa was to take off and changed into civilian clothes in a taxi back to L.A., intending to return home to his wife and openly resist the war. However, after talking by telephone to a male friend, he realized that he had "tried to hide my fear behind morality and principle." He returned to Norton, caught the next flight, and served out his tour as an infantry platoon commander and staff officer, even though he considered the war wrong and still does.[41]

Perhaps more charitably, my own paralysis could be ascribed to an innate and persistent difficulty in making up my mind about things. If I formed a more definite opinion, I might have to do something, so I avoided forming definite opinions. Viet Thanh Nguyen's nameless Vietnamese-French protagonist in *The Committed* agonized over his two minds and two faces—"Am I a revolutionary or a reactionary?"—but this did not keep him from taking dramatic, even violent, actions in service of one or the other.[42]

Perhaps I should be consigned to that Robert McNamara group who turned against the war but did nothing to stop it.[43] I do take some comfort from Myra MacPherson's characterization of the Vietnam War's "Haunted Generation": "Complex and confusing emotions and reasons were the motivations for being on either side of the barricade; there was nothing as simple as patriotism versus not serving in a war they couldn't support or cowardice versus getting killed for nothing."[44]

Bowing to my father's pressure, I completed the PLC program in the summer of 1966, surviving the notorious "Hill Trail" despite my history of heavy smoking and drinking at Harvard. For me, the Beatles' "Rain," with their first use of a backwards playback loop, always recalls that summer at Quantico.

After my second PLC camp, I was happy and grateful to do one thing my father wanted me to do: take a trip to Europe at his expense. I fell in love with Paris: drinking Heinekens at Fouquet's on the Champs-Elysées while watching the *boulevardiers;* swilling gin and tonics at Harry's New York Bar, one of Hemingway's hang-outs (only on later trips to Paris did I find Le Select in Montparnasse, a frequent setting in *The Sun Also Rises*); meeting by chance my CHA classmate David Wallace at Café Wagner near l'Opera and hanging out with him and a group of French students in discothèques and sidewalk cafés in St. Germain, where we loudly denounced the war for the benefit of American tourists passing by; and spending a warm afternoon by my open window at the Hotel du Ranelagh in the XVIᵉ, drinking a bottle of Beaujolais accompanied by a baguette and cheese, and reading Fitzgerald's great novella "May Day."

My Harvard roommate Warren, who had a summer internship in Paris, and I visited the chateaux of the Loire Valley and took the overnight train to St. Tropez, where we raced through the streets on Solex motorbikes and got sunburned at Tahiti Beach. In London, I stayed in the "Sunny South Kensington" of Donovan's song, bought the British version of the Beatles' new album *Revolver* (with "Eleanor Rigby" and "Here, There and Everywhere"), picked up a few shirts on Carnaby Street, had colloquies about the War with people of diverse political views at Hyde Park's Speakers' Corner, spent a lot of time drunk in various pubs, discovered Turner in the Tate Gallery, and, like Warren Zevon's werewolf,[45] stumbled aimlessly about Soho's rainy streets.

Nancy understood my predicament on the war and supported me throughout this difficult period. When I returned to Harvard for my senior year in the fall of 1966, my relationship with her gradually became more serious but I was still experiencing some periods of gloom, probably caused by my impending military service. As late as February 1967, I wrote a poem about a helpless person (me) being inexorably overtaken by an avalanche of misfortune and misery. It crudely prefigured Jackson Browne's 1974 song "Before the Deluge" and Fleetwood Mac's "Landslide" of 1977.[46]

Slowly but surely, Nancy helped me to emerge from my unhappiness: "It will be O.K.," she reassured me; "I'll be with you; We'll get through this together." I started seeing her every weekend. John and I had been granted one of Harvard's rare permissions to live off-campus for our senior year, based on John's concern that his piano practicing might disturb neighboring students in Adams House—John didn't even play the piano. We rented the third floor of Mr. and Mrs. Flaherty's "three-decker" in North Cambridge (31 Buena Vista Park or 31 BVP, as we called it). I have driven down that short street quite a few times recently; the house still looks the same and I have clear and fond recollections of our times there.

The Flahertys, immigrants from the Connemara in County Galway just after World War II, were not the sort of Irish people who inhabit so many of those depressing plays. They were great landlords, tolerant of the female comings and goings and of our late-night escapades, such as when John invited the entire Chambers Brothers band ("People Get Ready," "Time Has Come Today") over for a post-concert party. (On seeing John's shelves of books for his thesis research on Black youth in Roxbury, one of the Brothers asked, rhetorically quoting one of the titles: "Who *is* the American Negro?")

When Nancy and I later returned to live at 31 BVP while I pursued my PhD, Mrs. Flaherty used to invite me downstairs to her kitchen for lunch during the breaks in the Senate Watergate hearings, which I was watching to avoid writing my doctoral dissertation. On Nancy's and my first wedding anniversary, Mrs. Flaherty comforted us in her Irish brogue that "Ah, the first year is the worst." She updated this same advice on the next three anniversaries that we lived in her house ("Ah, the first two years are the worst," etc.).

Nancy was a good Catholic girl. On Sunday mornings that winter-spring of 1967, I waited for her at Tommy's Lunch on Mount Auburn Street, where I also worked as a short-order cook, while she went to Mass at St. Paul's around the corner. Tommy's was a fun place with a great jukebox (for some reason, I remember especially the Stones' "What a Shame" repeatedly playing) and pinball machines with expert players. Like the Childs in Columbus Circle in Fitzgerald's "May Day," and the Hayes Bickford and Waldorf cafeterias in Harvard Square, Tommy's was always full of various carousers and interesting characters late at night.

By full spring, soon before I was to graduate and begin my three years' active duty in the Marine Corps, which would almost surely include

13 months in Vietnam, Nancy and I began to sense that, maybe just maybe, we were in love. I had reversed my schedule with the help of quantities of Dexamyl, writing my undergraduate history thesis all night and sleeping most of the day. Nancy would take the MTA from Wellesley, arriving at my apartment in the afternoon, perhaps taking a North Cambridge bus operated by our landlord Mr. Flaherty.

My Harvard class had its very own band, the Forerunners. Nancy and I danced to their music many times. I remember with particular fondness drummer Eric Valdina's rendition of the Beatles' "You've Got to Hide Your Love Away." It captured my mingled joy, sadness, and dread that spring of 1967.

One very late night in early June, Nancy and I spontaneously drove from Cambridge to Rockport, on the Cape Ann seacoast north of Boston, in a "swift blue" (as I later termed it in a poem) Ford Mustang borrowed from John Ballard. Sitting together in that car by the ocean in the pre-dawn transition from darkness to light, I told Nancy for the first time that I loved her. She was the first and only woman I have ever said that to. My recollection is that she replied that she loved me, too. Nowadays, crossing the Tobin Bridge on the way to our summer place in Maine still reminds me of crossing the Mystic River Bridge, as it was called then, on that drive to Rockport with Nancy in June 1967.

I received my commission as a second lieutenant on the very hot day before Harvard commencement. I sweated in my Marine Corps dress whites, which I likened to an ice cream man's suit. Despite her opposition to the war, my mother helped to pin on my new gold bars. I had spent the previous weeks since I submitted my thesis listening almost non-stop to *Sgt. Pepper's Lonely Hearts Club Band*, drinking cheap scotch, and reading Thomas Wolfe's *Look Homeward, Angel*. I was waiting for Nancy to arrive for my graduation and for my father's contemporaneous 25th reunion. Nancy attended my commissioning ceremony and helped my mother pin on my bars, although she had also turned against the war. If my father was proud of me, he didn't say so. No doubt, he was still angry about my opposition to the war.

Soon after, I reported to the Basic School, the four-month initial training for new Marine lieutenants, where it was now clear what we were being prepared for: a tour of duty in Vietnam, most probably as an infantry platoon commander. If it wasn't obvious already, it soon became crystal clear that I would not be a model Marine officer. I lip-synched the growls we were supposed to let out when we stabbed the straw-filled dummies in the bayonet drill. I laughed at the instructor who referred to the Viet Cong in their spider holes thinking about "dialectric [sic] materialism." My platoon mates teased me about my unorthodox views and my taste in music, in which at that time the Doors (for example, "Love Me Two Times" from their second album *Strange Days*) figured prominently. Other songs that marked my time at Basic School were Otis Redding's "(Sittin' on the) Dock of the Bay," Van Morrison's "Brown-Eyed Girl," and the Box-Tops' "The Letter."

My friend Bill "Roc" Ganter, later wounded at Hue, labeled me the "Harvard Hindu." Captain "Dangerous Don" McMaster, our platoon commander, gave me no end of grief about my poor shaving ("Lieutenant Hammett, did you shave this morning? Next time, stand a little closer to the razor"), even though I hardly had a beard, as well as my uniform screw-ups and other foibles. One time I put my USMC eagle, globe, and anchor lapel pins on backwards with the anchors "outboard" instead of "inboard." My memories of Basic School include being hopelessly lost during the "land navigation" and the "three-day war" exercises. I essentially faked my way through the program.

Towards the end of Basic School, we could list three preferred military occupational specialties (MOS)—I selected supply ("why die, go supply"), motor transport ("motor T and out in three"), and communications. I had lingering doubts as to whether these choices reflected more cowardice than a principled wish to avoid combat in a war that I opposed. In any case, I would have been a terrible infantry platoon commander. In its wisdom, the Marine Corps recognized this and assigned me to supply. When I informed my father, his disapproval was palpable.

During Basic School at Quantico, I saw Nancy as often as possible—pretty much every weekend in Washington during the summer and then for several weekends after she returned to Wellesley in the fall for her senior year. These included a "phantom" weekend when she flew to Washington without informing her family. We had a nice dinner at Blackie's House of Beef near Dupont Circle, but Nancy was terrified that she would see someone she knew who would report her presence to her parents. She had already had battles with her father about the shortness of her skirts.

After supply officers' school at Camp Lejeune, I had three weeks' leave before going to Vietnam. I spent most of it with Nancy. We went to a wonderful concert by Ian and Sylvia at Wellesley. We danced a lot and held each other close. Before dinner at my mother's house outside Providence, she prepared a champagne fountain for Nancy and me to celebrate our "unofficial" engagement. I had a sense of gathering dread as my day of departure for Vietnam drew closer and closer. I would have to leave Nancy and go off to who knew what. In a novel of London during the Blitz, Elizabeth Bowen wrote of what "must always have been true of lovers.... Their time sat in the third place at their table. They were the creatures of history, whose coming together was of a nature possible in no other day."[47]

Nancy came to Philadelphia to see me off. The night before I left, my father and I drank a quantity of Schlitz beer and he, unaccountably, became morose and lamented how hard it was to send a son off to war. I guess he had forgotten the history of the past several years. Nancy was furious at his hypocrisy. On the cold, drizzly morning of March 12, 1968, I was delivered by Nancy and my father and stepmother to Philadelphia airport for the flight to Los Angeles, the first leg of my trip to the war.

In her first letter to me the night of my departure, Nancy wrote that

> we all watched 'til your plane got off the ground.... I was very mature about the whole thing ... as soon as you got on board, I began stuffing myself with coffee and pastries, which serves instead of weeping, I guess.... Having you fly out of telephone range is like losing some crucial appendage.... I don't feel all here.

Knowing nothing of the geography of Southern California, I took a taxi from LAX to Norton Air Force Base in San Bernardino (almost $100 even in 1968) and spent the afternoon and evening drinking gin and tonics in the officers' club as I waited for my midnight flight to Okinawa. (Unlike William Broyles, I never considered deserting to protest the war.) On a brief refueling stop in Honolulu, I heard the news of Eugene McCarthy's strong showing in the New Hampshire Democratic Presidential primary and I sent Nancy a postcard: "one day down, 394 to go." In the terminal, the Doors' "Light My Fire" was playing on the public address system.

My orders to a specific unit in Vietnam were delayed and so I had an unusual week-long layover at the Marine transient facility at Camp Hansen, Okinawa. Every day, I attended grim briefings about the situation in Vietnam, including the ongoing plight of the 26th Marines at Khe Sanh. These briefings did not cover the events of March 16 in My Lai-4 and three neighboring hamlets of Quang Ngai Province where soldiers of the U.S. Army's American Division slaughtered more than 500 unarmed Vietnamese people, mostly women, old men, and children. The full facts of this horrific event would not be known for several years and no one was ever deservedly punished for it.[48]

At the officers' club, I discovered San Miguel Beer and lost quite a lot of money in poker to a group of permanent personnel who preyed on young officers en route to and from Vietnam. When my orders finally came through, I found that I was assigned to 3rd Marine Division, in which my father had served in the Pacific in World War II. The 3rd Marine Division operated in northern I Corps, the northernmost part of South Vietnam and the scene of some of the bloodiest fighting of the war. I wrote to my father that "You will be happy to know that I am going to your old outfit.... I only hope that I do a good job regardless of my personal feelings. But that doesn't really make any difference now—I *have* to do a good job."

After arriving in Danang, I had no idea how to get to Quang Tri where I was to check in at 3rd Marine Division headquarters and receive my specific duty assignment. One just waited at the Marine Air Terminal until a flight was announced going to or near your destination. Late in the afternoon, I finally got to Dong Ha, four miles north of Quang Tri and about six miles south of the Demilitarized Zone dividing North from South Vietnam. (Dong Ha is now the provincial capital of Quang Tri Province and there is no more DMZ.) I got a cot for the night in an old French building in what I was told was the "v-ring," the bull's eye in the target of North Vietnamese artillery aiming for the airfield. In fact, the next morning while I was shaving, a few rounds came in, causing a quick jump into a nearby trench.

I hitched a jeep ride to Quang Tri and reported to 3rd Marine Division, where I was further assigned to become the Marine supply officer of 3rd Medical Battalion, which operated the division's field hospital in Phu Bai, just south of Hue, and two other medical units at Dong Ha and Khe Sanh. When I first reported to 3rd Marine Division, I was very mindful that my supply MOS might not matter; the Marine Corps often assigned new lieutenants arriving in-country to be infantry platoon commanders if there was a shortage in this most critical role, which was often the case. Indeed, one month after I arrived, the 3rd Marine Division instituted a policy of assigning *all* new lieutenants as platoon commanders, regardless of MOS, for their first six months. This was the result of high casualty rates.

I got to Phu Bai and found the hospital right next to the airfield, which is now the commercial airport for Hue. I would land here again in 1997 during my first post-war trip back to Vietnam.

For me, getting through my wartime tour in Vietnam was not so much about physical survival as about "passing time," as W.D. Ehrhart titled his memoir of the years immediately after his Marine Corps service in the war[49] and retaining what I could of my sanity. The main elements of my psychological survival were my girlfriend, my political views, my music, and, sad to say, my heavy drinking. February 1968—the month before I arrived in Vietnam—saw the highest U.S. death toll in the war—about 2,150—which was almost matched by the 2,100 killed in May. On the single day of March 16, almost a quarter of this number of Vietnamese civilians were massacred by American troops at My Lai.

Just a few days after I landed in Vietnam, the so-called "wise men"—Clark Clifford, Dean Acheson, George Kennan et al.—had advised Lyndon Johnson to stop the bombing of North Vietnam and seek negotiations to end a war they deemed unwinnable. Johnson rejected this advice, for the time being. Based, as he later said, on "everything I knew about history," LBJ was determined not to be an appeaser of aggression as Neville

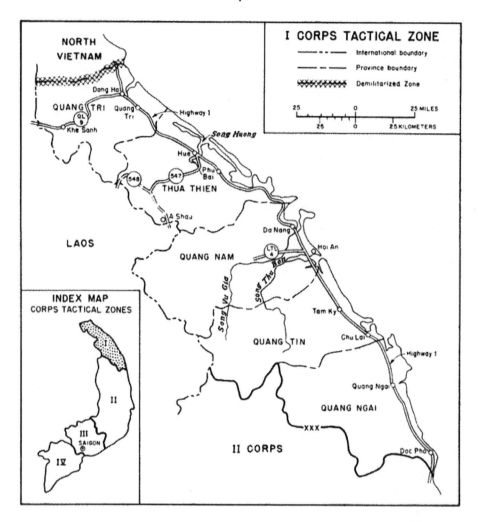

I Corps Tactical Zone, South Vietnam—Third Marine Division's Area of Operations (Citizendium).

Chamberlain had been: "Once we showed how weak we were, Moscow and Peking would move in a flash to exploit our weakness." At the same time, U.S. military strategy must be moderated, Johnson thought, to avoid triggering treaty obligations that he worried may have existed among North Vietnam, China, and the Soviet Union that could have begun World War III.[50] In the compelling context of the Cold War, LBJ's impossible strategic dilemma was that, in the words of David Halberstam, "nothing that could be truly effective against the North Vietnamese could be tried without the fear of a much larger war which Johnson wished to avoid."[51]

American strategy was trapped in a vicious tautology: bombing could only succeed in killing the North's will to continue fighting if the ground war in the South proved that the Viet Cong and North Vietnamese Army could not win there. But, conversely, the success of the ground war in the South seemed to depend on escalation of the air war in both North and South. Thus, in Philip Beidler's formulation, "The American war had become its own justification."[52]

2

Supplying 3rd Medical Battalion

While I saw no combat myself, I did see plenty of carnage. My first night in Phu Bai, March 26, 1968, an enemy rocket attack hit a ward of the hospital and several other buildings on the base. I banged my head getting into the bunker and later witnessed a bloody and chaotic scene in the hospital. At first, I was troubled by the behavior of some of the doctors and corpsmen. I wrote to Nancy: "here were these guys lying on the tables all shot up and people were standing around joking and laughing… 'Here today, gone tomorrow,' 'Sorry about that,' etc." As I saw more, however, I came to realize more compellingly that the medical staff had to take this approach in order to do their grim work with focus, skill, and speed, and to survive it psychologically.

Indeed, these scenes were repeated many times during my tour, as the hospital received mass casualties from firefights and North Vietnamese Army (NVA) attacks on Mutter's Ridge, ambushes near Con Thien, the Battles of Dai Do near Dong Ha, and NVA assaults on Fire Support Base Russell and other outposts in the mountains south of the DMZ. In August 1968, I wrote to Nancy that "you aren't learning too much about the Marines over here because they're getting their asses kicked almost every day—that's a secret, though."

Luckily for me, I spent my entire 13-month tour in Vietnam with 3rd Medical Battalion in Phu Bai and later in Quang Tri. The Marine Corps considered itself tougher than the other U.S. service branches, so our tours were a month longer than theirs.

Third Medical Battalion operated the 3rd Marine Division's main hospital. In Phu Bai, we received casualties through our "Delta Med" unit in Dong Ha but later when we moved to Quang Tri, we received casualties directly from the field by helicopter. The hospital complex included large plywood buildings which housed "triage" (it was the first time I'd heard this French word, meaning "sorting," for the room into which all casualties were first brought and treatment priorities set), X-ray, laboratory, operating rooms and wards that combined hardback hooches, like the ones we all lived in, and inflated rubber "MUST" units. The facility was like the one depicted in the movie and TV series *M*A*S*H*—although without quite the same range of odd-ball characters. We did have some of these, including the twinkly-eyed Irish Catholic chaplain, the sensitive psychiatrist, some aggressively non-military, even anti-military doctors, and a few right-wing supporters of the war, with whom I sometimes argued the merits after too many drinks had been consumed.

During times of mass casualties, chopper after chopper would land on the pad in front of the hospital and stretchers bearing the wounded, the dying, and the dead, all brought in for triage. Graves Registration personnel would take care of the dead. The doctors and corpsmen would decide which of the wounded to treat first and which to put aside for later, based either on the perceived hopelessness, relative seriousness, or stability of their conditions. These were necessarily quick but rarely erroneous decisions. The medical staff, despite their seeming callousness, were remarkable in their professionalism, dedication, and overall effectiveness.

Because of the relative rapidity of getting casualties to care, death rates among American casualties in Vietnam were much lower than in previous wars. But, of course, many, many—indeed, far too many—did die, and countless others suffered permanent physical and psychological injury and the scars of post-traumatic stress disorder for years to come.

Apart from the blood and suffering, what I remember most about the Marines who were brought to the hospital during times of mass casualties was their frequent bitterness about the encounters in which they had been wounded. "No one knew what the fuck was going on" was a common complaint; there was often no warning before they were hit; it was complete confusion; coordination among infantry, artillery, and air power was all too frequently absent. Far too many times, we received Marines wounded by our own forces. One of the doctors in our hospital estimated that 30 percent of the casualties we received were due to "friendly fire." After Army sergeant Michael Mullen's death from a misplaced "friendly" artillery round, his parents discovered that such "non-battle" fatalities were omitted from U.S. official casualty counts.[1] The Army was accidentally killing not only its own but also Marines. In April, I wrote to my father that U.S. Army units had killed about 20 Marines and wounded about 50 more in the last week when they inadvertently opened up with artillery and helicopter gunships—"this is a very well-run war over here." To Nancy, I elaborated: "The 'other war' you hear about appears to be less 'winning the hearts and minds of the people' than the battles between the Army and the Marine Corps."

I was not required to attend mass casualty events at the hospital but, I guess through some morbid fascination or desire to have my opposition to the war reinforced, I almost always made my way to triage when the alarm was sounded. Sometimes, I tried to help by carrying stretchers or talking to wounded Marines. During my first month, I wrote that "I feel much better working in a unit whose job it is to care for the wounded than I would in one whose job it is to inflict casualties on anyone."

Regardless of the rightness or wrongness of the cause, the Marines who served in the field in Vietnam were generally, like their NVA and Viet Cong opponents, incredibly resilient. Marines were brave and tenacious for whatever reason, noble or ignoble: for love of country, belief in the Domino Theory, for their buddies, for revenge, or out of racist hatred of the enemy.

Field Marines were often bitter and angry about unreasonable or suicidal orders or tactical errors from above. Some of the troops were certainly ruthless and crazed, following the unstated guideline to "kill anything that moves," the title of a 2013 book by Nick Turse on American war crimes in Vietnam.[2] Nico Walker describes an eerily similar directive in his novel's account of the Iraq War: "The curfew was sundown and our ROE [rule of engagement] was to shoot anybody we caught out after dark."[3]

Some of the Marine "grunts" in Vietnam could be pretty scary. I remember catching a ride in Danang with a couple of Marines just in from long stints in the bush. They and their uniforms were filthy, and their eyes had that telltale thousand-yard stare. They were talking about some firefight and who got blown away by whom. I was a "rear-echelon motherfucker (REMF)," whom they no doubt held in contempt or worse, so I was happy to get off that truck before they blew me away.

Marines could be cynical or at least ambivalent about things in the war. "Wasted" was a common synonym, arguably either literal or figurative—for "blown away." People were also said to have "bought the ranch" and an attack could "ruin your whole afternoon." Iraq war slang was similarly acerbic but perhaps more obscurely sophisticated: instead of being "wasted," an Improvised Explosive Device "Ate The Fuck Up"; "They'd died and gone to the Internet."[4]

"Eat the apple and fuck the Corps!" was a commonly voiced summary of Marine Corps life in "the Nam." Understatement was a feature of Marine parlance. Many things that were surely more important than this were only pronounced "decent"—maybe because there were no other words for their enormity. A Marine interviewed at Khe Sanh said that "it'll be really decent to go home."[5] "There it is!"—the classic American troops' slang line of the war—could be used simply to agree with something someone said but more deeply it also captured the mingled resignation and determination most of these Marines felt and displayed—the rough equivalent of today's overused "It is what it is." (Both these expressions fit nicely with my own understated opposition to the war.) Still and all, however they felt about the war and the totally fucked up situations in which they were so often placed, these young Marines largely persevered and did their duty with guts and distinction.

As Marine supply officer, I had no direct responsibility for the operation or provisioning of the hospital, except for clothing and some equipment like air conditioners. A Navy supply officer oversaw all medical supplies, and all the medical staff were Navy personnel. My primary role was to ensure that the Marine elements of the 3rd Medical Battalion—motor transport, perimeter security, administration, and supply—as well as the Navy medical personnel, had the weapons, "782 gear" (such as packs), helmets, flak jackets, clothing, furniture, and clerical supplies that they needed. Upon my official ascension to battalion supply officer, I wrote to my college roommate Warren Bowes that "I am now the omnipotent supply officer of this battalion with immense responsibilities and great influence with the commanding officer on matters of the highest importance." In short, "a total of nothing," as the Marines would say.

Most of the time, my supply duties were tedious and boring, with endless paperwork. Often, I just sat at my desk with my feet up, reading magazines, and smoking cigarette after cigarette with the fan playing on me. In August, I wrote Nancy:

> And so the days go on—I don't feel that I've written you anything significant in quite a while. Everything is hard to tell—every day is the same. I usually don't even know what day it is—and I cross them off one by one on the calendar— each one brings me closer, I guess. But it's still such a long way.

We experienced frequent shortages and persistent difficulty obtaining needed supplies. I did the best I could to address these problems and, in fact, thought that I did a pretty good job under the circumstances. Was I a lazy and disaffected drunk or an exemplary performer of my duties? I guess I tried to be a combination of the two but ended up not convincing my superiors that I was more of the latter than the former.

The problems obtaining air conditioners for the hospital wards lasted for months. I noticed that in rear areas plenty of clubs and living quarters had air conditioners "but you can't get them where they are really needed." One of our hospital's patients had gone into shock after he came out of the operating room and was put into a ward where the temperature was 120 degrees. When requisitions for air conditioners and other supplies went unfilled for too long, we took truck convoys to Danang to speed the

At work in Quang Tri, 1968.

process. On one of these trips, we succeeded in obtaining several air conditioners that had been on order for months without result.

We also resorted to stealing and trading to get what we needed. The Army had "shelves and shelves of all the stuff we can't get." For two lister bags (for water storage) and two old Marine Corps–issue watches, I obtained from the Army three cases of green skivvies (underwear), some jungle boots, and jungle utilities ("fatigues" in the Army), which were much needed. I considered this a "fairly good deal." Another time, I was able to scrounge 30 cots from the Army to help accommodate an overflow of malaria patients.

When the battalion moved to Quang Tri in August 1968, we were assigned an area where rice paddies had been filled in with sand. We lived in tents before our hardback hooches were built. I wrote that "when the monsoon comes, I fully expect us all to sink right down some night and never be heard from again." To avoid being flooded out, we wanted to build plywood floors in our tents. However, no plywood was to be had for this purpose through normal supply channels. Intelligence was received that the 3rd Engineer Battalion had many pallets of plywood in their equipment yard in Dong Ha, so much that they might not miss a few. We took a truck over there and hoisted about four pallets while one of our enterprising men distracted the Marine in charge of the yard. We thought we had made a clean escape, took the plywood back to Quang Tri and built the floors in our tents. However, we were found out somehow and an angry representative of the Engineers paid us a visit and told us we had to rip up the floors and return the plywood to them. Negotiations ensued, whereby we were able to keep our floors in return for several of the highly coveted combat knives called "K-bars."

K-bars also figured prominently in our frequent trading with the Navy's Seabees for beer—of which we were often short, and they were almost always flush—and for the construction of our officers' club in Quang Tri. The amazing Seabees (short for Mobile Construction Battalions) built our club for us in about two days, complete with patio and full bar. When we were able to get them ourselves, camouflage utilities were valuable trading commodities with the Army who did not yet have these in their official supply chain. We obtained much of the lumber for our officers' club in trade with the Army for camouflage utilities.

Sometimes I resorted to lies to get necessary supplies. When we needed a last ten sheets of plywood to complete the floor of our new warehouse in Quang Tri, I submitted a request to a special program of the Division engineer requesting plywood to build "bins for medical supplies in the hospital wards." I gave this story to the colonel in charge and he approved the request. The appeal based on medical supplies was, as I suspected, more compelling than our more prosaic desire to have a finished floor in our supply warehouse.

Once, I got into big trouble at the in-country R&R center at China Beach in Danang. We had convoyed to Danang for supplies and spent the afternoon drinking on the beach. Lewis Puller brought his platoon to China Beach for a day after a particularly rough stretch in the bush and one of his Marines threatened to dive into the South China Sea and swim home.[6] None of my men tried this but many of us were quite drunk and when we were denied beds at the R&R center, we determined to steal some mattresses and sleep in our trucks. We were caught by the MPs as we tried to leave the compound with the mattresses and I mouthed off obscenely when brought before the Navy officer of the day, referring to him as a "fucking asshole," among other things. Later, I was called in by Colonel "Stormy" Sexton, Chief of Staff of the 3rd Marine Division, and given a verbal reprimand for my behavior. However, Sexton did praise me for the concern I had shown that my men have decent places to sleep. Nancy thought the whole episode was a "positive reflection on your character." I did a lot of things with a certain impunity because, as another favorite Marine saying went, "What are they going to do, send us to Vietnam?"

Sometimes the Navy doctors made unreasonable demands for supplies. Upon arrival, one demanded a proper bed and mattress rather than the standard army cot. When informed that these were not available in a war zone, he angrily stormed out threatening to complain to the commanding officer. On another occasion, one of my men caught several doctors stealing gear from our supply warehouse. The doctors became incensed when caught and began "cursing and screaming at the poor kid." I reported the doctors' behavior to the commanding officer, but nothing was done. I complained to my father that some of the doctors "think they rate all sorts of special treatment and coddling.... They never ask for things, they demand them." The supply officer, I concluded, "is the most hated person around."

When our hospital moved north from Phu Bai to Quang Tri in early August 1968, I was in charge of the move by truck convoy and air, after I had spent a month at Embarkation School in Okinawa learning how to load ships and planes. The move was quite a complex operation that I had feared "will surely be the biggest mess in history" but actually went off quite smoothly. We had to close the hospital in Phu Bai one day, transfer non-ambulatory patients to facilities in Danang and a hospital ship offshore, fly ambulatory patients to Quang Tri, and be prepared to reopen the very next day in the new facility. The move was accomplished with six C-130 transport planes carrying the most critical equipment and supplies for the hospital, with convoys involving 60 five-ton trucks hauling the less essential gear. We had moved everything into place at the new hospital on time, but its opening was delayed by a week due to problems with electricity and plumbing. Luckily, there were no mass casualty events during that interval.

Ours was a very different type of move from that of a Viet Cong unit's makeshift hospital threatened by American forces. As described in Max Hastings' *Vietnam*, "a long column of fighters, porters, and medical staff set forth, carrying the sick and wounded on stretchers, together with as many medical supplies as they could hump." Dr. Đặng Thuỳ Trâm described the evacuation: "We trudge up the hill, sweat pouring down our faces, not daring to pause to rest. We are so exhausted I have to cajole some men to return and bring out the last three stretchers.... If we have to leave this place, when can we enjoy such treatment facilities again?"[7]

Many years later, I learned that the father of one of my Vietnamese friends—Ngụy Khanh, a leading environmentalist for whose NGO Nancy volunteered when we lived in Hanoi—had worked as a nurse in one of these Viet Cong field hospitals near Bien Hoa, the site of the largest American base.

In contrast to the horrors and hardships suffered by the Viet Cong and NVA and our own field troops, a lot of my time was spent in boredom, loneliness, and misbehavior. Days were marked by the malodorous "burning of the shitters" each morning, in which 55-gallon drums with their accumulated feces and urine were torched with diesel fuel.

Another constant, remembered by so many Vietnam veterans, was the "thunk-thunk-thunk" of helicopter rotor blades overhead. This soundtrack figures famously in the "Ride of the Valkyries" scene in *Apocalypse Now* (Robert Duvall's Lt. Col. Kilgore: "I love the smell of napalm in the morning!") and can be frequently heard on the audio tapes I recorded for Nancy. I still immediately think of Vietnam when I hear a helicopter above, even if it is just there to give traffic reports.

I had a good group of enlisted Marines in the battalion supply unit. We passed the time and tried to do our jobs. We played volleyball and football with the motor transport guys in the often-muddy yard behind our office. Once, I reported to Nancy that I was exhausted after six volleyball games, "but not too tired to lift the beer can." Another time, after a spirited tug of war between the Marines of supply and motor transport, the enlisted men threw motor T officer Tom Sweeney and me into a water trailer filled with ice and beer. On these and other occasions, I drank with the men, which I shouldn't have done. This led to some awkward and embarrassing moments. At one party, I was quite drunk and got into conversations in which some men complained about the supply sergeant and others in the unit. Afterwards, the supply sergeant, a longtime Marine veteran, told me in no uncertain terms that it was inappropriate for an officer to behave in this way with the enlisted men. I was chastened and tried to take his advice to heart but it did not stop my drinking.

As I had always known and was in fact proud of, I was not a model Marine officer. At one point, Nancy asked "Are you turning into a hard-nosed Marine lieutenant?" This was hardly the case: "I'm not very good at issuing orders or handling troops," I wrote. And again, "I guess I'm supposed to feel and act superior to them—but I can't. To some extent, I'm afraid of them. I'd just like to be buddies with them except I have to be the boss and can't get too familiar—the system, of course; I hate it."

In April, after I conducted an inspection that found many of the troops with filthy weapons—one had a pistol covered with rust and another had a spider web in his rifle barrel—I reported to Nancy: "Boy, did I chew them out. Are you kidding? All I could do was laugh." Once in a while, I felt that I was learning something from my relationships with the troops. I wrote to Nancy that

> It's a real education learning to deal with these kids—in a way it's rewarding. I hate it here just like everybody else and as often as I think it's all a complete waste—from the point of view of learning about people and broadening my experience—it can be an interesting and challenging job.

When our commanding officer sent a harsh message to the commander of the supply center in Danang complaining of inadequate provision of ordered medical supplies, the resulting brouhaha was more about a violation of the chain of command than about the substance of the problem. I wrote to Nancy that "the petty politics involved in the higher ranks are shocking—they seem to care more about their personal reputations than about the welfare of their men."

As a collateral duty, I served as defense counsel on several courts martial. One case involved three enlisted Marines from the motor transport section who went into a "vil" in search of female companionship. Once these Marines had completed their business, they tried to hitchhike back to the base and, when nobody would stop, one of them fired off several rounds at an Army jeep, blowing out a tire. Other cases were brought against a Marine who pulled a loaded .45 pistol on another Marine and a Marine who got drunk and totaled an ambulance, luckily empty at the time. The "fragging" of officers and NCOs was just beginning towards the end of my tour. In fact, one of my friends had to return to Vietnam to testify in a court martial for a fragging incident.

I reported to Nancy that

> this outfit is so screwed up … morale is at an all-time low. There is absolutely no discipline. On New Year's Eve, one of my men got drunk and went out of his mind—telling everybody he was going to commit suicide.… The commanding officer has no idea what's going on and consequently nothing is done.

A "hard-nosed Marine lieutenant": Quang Tri, 1968.

In my disaffection, I was more an observer of the poor morale than someone committed to trying to improve it. Two months later, I wrote that "I won't have to play Marine much longer."

Late in 1968, I was summoned to meet General Leonard Chapman, Commandant of the Marine Corps, who was visiting Vietnam and wanted to meet Marine officers whose fathers had also been Marine officers. We waited in the blistering sun outside the briefing room for about two hours. Finally,

Meeting the Commandant, 1968.

Chapman came out and greeted us individually as we stood in a line at attention. When he got to me, he said that he'd known my father very well. "As if he'd even seen him," I wrote to Nancy, "It was so fake it was ridiculous."

Our supply unit's performance received some criticisms in a Commanding General's inspection, many of which I thought unfounded and trivial in that they focused more on the completeness of our paperwork and record keeping than on the quality of our supply support to the battalion. We passed the embarkation portion of the inspection, but only because I fabricated all the form entries the night before.

A few months before my departure, I received a "marginal" fitness report "with unfavorable comments" based primarily on the episode of the stolen mattresses in Danang and an alleged lack of initiative in addressing critical supply shortages. I told Nancy that "It hurt my pride a little bit. I didn't agree with the war and still don't; I didn't like military life and still don't. I came over here with the idea that, regardless of these feelings, I would do the best job I could." Tom Sweeney and I jokingly considered writing each other up for medals, but we never did. Obviously, I didn't get a medal; I don't know if Tom did.

While I disagreed with my fitness report, in retrospect I must own my disaffection and its detrimental effect on my performance. I wrote a three-page rebuttal and received a call from a Division staff officer saying that the Commanding General was concerned about my fitness report and asking if I wanted a transfer. I declined in view of the short time remaining in my tour but felt gratified that the Division had taken an interest. I was "never comfortable" with military life, I wrote to Nancy, and "I feel like a fool now for even trying to conform and do a good job if this is my reward."

With typical ambivalence, I was proud of my contrarian attitudes but didn't dare express them too openly. At some level, I was also ashamed and tried to do better in my job. When Navy enlisted men failed to salute me or speak to me respectfully, I wondered to Nancy "why do I care? I shouldn't because I hate the military, but somehow I do care." We need discipline in order to operate effectively and get things done, I said.

Nevertheless, my immediate superiors were not convinced of my dedication and my ability to perform my duties well. I guess I was ultimately unable to conceal my disillusionment and disaffection with the war and military life. Even my peers could see this. Soon after he arrived, my replacement told me "I'm fucked because of the job you've done." While I didn't entirely agree with him about the quality of my work, I clearly did have a bad attitude.

3

Being Apart

About halfway through my tour, Nancy sent me a recording of Jefferson Airplane's "Today" from *Surrealistic Pillow*. We had first seen the Airplane at the Unicorn Coffee House in Boston and this song had become "our song."[1] Earlier, she had sent me a "partial list, composed in a dull Econ. Meeting, of times when I love you the most." These included "when you remember the same Jefferson Airplane song (and the same Sunday morning) that I do." (Re-reading this list several times in recent days has brought me to tears.) I shared Nancy's recollection that something really had happened that Sunday morning—not a thunderclap but the culmination of a "gradual, easy, falling into something natural—something you suspected was there, and then was there." In the words of our song: "With you standing here, I could tell the world what it means to love…. It's taken so long to come true." Those feelings, I said, stood in sharp "contrast to the uselessness and senselessness of this over here."[2]

I purchased small reel-to-reel tape recorders for Nancy and me when I was in Okinawa for Embarkation School in May 1968. Our audiotapes and letters enrich my memories of being apart from Nancy in Vietnam and how much her emotional presence helped me to get through it. Vietnamese people, like Eric Nguyen's fictional Hương, who fled their country after the war also used audiotapes in an effort maintain connection with loved ones who stayed behind.[3]

In my first letter to Nancy from Okinawa before I even got to Vietnam, I apologized:

> I'm sorry I haven't written. I've tried to start so many times. If I write to you or think about you (which I do constantly, anyway) or look at your pictures, it only makes me miss you about 10 times more.

I wrote that I was "really lost" without her. In April, in response to one of Nancy's expressions of uncertainty:

> Don't use so many question marks. Please don't think I'll ever forget you because I won't—or that I'll ever not love you because I won't—or that I'm

not sitting here thinking about you 1000% of the time because I am—or that it won't be the happiest day of my life when I see you again—because it will. [These are among] the few certainties.

And later that month:

What memories! That's what I thrive on over here. I have been thinking recently about spring and all the wonderful things that happen—Rockport, 31 BVP, gin and tonics, the Sprints [crew races on Lake Quinsigamond in Worcester], the Fly Club Garden Party, *Sgt. Pepper's Lonely Hearts Club Band*. I'm living on memories and visions of the future, which make for hours of blissful daydreaming.

In my first audiotape to Nancy in May, lamenting that "I haven't talked to you in three months," I said we "have to start from scratch." Later in that first tape, I apologized "if I sound awkward and strained. I'm trying to sound natural, but it isn't natural." (This was a bit like concerns about the quality of Zoom meetings during the Covid-19 pandemic.) In a May letter, I noted the "very sad but very happy connotation of our memories—it all seems so far away but it gives me something to look forward to." In July, Nancy wrote to me that "writing is so unsatisfactory. I want you here where I can fuss over you and watch you shave in the morning and watch Johnny [Carson] with you at night."

Nancy: A picture posted in my hooch.

I replied that "Your letters are so beautiful. I love every one of them. It's sad and wonderful at the same time." The next month, I worried that "I'm having a hard time expressing myself. I have to start thinking again. I'm afraid I will lose myself. But I just have to get through. And knowing what I have to look forward to I know I will." In September, I wrote that "I want to go home and have it be like March 13—one day after I left but a year later. I just don't want your feelings to change. I know mine haven't. There are momentary joys and laughs—but nothing lasting without you." I was like the RAF "Bomber Boys" who war correspondent Martha Gellhorn wrote "want a future that is as good as they now imagine the past to have been."[4]

In September 1968, Nancy moved to Madison to start a PhD program in economics at the University of Wisconsin. I didn't hear from her for a few weeks and I was worried. But then I was very relieved to get her first tape from Madison. "The worst thing was that I didn't even know your address or where you are and what you're doing." A lot of U.S. troops received "Dear John Letters" while they were in Vietnam. These often came as horrible shocks, as was the case with Marine W.D. Ehrhart. Nancy never sent me one of those. She did date a few other guys in my absence, but she stuck with me, for which I am grateful.

In November, Nancy asked:

> Any chance you can come [home] a little sooner (like tomorrow)? I think I deserve it. That's the only thing I ask of God—he has enough solders fighting his battles in Vietnam, but I have to wait. Why the hell did you join the Marines in the first place? Why couldn't you stay home with me where you belong?

As the Kinks would sing in "Australia," I went on "holiday" (R&R) to Sydney, arriving there the sunny morning of Christmas 1968. I had told Nancy that I would miss her on Christmas and "I'll be thinking about you the whole day." I had a wonderful time with the welcoming and fun-loving Aussies and had a few purely platonic dates, but I was thinking of Nancy constantly: "It was funny being in a hotel without you. I missed you every night so much." I telephoned Nancy from Sydney, which was "very emotional," and bought her a kangaroo coat for Christmas and her birthday, which are three days apart. I couldn't afford to send the coat by air, so I had to wait for her to receive it by surface shipment more than a month later. It fit her perfectly. As my tour wound down in January and February 1969:

> These last days are so hard—so slow—all I can do is watch the clock and calendar and [they] never seem to move" [and] It's hard to write any more letters; all I want to say is I want to come home, I want to come home [and] just be with you for always and sleep until noon with you and laugh with you and listen to music turned up as far as it will go with nobody complaining—all the things that I remember and want so much again.

Nancy also wrote about home:

> I keep thinking about going home. And it's not home with my parents or my room at school or any office or any real place that I'm picturing. I keep

imagining some apartment that you and I live in and I think of that as home. I feel a little out of place everywhere I go.

I suggested "Let's get married the day I get home"—a nice but impossible idea. Anyway, my parents' getting married a week after my father's return from World War II had not worked out so well. In an August tape, I had predicted that "we'll have to get to know each other again" but concluded that "It's all going to be fine." On March 30, 1969, a week before leaving Vietnam, I wrote: "At last, at last, is all I can say."

4

The Politics of the War

After one night of mass casualties arriving at our hospital, I wrote that "they had a kid die right in triage. It was just horrible. It's all so completely senseless. It's just insane—it has to be stopped." I circulated a Eugene McCarthy chain letter sent to me by my mother and was pleased to see a Navy doctor wearing a McCarthy button on his jungle utilities. After an Australian USO show, I joined one of the Navy doctors, who I thought was a "decent guitar player," to sing several "rather bitter anti-war songs."

Nineteen-sixty-eight was one of the most tumultuous years in American history. I did not experience the tumult directly because I spent almost all of that year in the place that occasioned much of it. When I arrived in Vietnam in March 1968 the war was raging in-country and the anti-war movement was raging at home. My father dutifully wrote to me every week while I was in Vietnam, including the news that I had received a draft notice in the mail. We continued our political repartee by letter, and he kept me informed of his unfavorable views of McCarthy's supporters and the Poor Peoples' Campaign. After my father took a business trip to Cambridge, I expressed hope that "you were not accosted by any persons of radical persuasion." Rereading these letters now, I am struck by their amicability and good humor, even though I stuck to my antiwar arguments. Maybe I had repressed my anger at his pressuring me to join and stay in the Marine Corps. If so, these feelings would reappear later in my life.

I went to Vietnam just hoping to survive, physically and psychologically, and to avoid getting anyone else killed, whether Vietnamese or American. I didn't join any antiwar groups or participate in any demonstrations. I was happy for my Harvard friend Warren Bowes who was able to get a 1-Y classification that exempted him from military service: "the military is so ridiculous—nobody should have to come into it—I'm only sorry I was stupid enough to." I also expressed hope that my roommate John Ballard would be able to stay out of the service: "Nobody belongs here."

I just wanted to fly under the radar. In my first letter to Nancy from Phu Bai, I wrote that

being here makes many political arguments seem irrelevant. When I get settled, maybe I'll be able to be more objective. I still have my views, of course—
they haven't changed yet—but I just want to see as much as I can so when I
come home, I'll have some experience to base my opinions on.

I was very lucky in my duty assignment as a supply officer, which spared
me any real danger as well as any need to kill any Vietnamese or be responsible for the loss of any Marines. I remained against the war and increasingly convinced that it was a tragic waste of lives and treasure on both
sides. Following the Tet offensive, despite disproportionate losses among
the Viet Cong and NVA, it was clear that the highly respected TV news
anchor Walter Cronkite was right—it was a "stalemate" in which the other
side was far more willing to outlast us than we were to outlast them.

Many years later, I attended a reunion of my Basic School class, which
included a tour of several Civil War battlefields. At the site of repeated
Union attacks during the Battle of Chancellorsville in 1863, our guide pronounced what could also be an epitaph for the war in Vietnam, except
with a much larger number: "18,000 casualties, nothing gained."

In *Dispatches*, one of the very best books on the Vietnam War from
the perspective of American combat troops, Michael Herr wrote of the Tet
Offensive and its aftermath:

> Vietnam was a dark room full of deadly objects, the VC were everywhere all at
> once like spider cancer, and instead of losing the war in little pieces over years
> we lost it fast in under a week. After that, we were like the character in the pop
> grunt mythology, dead but too dumb to lie down. Our worst dread of yellow
> peril became realized; we saw them now dying by the thousands all over the
> country, yet they didn't seem depleted, let alone exhausted....[1]

Combat veteran Bruce Weigl's poem about Tet begins with these evocative lines:

> Year of the monkey, year of the human wave,
> the people smuggled weapons in caskets through the city
> in long processions undisturbed
> and buried them in Saigon graveyards.[2]

Soon after arriving in-country, I wrote to my mother about American
jets, dragonships, and assault helicopters hammering "suspected enemy
positions" about five miles from our base perimeter. I marveled that, being
constantly assaulted with

> such superior firepower [and] sophisticated weaponry, these people have been
> able to fight us so successfully for so long. I think it really says something for
> their courage and determination. The only good thing about [that nighttime
> air barrage] is that it might have saved us from getting hit with rockets.

Like many, I was surprised when Lyndon Johnson announced on
March 31, 1968, that he would not seek another term as president. He also

declared a halt to the bombing of North Vietnam and a willingness to enter peace talks with North Vietnam. Of course, it would be five more long years before there was a peace settlement. Even then, it was not really a peace settlement but rather a final exit strategy for the U.S., contingent only on release of our POWs and preservation of a "decent interval" before South Vietnam collapsed, and the Vietnamese people unified their country. More than 20,000 Americans died between 1969 and 1975 in service of this, apparently Nixon's "secret plan" to end the war. And it was implemented after he was elected president with the help of what we now know was a treasonous conspiracy to prevent South Vietnam coming to the peace table in November 1968. Unaware of this at the time, of course, I wrote to my mother just after the election, "if only Saigon would join the talks—they could very easily ruin everything with their pig-headedness."

Meanwhile, the war went on, and with particular savagery in Northern I Corps. Even after the April 1968 relief of Khe Sanh Combat Base—where almost 300 Marines lost their lives and 2,500 hundred more were wounded to hold it against three months of relentless North Vietnamese Army artillery and rocket attacks—the suffering of the troops that had been there did not end. One unit that had been at Khe Sanh for four months was flown to Quang Tri to spend several days in relative comfort on what was to be 3rd Medical Battalion's new compound. However, the compound was hit with rockets the first night the unit was there, killing six Marines. I wrote to Nancy that "these kids—dog tired, filthy, finally after interminable danger and suffering get to a place where they think they are safe at last and they lie down for their first good night's sleep—and boom! They get hit. It's just horrible."

In May 1968, a battalion of the 4th Marines was decimated in a three-day series of battles around Dai Do, near Dong Ha. Carl Gibson, one of the platoon commanders in the 2nd battalion, 4th Marines and a Basic School classmate of mine, was killed at Dai Do after only ten days in-country. Later that month I wrote to Nancy after learning that two of my Basic School classmates were already dead, "most people get mad [at the enemy] when their friends get killed—I'm just the opposite—I just want to see the thing end and see people stop getting killed and maimed."

On May 21, Raymond Davis took over as Commanding General of the 3rd Marine Division from General Rathvon Tompkins, who was considered too passive. Davis ordered more aggressive mobile operations, some of which were successful, but some of which also resulted in chaotic and bloody ambushes and encounters and costly NVA assaults on remote outposts just south of the DMZ. We frequently saw the fruits of this strategy in the triage room of our hospital at Quang Tri.

I followed the news from home of assassinations, riots, and turmoil in the streets. Martin Luther King was killed soon after I got to Phu Bai and I overheard several white Marines cheering this terrible event. A battalion party was postponed for the official day of mourning, but I was disgusted to hear several white Marines say that the party should go ahead to celebrate King's death. Robert Kennedy, who probably would have been the strongest antiwar presidential candidate, was assassinated while I was in Okinawa for embarkation school. I recall at least several fellow Marine officers exulting at this news over drinks in the Officers Club. I confessed to Nancy that "I allow my own personal sorrows [about having to be in Vietnam and apart from her] to somehow overshadow something really horrible like that. What the hell is happening, anyway? What a screwed-up world. God!"

It was the time when the Black Power movement appeared among enlisted troops in Vietnam. I began to see the clenched fist salutes and Black Marines aggressively cutting in front of white Marines in the mess hall line. Once, we had a USO show that ended with "God Bless America" and everybody stood up, but a group of about 20 Black Marines raised their clenched fists. I wrote to Nancy that "everybody thought it was in poor taste, but I thought it was quite impressive." At the time, I did not recognize, let alone acknowledge my own racism, but I tried to describe the racism I saw among the troops (I acknowledge the antiquated terminology, which I would not use today):

> Most of the whites can be good buddies with Negroes when they're working together or fighting together but let them get out of the Negroes' presence and the comments start. The same old stuff. A lot of the white Marines do have many Negro friends, but that friendship is a very narrow, individual type. It's not extended to the race as a whole. They just can't seem to make the connection. No matter how many outstanding Negroes they meet, they still feel the race in general is somehow "inferior."

On occasion, particularly after having a few too many drinks—a not uncommon event—I would get into arguments about the war and other issues. Most of the Navy doctors were, I suspect, at least skeptical about if not overtly against the war. A few were, however, rabid supporters. Sometimes, the battalion psychiatrist, a soft-spoken Georgian with whom I wished I had kept in touch in later years, would be an ally. We had many lively political discussions and arguments about the South. I jokingly wrote to my father that in one of my discussions with Steve, "you will be happy to hear that he accused me of 'sloppy thinking' [one of my father's frequent jabs at me].... I think you would like this guy. He seems to believe in property rights."

Usually, I was on my own in arguments about the war, however. On the 4th of July and later that summer during the Democratic National

Convention in Chicago, when Mayor Daley's cops engaged in a "police riot" against antiwar demonstrators, I got into it hotly with one of the pro-war doctors. We had previously argued over gun control legislation and he, as I reported to my father, had "denounced me as a hippie, among other things—I was very flattered." On the night of July 4, I stood on a bunker outside this doctor's hooch watching a "fireworks" display by an artillery battery and began sarcastically singing "America the Beautiful," to which he took angry exception. In the exchange that followed, his main message was that "you've got a lot to learn, buddy." So did he, apparently.

Later we clashed again when he opined that the Chicago police had in fact shown remarkable restraint in dealing with the violent and traitorous demonstrators outside the Democratic convention. In September, during my "wetting down" party for making 1st lieutenant, we staged a mock presidential election and, when I voted for McCarthy, everyone "booed and cursed lustily." In a September tape, I told Nancy that the time is "long, long overdue" for the U.S. to get out of Vietnam. I also commented on George Wallace's candidacy, cleverly appealing to Americans' "basest instincts and hatreds." (In retrospect, it is noteworthy how much Donald Trump's campaign resembled Wallace's.)

My own Marine hooch-mates seemed either agnostic about the war or didn't betray their views. Neither did they seek mine. My predecessor as supply officer had received a Purple Heart for a wound suffered in Hue during Tet and was too "short" (close to the end of his tour) to care much for political discussion during our one-month overlap period. We mainly talked about the handover of the job. Roland Ames, the motor transport officer, was a smart guy and quite a character with whom I had some interesting conversations about books but not, as I recall, about the war. He went on to a long career as a military historian and teaches a university course called "The Meaning of Vietnam." Ames appeared in several war memoirs by John Parrish.[3] Parrish, a 3rd Medical Battalion doctor who served in Phu Bai, Dong Ha, and with Marine infantry units in the field, went through a period of PTSD, became a noted physician at Massachusetts General Hospital in Boston, and helped to found an organization supporting "wounded warriors" of later American wars in Iraq and Afghanistan.

It was similar with my hooch-mates after we moved to Quang Tri: Tom Sweeney, who took over from Roland Ames as motor transport officer, and Andy Richards, who had been a platoon commander with 4th Marines and then became 3rd Medical Battalion's intelligence officer. We bantered and drank, and drank and bantered, about various things—girls, "the World [U.S. troops' slang term for where we would return at the end of our tours]," R&R—but rarely if ever about the war. Like most, perhaps, they had become skeptical about the war or were, at least, confused about its objectives and their achievability or value. But mainly, like me, they just wanted to mark off the days and go home.

Out of the blue, I received a letter from Tom Sweeney when I was living in Hanoi in 2009. Tom wrote that his son-in-law had researched my name on the Internet. Tom wondered if I was the same Ted Hammett who had served with him in the 3rd Marine Division in Vietnam in 1968–1969. I was briefly in touch with Tom by email, learning that after his time in the Marine Corps he went on to a long career as a high school football coach in California. Shortly after I reconnected with Tom, however, his wife wrote to tell me that he had died of cancer. I never saw Tom or Andy Richards after leaving Quang Tri.

While in-country, my opposition to the war was not unalloyed. After LBJ announced a halt to the bombing in North Vietnam in March 1968, I wrote to my mother that "It's very hard because if the North Vietnamese do use it to their advantage it places our people here in much graver danger." Still, "I hope it is a risk that will pay off." When a further bombing halt was announced by Johnson in November 1968, I confessed again to mixed feelings. I wrote to Nancy that

> it is funny, though, when you're over here you aren't quite as anxious to see the bombing stopped because, if it turns out that the North Vietnamese don't really want to talk but merely want the chance to move up more supplies then we all may get hit harder and more frequently—it may just make it that much more difficult for the people in the field…. Over here, you realize a lot more clearly how much of a risk in terms of lives it is to stop the bombing.

David Halberstam paraphrased LBJ's more crudely stated concern: "I'll tell you what happens when there's a bombing halt: I halt and then Ho Chi Minh shoves his trucks right up my ass."[4] Still, I again concluded that "I think it's a risk that probably has to be taken in the hope that some settlement may result."

Of course, plenty of bombing continued in South Vietnam after November 1968. We could feel the ground under us tremble for several minutes as fearsome B-52 "Arc-lite" carpet bombing strikes occurred some distance away. I remember standing on a bunker watching the jet fighters working a few miles off our perimeter and joining my compatriots in yelling "get some!" as we saw the explosions. They may well have been killing innocent civilians, even women and children, but in our minds, they were also protecting us from rocket attacks and helping to ensure that we safely saw the ends of our tours.

As I grew shorter and shorter, I longed for home and my reunion with Nancy, who was involved in antiwar and related political activities in Madison. She may have appeared in the crowd scenes in *The War at*

Home, a documentary film about Madison in those years. It was a turbulent time. Nancy's former views were being challenged and she was changing. In February, she told me that "this whole year has been an identity crisis. I feel a lot more militant." In response, I sadly commented:

> My views haven't changed—but I feel out of it. I get your tapes about political issues, lectures, movies, plays—nothing like that here. I don't know if I can even engage you in intelligent conversation—you're so excited about what you're doing. I have nothing to be excited about—except coming home.

I voiced some criticisms of the antiwar movement in the U.S., who I thought sometimes

> overemphasize the loss of Vietnamese lives and do not mention enough the tragedy of so many of our own people dying over here. Of course, it's horrible when the Vietnamese die but just as tragic, I think, is the plight of Americans.

A former antiwar activist admitted that "we were naïve. We idolized the 'noble Vietnamese.' ... If America was wrong, then they *must* be right."[5]

I had voted, reluctantly, for Hubert Humphrey in my first exercise of the franchise. I thought he had shown at least some willingness to move away from LBJ's war policy. To me, the New Left's opposition to the war was justified but I sometimes quarreled with their methods—such as taking over buildings or shouting down opposing voices. Perhaps naively, I believed that polite behavior might be enough to end the war. In Madison, Nancy joined the Union of Radical Political Economists, supported a student strike in support of Black students, and used the economics discussion sections she taught to consider their demands. In a February tape, I told Nancy that "I've missed a lot of changing political philosophy since I've been here—you'll have to take me by the hand" and help me understand these changes. I longed to discuss with her the arguments pro and con on violence and disruption, conflicts of rights and whose rights take precedence, and when violence is justified. "I'm considered the radical of the outfit here," I wrote, but I will seem like an "old fogey" there.

5

The Vietnamese People

I am ashamed to admit that I did participate in mistreatment of Vietnamese people. I didn't shoot any civilians (or anyone, for that matter) or burn any villages. In Bruce Weigl's possibly autobiographical poem, a soldier mutely watched a driver bludgeon an old Vietnamese woman with his M16:

> I have no excuse for myself.
> I sat in that man's jeep in the rain
> and watched him slam her to her knees.[1]

My acts were a bit more prosaic but nonetheless cruel and thoughtless. On helicopter rides, we sometimes strafed, without shooting, farmers working in rice fields and we (and I) laughed to see the terrified faces below. To Vietnamese people, helicopter attacks were particularly "'terrifying' because they were so intimate, flying low enough that 'I even saw the face of the door gunner.'"[2] We (and I) also deliberately splattered Vietnamese people with mud as we drove by them in our trucks and jeeps. "I have no excuse for myself." At the bottom of one letter to Nancy, I wrote simply: "Vietnam sucks."

During my first tour, I knew little about the Vietnamese people and didn't care to learn any more. Although I opposed the war and should have sympathized with the plight of the people on both sides who were being victimized by the Americans, I came to hate and casually mistreat these people whom we were supposed to be helping. I don't remember whether I ever actually referred to any Vietnamese people as "gooks," but my thoughts were certainly in that racist vein. Troops in the field saw their buddies killed by the Viet Cong and NVA and most felt that the ARVN were cowardly or corrupt or both. Karl Marlantes powerfully describes his own dehumanization of the Vietnamese enemy: "I didn't kill people, sons, brothers, fathers. I killed 'Crispy Critters.' This ... is a kind of pseudospeciation. You make a false species out of the other human and therefore make it easier to kill him."[3] Rodger Jacobs' letters home frequently relate his avidity, even joy, in killing "gooks." In his inter-letter commentary, Jacobs says that without this correspondence with his parents, "the savagery of war would have overtaken me right away." Those who did not get mail succumbed to that savagery sooner, but ultimately it "got us all."[4] Grunts like Marlantes and Jacobs had much more reason to hate the Vietnamese than I did, with my safe job in the rear.

I wrote to Nancy that most Americans think the Vietnamese are "untrustworthy, dirty, uncivilized and generally good for nothing. I don't know why we are fighting for them or fighting them or whatever we're doing in that case." To my mother, I wrote: "Most American troops dislike the Vietnamese, North and South, and just want to get their tours over with and go home." Wittingly or unwittingly, I shared these views. I felt the Vietnamese people were to blame for our wasting more than a year of our lives and, for many, risking our lives and being killed or wounded. I thought much less about the human and material ravages of the war on the Vietnamese people.

I did not have occasion to face the NVA or Viet Cong in combat. However, it was clear and often remarked upon by Americans who did see combat that their soldier foes, and the civilian populations behind them who lived under U.S. bombing, were remarkably determined and courageous. They suffered horrendously yet ever persevered against astronomical odds. Mary McCarthy, an outspoken critic of the war, observed these qualities during a visit to Hanoi in March 1968, just as I was arriving in South Vietnam. To the North Vietnamese,

> everything is now a symbol..., expressing the national resolve to overcome.... Growth statistics, offered everywhere, on bicycle ownership, irrigation, rice harvests, maternity clinics, literacy are the answer to the "the war of destruction," which began February 7, 1965,... [and] ... carrying a secondary meaning—defiance.

McCarthy also described the nationalism underlying Vietnamese resolve: the people's

> root-attachment to ... the sacred, indivisible unity of the fatherland ... going deeper than politics, into some sphere of immanence the foreigner is almost embarrassed to name.[5]

Although I disliked the Vietnamese, I too occasionally marveled at their strength. Taking a ride into Hue about three weeks after the battle there had ended, I found a city in virtually complete devastation with the people picking among the rubble and ruin for something to sustain them. In the face of this misery, I wrote to my mother, the residents seemed exceptionally "brave and cheerful." In general, too, I thought the Vietnamese kids we encountered along the roads and in the villages were "adorable." "They have so little," I wrote, but "they are so cheerful and funny, always clowning around and trying to hug you." There may, of course, have been ulterior motives but I was, perhaps naively, reluctant to see such designs in the kids. And I never experienced any hostile acts from children, as some American troops did.

While unintended, the terms I used to describe Vietnamese people during the war seem retrospectively to fall into the romanticized "noble savage" and "poverty porn" framing of poor, foreign communities often used by and for Western audiences, tourists, and donors. The use of such descriptors, however meant, is receiving increasingly sharp scrutiny in current efforts to confront and overcome anti–Asian racism.

I didn't learn Vietnamese and had no interest in doing so. I and most of my colleagues mastered only a few pidgin Vietnamese phrases like "di di" ("go!" or "fuck off!") and slang words, some dating back to the Korean War or World War II and the occupation of Japan: "numbah one" (the best), "numbah 10" (the worst), "mamasan"/ "papasan" (old woman/man), "beaucoup" (from the French War), and of course the ubiquitous racist slurs: "gook" (a supposed descendent of a derisive Korean word for "people"), "slope," "slant," "zip," and "dink." According to Philip Beidler, such pan-Asian terms suggest that "One Asian war ... came to look like just another Asian war. One Asian people ... came to look like any other Asian people."[6] Conflation of Asian groups continues to this day. Vietnamese people in the U.S. complain that white Americans, even intending to be cheerful and friendly, often greet them with "ni hao." Of course, the lumping together of all Asians as somehow responsible for the Covid-19 pandemic can have even more dangerous outcomes.

I never had any real interaction with Vietnamese people. Some Americans, particularly those who served as advisors to ARVN units or worked directly with the South Vietnamese government, did have the chance to meet and know more Vietnamese people. However, as aptly put by Max Hastings in his 2018 history of the war, "...the vast majority of the three million Americans who ... served in the country departed without holding any more meaningful interaction with its inhabitants than a haggle about the price of sex."[7] The fact that I didn't even have that experience by no means diminishes the dehumanization, fetishization, and sexual exploitation by American troops of Vietnamese women during the war and by all manner of Westerners of Asian women and other women of color in wars and colonial occupations through history.

Shortly after the first Marine combat units arrived in Vietnam, the Southeast Asia Religious Project was initiated at the request of the Commanding General of Fleet Marine Force, Pacific. This project produced a set of materials, first disseminated in 1967, on Vietnamese religion and culture that was intended to be conveyed to American troops being deployed to Vietnam. The materials covered the major strands of Vietnamese spirituality and the cultural principles associated with them. The cover letter from the Navy Chief of Chaplains made the important point that "lack of information ... about the religious and value systems of a host country ... can create alienation of local peoples, decrease in security, and a potential increase in casualties."[8]

It seems clear that few if any American troops in Vietnam ever received any training on these matters. I know I never did. The results were predictable. American troops knew little if anything about Vietnam, its people, culture, or history: According to Max Hastings, "The main thing those Americans who really knew about Vietnam knew was how little they knew."[9] This lacuna has remained ever since. Afghanistan veteran Erik Edstrom writes of a worse than useless "cultural sensitivity training" he attended before deploying. It was led by a sergeant whose principal message was "You can't treat 'em like people 'cause they're not." As during the Vietnam War, the more nuanced written material was ignored and untaught.[10]

American policy makers displayed a similar ignorance or blindness, as effectively shown by Frances Fitzgerald in *Fire in the Lake*.[11] For example, if we had known of and considered Vietnam's ancient enmity with China, would we have assumed that a North Vietnamese victory would lead inevitably to Chinese domination of Southeast Asia and beyond? Philip Beidler points out that McCarthy-era purges had deprived the State Department of many Asia experts who might have been able to demonstrate the fallacy of this view and more broadly attune U.S. policy to Vietnamese history and culture.[12]

The Southeast Asia Religious Project's materials include this statement, which is intended to educate American troops about the cultural differences between the U.S. and Vietnam, but which also employs what would today be considered "othering" language:

> worship of the land ... tended to create in the Vietnamese peasant an almost fanatical attachment to his birthplace which nourished him during life and becomes his grave after death. It is the combination of worship of the land and ancestor veneration which creates the ... numberless graves ... scattered throughout the farming areas of Vietnam.[13]

If the U.S. leadership and its troops had understood and respected the Vietnamese people's weddedness to the native soil of their home villages and the burial sites of their ancestors, would we have implemented large-scale forced resettlement programs and then been surprised at the hostility and opposition they evoked? Of course, white Americans have not exactly respected Native Americans' similar dedication to their sacred soil so this disregard in Vietnam followed an historic pattern.

An American officer famously capsulized the inevitable results of our war strategy when he told a reporter during the Tet Offensive that "we had to destroy this village in order to save it." One of the most moving such accounts is in Marine veteran Allen Glick's early novel of the war, describing the forcible evacuation and destruction of a village and the slaughter of its animals after it had in fact been at least temporarily saved from Viet Cong takeover by Marines and local militia in a bloody battle:

> Schrader was shaking with rage and shooting and smelling the blood and the animals shitting in fear. His hands were white and bloodless on the rifle and the animals kept dropping and the fires burning stronger, and Schrader was shaking badly, very, very badly, and he wanted to cry.[14]

W.D. Ehrhart described his unit's senseless destruction, just for the fun of it, of a small temple they came across during a patrol.[15] As a poet, Ehrhart spoke for many, many Vietnam veterans:

> We are the ones you sent to fight a war
> you did not know a thing about—
> those of us that lived
> have tried to tell you what went wrong.
> Now you think you do not have to listen.[16]

One "voice crying in the wilderness" as early as 1963 was the rookie foreign service officer Richard Holbrooke whose first posting was in the Mekong Delta of South Vietnam. According to George Packer, Holbrooke was not at that juncture ready to question the reasons for the U.S. presence in Vietnam—that would come later—but he clearly perceived the fatal flaws of our strategy in a war that did not yet have American combat units involved:

> We arrive here with no knowledge of the country or of the situation and we immediately start giving advice, some of which we can turn almost into orders because of the materials and money and transportation that we fully control. I think that no American would stand for such a deep and continuing interference in our affairs.

Furthermore, Holbrooke said, "'one division of Americans would clean this place up' is a common statement, and nothing could be more wrong: a division of Marines would be bled to death in the swamps and paddies here, and never make a dent against the VC."[17] Also, Americans never understood or appreciated the critical roles played by Vietnamese women in the war, as intelligence agents, couriers, carriers of supplies down the Ho Chi Minh Trail, and, yes, some as combat troops.[18]

In Robert Stone's novel *Dog Soldiers* (brought to the screen as *Who'll Stop the Rain* after Creedence Clearwater Revival's great song[19]), John Converse, an alienated journalist in Saigon, refers to Vietnam as "the place where everyone finds out who they are." "What a bummer for the gooks," comments Ray Hicks, whom Converse has hired to bring the war home to Berkeley in the form of a brick of pure heroin.[20] Hicks provides what historian Christian Appy terms a "witheringly sardonic" summary of the impact of the American war on the Vietnamese people.[21]

The only Vietnamese people I saw were the "house-mouse" who cleaned our hooch in Phu Bai and did our laundry (actually, we complained, lost or more likely stole a lot of it), and then disappeared into the probably VC-controlled countryside for the night, the vendors of (possibly adulterated or poisoned) warm soft drinks and beer, cigarettes, and chewing gum along village streets; the old ladies with their betel nut-blackened teeth squatting by the side of the road; the kids who always ran out to beg for candy (often very cute, but also potentially dangerous); and the hookers in front of their places of business in shanty towns outside American bases such as Danang's "Dogpatch." Farther South, many Americans frequented Vietnamese villages for sex and other goods and services but in Northern I Corps where I was stationed, this was more strictly forbidden and severely sanctioned. Once in a while, we would get a Viet Cong or North Vietnamese Army casualty or a wounded or sick civilian in our hospital, but these were normally dealt with by intelligence staff and interpreters in an effort to obtain useful information about the enemy and its plans.

So, in my first tour I viewed the Vietnamese variously as the reason for my misery, interested only in their own survival and ability to purloin anything of value from their ostensible protectors, and profoundly ungrateful, even hostile to the protection we were providing. My only countervailing views were the cuteness of the children and the courage and resilience of the people, including our enemies, in the face of almost incessant suffering and danger.

More clearly understood in the context of the origins, strategies and political context of the war, the attitudes and priorities of the Vietnamese were entirely understandable. And, as Americans, our attitudes and behavior towards them were racist, misguided, and insensitive. Moreover, those attitudes and behaviors were based, as we now more clearly understand, on systemic rather than simply individual racism.

To be fair, individual Americans serving in combat in Vietnam had every reason to be angry about their sufferings and plight and so their misplaced hatred and mistreatment of the Vietnamese is at least more understandable. In my case, I really had no danger to blame on the Vietnamese, only a wasted and unhappy 13 months away from my girlfriend and my pursuit of a career in history, so I had really had "no excuse" for my feelings and behaviors.

6

Culture from Home

Seated on the back steps of my hooch in Quang Tri with "a lot of stars and flares and a lot of enemy persons out there," I listened to the recording of Tom Rush's instrumental "Rockport Sunday" that Nancy had sent me. I attempted to capture in a poem the sound of Rush's guitar and our spontaneous drive to Rockport in June 1967. There is little in this poem worth noting or quoting, but here are a few lines (if I can even make them out now from my drunken scrawl of the time):

> And so the song begins again—over and over—lyric and rollicking—
> the range of notes bespeaks the range of emotions that I feel—
> in these days that sometimes drag in endless desperation—
> waiting for the day that will fulfill all this—
> that will make it all well again....
> the joy, the beauty, the almost insane happiness of a moment when all is what
> it cannot be and yet is—
> as we hold each other—
> as we look into each other's minds—
> and we hear the surf;
> the sun beats down and the moon beats down—
> and it is, really and truly, a Rockport Sunday.

The most indelible element of culture for me during my first tour in Vietnam was the music. And it was all about the music from home. I think almost all Vietnam veterans remember their songs and what they meant to us at the time, whatever we did and wherever we were—turning against the war, leaving home and going to war, being in Vietnam, returning home, living with what we had done or not done. As Philip Beidler wrote, "Now, as then, the war lives on in the music of the Nam ... the sound track of before, during, and after."[1] Doug Bradley and Craig Werner's book "*We Gotta Get Out of This Place*": *The Soundtrack of the Vietnam War* captures well the importance of music to Vietnam veterans and to the Vietnam War generation. Its title refers to a 1965 hit by the Animals that became an anthem of American troops in-country.[2] Admittedly, for an REMF like me, that song's plea paled in power to its title words being screamed almost verbatim by Marine grunt Ron Kovic as he lay alone on the battlefield, his body shattered by NVA gunfire, or later befouled by his own urine and feces after being maltreated and abused for months in the squalid Bronx VA Hospital.[3]

Many of us came to believe that our wartime had a unique intensity of feelings and a musical soundtrack of a quality and resonance unlikely to recur.[4] This may or may not be true. After all, our parents' generation felt the same way about their World War II soundtrack—Glenn Miller, Benny Goodman, the Andrews Sisters, et al. No doubt, veterans of Afghanistan and Iraq feel the same way about the music with which they went to war.[5]

America's 21st century has so for been a time of distant relatively small-scale but persistent military involvements and highly polarized and toxic domestic politics. Nitsuhe Abebe argued that the music of the U.S. in 2019 reflected an "oddly strong … in-the-moment consensus on how everyone is feeling these days, and it is not good." Abebe's proposed body of 25 songs "that matter right now" projects a

> very earnest, very serious desire to find the right reaction to a world that feels tense and high-stakes—an ambient conviction that music should be looking for ways to cope, ways to protect ourselves, moments of escape, hard reckonings with our collective responsibilities, ideas for how to make the world feel less brutal.[6]

Many of these qualities could apply equally well to the Vietnam War era, absent the millennial or post-millennial terminology. Not being of either of those generations and being unfamiliar with the artists and songs in Abebe's top 25, except for Bruce Springsteen's version of "Born in the U.S.A." from "Springsteen on Broadway," it is hard for me to judge the veracity of his argument. I do believe, however, that in the music of our generation, there was an affecting originality, innocence, and lack of pretention. Whether the songs of the Vietnam War era delivered a coherent message, revealed a peculiar intensity, were uniquely great or not, however, cannot diminish the depth of our feelings for the music of that time and during that time.

Indeed, my Vietnam soundtrack remains etched in my ears and mind. I and no doubt most other members of my generation could easily come up with our lists of 25 songs that really mattered. Some of the songs on my list seemed directly relevant to my times and places but others were just what I remember listening to in those times and places. Qualitatively, some were clearly great and have aged very well and some were pretty bad, but I remember and cherish them all the same.

Moreover, songs that I didn't even know of or listen to during my wartime but happened to have been recorded during that time have, by their simple contemporaneity, become intensely important to me now. These songs come from albums such as the 13th Floor Elevators' *Easter Every-where* (1967, with "I Had to Tell You"), Van Morrison's *Astral Weeks* (1968, including the title track, "Cyprus Avenue," and "Madame George"), and Fairport Convention's *What We Did on Our Holidays* (1968, with "Meet on the Ledge") and *Liege and Lief* (1969, including "Farewell, Farewell"). I have almost come to believe that I did in fact hear and love those songs back when they first came out. Oddly enough, as a teenager I had gotten very interested in my parents' World War II era music, almost developing a nostalgia for a time before I was even alive.

Many songs I am sure I do remember. At the time of my going to Vietnam in March 1968, there was Peter Paul and Mary's highly relevant "Leavin' on a Jet Plane,"[7] the Troggs' "Love Is All Around,"[8] Manfred Mann's "The Mighty Quinn" (written by Dylan as "Quinn the Eskimo") and, of course, The Doors' "Light My Fire." During my early months in Phu Bai and in Okinawa for Embarkation School, I listened to Aretha Franklin's "Think," Merilee Rush's "Angel of the Morning," Archie Bell and the Drells' "Tighten Up," and some lightweight "bubble-gum" songs like the Ohio Express's "Yummy, Yummy, Yummy (I Got Love in My Tummy)."

While in Okinawa in May, I recorded some songs from the radio and commented on them in a letter to Nancy, including "The Mighty Quinn," "Love Is All Around" ("which reminds me of our wonderful 3 weeks before I left"), and the Young Rascals' "A Beautiful Morning" ("which reminds me of 'Groovin' [on a Sunday Afternoon],' which reminds me of Cambridge in the spring, and you, of course, most of all.") Also evocative of that Cambridge spring of 1966 was the Lovin' Spoonful's "What a Day for a Daydream." WBZ radio in Boston included all these songs in a genre it labeled "springtime music." WBZ had a great lineup of DJs in the mid–1960s: Jefferson Kaye (who also did a weekly folk music program), "Juicy Brucie" Bradley, and especially Dick Summer's all-night "Night-light" show, with his recitations of "The Highwaymen"; his manufactured contention that the sandwich should be called the "Shrewsbury" because it was really invented by the Earl of Shrewsbury rather than the Duke of Sandwich; and his "Comedy Hour" from 3:00 to 4:00 a.m. On the comedy hour, Summer played World War II Marine veteran Jonathan Winters, among other greats.[9] My roommate John and I committed to memory many of these classic Winters routines—Maudie Frickert and the Wright Brothers, Football Game, Prison Scene, and Marine Corps (particularly relevant, as his father said when he enlisted: "Go get 'em, Tiger" and Jonathan sarcastically replied "Yeah, Dad, sure")—and repeated snatches of them at the appropriate moments of many real-life situations.

The 3rd Medical Battalion had its own rock 'n' roll band, "3rd Med's

Music Men," outfitted with instruments from Special Services. They played at parties in and outside the mess hall, depending on weather, and offered a typical assortment of party classics such as "Louie, Louie,"[10] "Shout," "Walkin' the Dog," "Twist and Shout," and, of course, "We Gotta Get Out of This Place."

Starting in the summer of 1968 and into early 1969, Nancy sent me several music tapes that I listened to constantly: "The beauty of the music brought me back" to cherished memories and a "way of feeling and thinking that I'd lost a lot of since I've been here." I apologized to her for requesting so many songs ("I know this is a lot, but I need to hear music"). The first tapes she sent included many of the songs I had requested, such as Cream's "Strange Brew" (from the album *Disraeli Gears*, that we had given to each other by mistake for Christmas 1967), folk songs by Judy Collins (Joni Mitchell's "Both Sides Now"[11]), Ian and Sylvia (Gordon Lightfoot's "Early Morning Rain"[12] and "You Were on My Mind"[13]), Buffy Sainte-Marie ("Universal Soldier"[14]), Steve Gillette ("Darcy Farrow"), and Tom Rush (Joni Mitchell's "The Urge for Going,"[15] "Joshua Gone Barbados," "No Regrets,"[16] and "Rockport 'Sunday'") that we had loved during our times together. Sometimes, she threw in songs she had recently heard but were not familiar to me. From her first months in Madison, she sent a few tracks from Jeff Beck's album *Truth*, which I didn't much like. Nancy was a little offended when I referred to it as "just noise" and suggested that she had included it as a "joke." I guess I *was* a bit out of it sitting there in Quang Tri.

Nancy included Dylan's "Subterranean Homesick Blues"[17] on one of the music tapes she sent. I loved playing it at high volume for my hooch-mates, who hated it and typically "stomped off" as soon as it started. The song provided the name for the Weathermen ("You don't need a weatherman to know which way the wind blows"), a splinter group of the Students for a Democratic Society (SDS) who engaged in violent acts of resistance in the late 1960s and early 1970s. Many years later, I noticed in the guest book at the museum on the site of Khe Sanh Combat Base an entry that consisted simply of this injunction from Dylan's song: "Don't follow leaders, watch the parking meters."

Listening to Tom Rush's "Rockport Sunday," and writing that poem about it, brought me some solace in addition to the warm memories "Nights like this I am sure—very sure—that it hasn't all gone. I feel sure I still have something—some feeling for beauty, some appreciation, some sensitivity left—amid all this confusion—amid all this bitterness and apprehension." Although I had expressed my gratitude to Nancy that she was "always there to listen to my stupid ideas," I don't know if I actually sent Nancy the tape of my "Rockport Sunday" poem then, or whether she's ever listened to it since. At the time, she kept asking for the poem. I had been drunk during the writing and the recording, and maybe I was too embarrassed for her to see or hear it.

Nancy and I attended a Tom Rush concert in May 2019, and I hoped he would play "Rockport Sunday" for us, but he didn't. Instead, he played a new instrumental called "Lullaby in E," which sounded to me quite a bit like the one we wanted to hear. At the meet and greet (and sell CDs) session after the concert, I almost—but didn't—tell Rush how much "Rockport Sunday" had meant to us and to remind him that I had made him tuna sandwiches (on toast) at Tommy's Lunch, back in my short-order cooking days when he was still playing at the Club 47. All these years later, at the age of 80, Rush has a wonderful weekly podcast of songs and stories called "Rockport Sundays."[18]

One of my favorite movies of that wartime, even though it didn't explicitly mention the war, was *The Graduate*, with its Simon and Garfunkel songs. Nancy and I saw it in Cambridge when it came out in 1967. While on R&R in Sydney at Christmas 1968, I saw it again *twice* and then particularly embraced the song "April, Come She Will," because that was the month I was to leave Vietnam.

Early 1969 brought the best music tapes of all from Nancy: the Beatles' "White Album" and Judy Collins's *Who Knows Where the Time Goes*. I remember very clearly another night sitting on the steps of my hooch simulating "field goals" by shooting pencil flares (miniature signaling flares meant for use in combat situations) over an electric wire between two poles, while listening to the Beatles' "While My Guitar Gently Weeps." The White Album includes other songs that immediately and sharply bring to mind that specific time and place whenever I have heard them since: "Back in the USSR," "The Continuing Story of Bungalow Bill," "Rocky Raccoon," "Happiness Is a Warm Gun" (maybe intended to be about Vietnam, at least in part), and "Blackbird."[19]

Nancy and I had both attended Judy Collins's December 1964 concert at Jordan Hall in Boston, although with other people, as also the Stones' Boston Garden concert in November 1965. I had also heard Collins at the Philadelphia Folk Festival the next summer. Her album *Who Knows Where the Time Goes* came out in late 1968. It included songs that had immediate meaning for me: Ian Tyson's "Someday Soon," Collins's own "My Father," and the title song by Fairport Convention's Sandy Denny. It is very evocative for me just to type out the titles of these songs on the page while listening to them. Collectively, the songs on *Who Knows Where the Time Goes* spark a wistfulness that I felt at the time and still feel about the experience of being lost and apart yet yearning for the great joy of coming home. The title song becomes particularly apt as I grow older but back then it also reminded me of what I was returning home to and for: "I am not alone,/ while my love is near me."[20] I was beginning to believe that, in the words of Denny's song, "I do not fear the time," and I was counting the days, as all short-timers did. My fill-in calendar depicted a Marine who was so short that his helmet virtually covered his body. I wrote to Nancy that "I don't know how I ever could have gotten through this without your tapes.... My buddies don't like my music but that's tough. It's 'ours' anyway.... I'm glad we both like loud music!"[21]

I tried to continue reading books while I was in Vietnam. I was already planning to go to graduate school in American history after I got out of the Marine Corps and so I wanted to keep up with history reading. At my request, Nancy and my mother sent me a bunch of books—mostly biographies of Woodrow Wilson and Theodore Roosevelt and straightforward political histories of the 1920s and 1930s. I also had a biography of John Reed, the kind of tragic cultural revolutionary or doomed romantic (as in J.D. Salinger, F. Scott Fitzgerald, Eugene O'Neill, and Thomas Wolfe) to whom I sometimes presumptuously compared myself. Reading Richard Hofstadter's *Anti-Intellectualism in American Life,* I wrote, "makes it more difficult to succumb to the military propaganda." I also asked my father to send me Barton Bernstein's *Towards a New Past,* a collection of essays by New Left historians, but he failed to do so—probably because he objected to the book's political stance. On one occasion, I wrote to Nancy that "reading is really a tremendous escape over here. I can just lose myself in it." But to be honest, I never got through many of these books, let alone got lost in them. Maybe I wanted Nancy to think I had it more together than I really did.

In fact, I spent a good deal of my off hours, and even some on-duty hours, getting and being drunk. I worried that I was losing my mind and my intellect and, as I have said, that my sensitivity to feelings and people was deserting me. In July 1968, I wrote to Nancy that "I have been commiserating on the deterioration of my mind in Vietnam with several of my associates, namely the shrink." Despite these conversations, I worried that "This place is horrible on my mind and my nerves."

We got to see current movies regularly, although it's unclear how and by whom these were chosen. I tended to like movies about rebellious or alienated youth—a favorite was *You're a Big Boy Now,* a tragicomedy about a failed love affair between a shy New York City library assistant and a go-go dancer. I loved the title tune and several other songs in the soundtrack by the Lovin' Spoonful, including "Darlin' Be Home Soon." I had a long conversation after the film with a lieutenant who had recently joined our battalion. He seemed to be someone who, like me, "doesn't know why he got into this Marine Corps and likes things which are a little 'different.'" I wrote to Nancy: "I just discovered tonight how much I want to grow my hair long again, put my blue jeans and cowboy boots on again and get the hell out of this and do crazy things with you again like we did before but this time for always."

I listened regularly to Armed Forces Radio Vietnam (AFVN), the home of Robin Williams' Adrian Cronauer in the film *Good Morning Vietnam*. AFVN played some up-to-date music, which was good, but its reporting on the war was always overly optimistic. In every battle, enemy losses were exaggerated and "ARVN casualties were described as light." We didn't have a television set until we got our new officers' club in Quang Tri. The armed forces TV station featured a lot of old westerns, sitcoms, and detective series but it also, somewhat surprisingly, aired *Rowan and Martin's Laugh-In,* an innovative and irreverent comedy show featuring Lily Tomlin, Henry Gibson, Arte Johnson, Ruth Buzzi, and Goldie Hawn. I don't recall that *Laugh-In* explicitly took on the Vietnam War, but its tone and content were clearly anti-establishment and made fun of the military—such as in Arte Johnson's portrayal of the German soldier always saying, "Very interesting, but stupid!"

I wasn't yet much of a Boston Red Sox fan in those days but had followed their "Impossible Dream" season of 1967. In fact, I didn't really pay much attention to professional sports. I guess I knew about Joe Namath's Jets' upset of the Colts in Super Bowl III but had no particular feelings about it. However, I was still interested in Harvard football and was excited to receive in the mail from my Harvard roommate Warren Bowes clippings from the *New York Times* on Harvard's 29–29 "win" over Yale in 1968's edition of "The Game." Both teams came in undefeated, but Yale was heavily favored, with its powerhouse team featuring Brian Dowling ("BD" of *Doonesbury* fame) and Calvin Hill. Down 29–13 with 42 seconds remaining, Harvard miraculously scored 16 points to secure the tie (there was no overtime in those days) and break Yale's heart. Pat Conway, a Harvard defensive back in that game, had been a Marine at Khe Sanh only nine months before.[22]

Religion was not an important part of my getting through my first Vietnam tour. Being in little or no danger, I had no need for the proverbial "foxhole conversion." Although my parents didn't attend church, my mother used to drive me and my sisters to St. Paul's Episcopal Church in Chestnut Hill on Sunday mornings with a raincoat thrown on over her nightgown. As a young boy, I loved the ritual and the music. I was baptized, but not until I was ten (along with my father, mother, and two sisters), reportedly because my father was considering running for political office in Philadelphia and thought it would help if he and his family had an official church affiliation. I went to Sunday school, attended youth groups, and served as an acolyte. At home, I pretended to be a priest celebrating Holy Communion with a kitchen tray and some stray coffee cups and wine glasses. On a visit to New York City, my grandmother took me to a service at the Cathedral of St. John the Divine presided over by the iconoclastic Episcopal Bishop James Pike, who later killed himself by driving a rental car into the Jordanian desert with his wife and two bottles of Coca-Cola.[23] While it may not have saved Bishop Pike, church was a vital comfort to me as my parents separated and divorced. My mother also found her faith amid the wreckage of her marriage to my father.

Like many people moving through adolescence and into adulthood, I began "losing my religion," as R.E.M. would later sing. For me, the break came after the assassination of President Kennedy in November 1963, my freshman year at Harvard. On that day, I received communion for the last time in more than 20 years. For those next two decades, I only entered a church for the occasional wedding or funeral. When I joined the Marine Corps, I specified only that my dog-tags say that I was a "Protestant."

On Easter Day, 1968, less than a month after my arrival in Vietnam, I wrote a poem with an epigraph from a Randy Newman song that I'd heard by Judy Collins: "human kindness is overflowing and I think it's going to rain today."[24] My poem lamented that

> In this day of joy and so-called happiness
> there is nothing to believe in really
> ...so here we are with nothing to praise but the inexorably ugly progress of
>   inhumanity
> in the name of love and hatred in the name of peace
> And for this we rejoice this day.

My fall from faith was pretty complete but not so sudden or dramatic as that of the fictional British chaplain who, watching "half of England" slaughtered on the first day of the Battle of the Somme in 1916, "pulled the silver cross from his chest and hurled it from him ... he fell to his knees but he did not pray.... Jack knew what had died in him."[25]

In June 1968, at the behest of a new Episcopal chaplain, I did attend one Sunday service. "I rather surprised myself," I wrote to my father, and "I thought that might amuse you." As far as I recall, that one service was my only formal religious observance during my tour except for playing poker frequently with the Catholic chaplain.

7

LRP Rations
and Warm Beer

Shortly before my departure from Vietnam in early April 1969, Tom Sweeney, Andy Richards, and I got very drunk and trashed our hooch. This was during a blackout ordered in anticipation of an enemy attack, which, luckily, never came. This episode, recorded on tape with narration by me and several Navy officers who came by during the proceedings, included turning over all the cots, spraying beer all over each other and everything in the hooch, and various confused wrestling matches on the floor. With the Beatles' "Why Don't We Do It in the Road" blasting in the background, one of the Navy lieutenants reported to the "folks back home" that

> We are now in the Marine hooch in Quang Tri by the '[DM]Z...Theodore is in the rear trying to come out from under several racks.... They're pouring beer over poor Theodore now.... They are remonstrating one with the other.... These are Marines, we'll have to excuse them.

Another participant commented that "The 'Nam does strange things to strange people.... You could get a lot of money for this tape" Later, he reported that "We're under attack here and emergency conditions are in effect ... we're getting low on liquor! I was able to snap open one last can."

My periodic comments suggested how mistreated I felt by my fellow Marine officers: "I think they've fucked with me enough for one night!" and my determination to retaliate: "They fucking wrecked my area, I'll fucking wreck theirs!" At one point, I donned my helmet and flak jacket, "trying to avoid these missiles being thrown at me. I have to flee from you now to duck behind the nearest revetment." When, in response to my assertion to this effect, I was asked, "Are you a pacifist?" I went into a parody of radio communications by infantry units in the field: "That's a great big affirmative on that last." Continuing to describe the situation: "Lt. Richards has mounted a very heavy attack on my pos and has been repulsed with moderate to heavy losses of friendly troops. ARVN losses were described as light." My narration went on:

> This is the real 'Nam, this is the way it is, fighting the Communist insurgents from door to door, from street to street, from hooch to hooch. This is the real war over here, gentlemen. We have a man wounded, the corpsmen are up. A desperately courageous Marine rushes to the rescue; he's opening another beer, I mean pulling the pin on a grenade; he's emptying the beer out of his boots, I mean he's trying to chamber a round in his M16. Oh my God, the whole world has erupted in chaos. This is the real 'Nam!

Finally, I had an announcement:

> At this time, the Paris peace talks have come up with a solution to the battle for Hooch 14.… The battle is hereby terminated. All parties, combatant and non-combatant, will immediately and without delay return to their respective areas.

During the trashing of the hooch and throughout my wartime tour, I was consuming American alcoholic beverages. Probably like most American personnel, I knew nothing of Vietnamese food except for rice. I had heard of 33 (ba mươi ba) Beer, whose name was mysteriously changed after the war to 333 and still exists, brewed in Ho Chi Minh City.

My only direct experience of Vietnamese food was during the only Vietnamese meal I had during 13 months in-country. Mr. Liêm was a businessman of multiple enterprises, including an ice plant, and probably multiple political loyalties. This was a common and necessary strategy for Vietnamese people living in communities that were divided and governed by parallel forces sometimes alternating by day and night. Businessmen like Mr. Liêm no doubt had to pay taxes and other forms of protection to both the South Vietnamese authorities and the Viet Cong.

We wanted to see if Mr. Liêm could help us to obtain traps to capture rats alive so they could be tested for plague—there had been a suspected case of plague in a Marine at Cam Lo, west of Dong Ha. Mr. Liêm was unable to help us get these traps but he invited me, Tom Sweeney, and several Medical Service Corps officers to join him for lunch at a restaurant in Quang Tri City. I liked the food very much, especially the crab and asparagus soup, a classic Vietnamese dish that I've enjoyed many times since, and the 33 Beer. We also had whole crabs cooked with garlic and spices to be cracked and pulled apart by hand, grilled chicken and shrimp, and fried rice. Mr. Liêm was a garrulous storyteller and warm host. However, I suspect that his shrewdness and resourcefulness enabled him to survive and even thrive in the changing circumstances.

During my tour with 3rd Medical Battalion, I subsisted on the mess hall food, which was of pretty poor quality (our mess sergeant was a particularly bad drunk) but Michelin-rated compared to the C-rations the grunts got in the field. There was a turkey dinner for Thanksgiving, which was even delivered to some units in the bush. Occasionally, we procured steaks through trades with the Seabees and grilled them in halved 55-gallon drums over scrap lumber dowsed with diesel fuel. My hooch-mates and I also obtained a supply of long-range patrol (LRP) rations, newly introduced freeze-dried meals that needed only to be mixed with water and were quite delicious, especially the beef stew and beef with rice. I recall that there was a beef stroganoff LRP, but that may just have been a dream. While the LRP supply lasted, we dined in our hooch and shunned the mess hall delicacies.

I was a 2½ pack-a-day cigarette smoker, encouraged by the PX price of 10 cents per pack, and probably would still be smoking if it weren't for an uncontrollable cough that was the combined result of the cigarettes and the dusty environment at Quang Tri Combat Base. The doctor I saw said that there was nothing to be done except to stop smoking. Which I did, with the help of prescriptions for the tranquilizer Valium and a "mood elevator" (which one, I don't recall), about two months before I was due to go home. If I had been able to endure the cough for those last two months, I would probably have continued to smoke for much longer.

Other than alcohol and nicotine, I did avoid drugs in Vietnam. This was because I was an officer and officers were meted out very harsh punishments if caught using drugs. Later, I met some lieutenants at Camp Lejeune who said they had regularly been stoned while serving as artillery forward observers in Vietnam, one of the most dangerous combat assignments. Marijuana use was becoming widespread during my first tour, but I was not aware of the incipient epidemic of heroin addiction that marked the last few years of American military involvement in Vietnam.

As Oscar Wilde is supposed to have said and my later dear friend and running buddy Martin Duffy assured me that he *did*, in fact, say: "work is the curse of the drinking classes."[1] That was my story in Vietnam during my first tour. I basically stayed drunk as much as I could, both on and off the job, and was pretty clearly headed to alcoholism. I drank whatever beer we could get: Budweiser (my father derisively called it "girls' beer" but we happily swilled it), Hamm's, Piel's (I remembered the funny TV ads in which Bob and Ray played Bert and Harry Piel), Pabst, Schlitz, and Olympia ("Oly, It's the Water"). My Californian hooch-mate Tom Sweeney sang the praises of Coors, but we couldn't get it in Vietnam, and I was only able to try it much later. I told Nancy that most of the year, it was so hot that "you have to drink a can of beer in 10 seconds or it gets warm on you." At least, in the rear, we were lucky to be able to have beer most of the time, even if it meant getting used to "drinking lukewarm beer with a fan blowing hot air in my face."

I also drank hard liquor, whatever was available: rum and cokes, gin and tonics, and 7 and 7's in the officers' club. When my mother asked me if I needed "anything for your comfort or entertainment," I responded "Yes—to come home; maybe a bottle of whiskey." Dutifully, she sent me a bottle of Cutty Sark protectively encased in a loaf of bread. The bread was moldy upon arrival, but the Scotch was fine.

Troops in the Iraq and Afghanistan Wars were forbidden not only drugs but also alcohol. However, these substances were apparently often provided through the mail by friends and family. Troops also resorted to sniffing "air dusters" whose intended purpose was to clean their laptops.[2]

My drinking was a mixed blessing. Although I was largely safe, I was pretty miserable, probably depressed, and I drank as a way to get through it. My drinking was clearly a form of self-medication that was very harmful. In July, I wrote Nancy:

> I realize I shouldn't drink and that it's a crutch but over here I do have a need of a crutch—there's really nothing else—Back there I have you and I don't need to drink at all to feel content. It's bad to be dependent on it but it does help to some extent. I love you and miss you so much that I have to have something to fall back on sometime or I will go out of my mind. [And in October:] Now I'm sitting here drinking a scotch and water and letting my thoughts go. If I had Fitzgerald's "May Day," I would read it again for the 500th time. Those were the days, weren't they?

This was more of my bullshit scenario of the doomed romantic. In fact, the days depicted in that Fitzgerald story were not so great and it has a tragic ending produced in large part by excessive drinking. I loved and missed Nancy and my drinking helped me to get through the time until we could be together again. But it also played to some darker and more neurotic notes, what my sister Janet sometimes called my "crepe-hanging."

I was drinking so much and was so dependent on it that I was unable to resist sneaking into the hooch and having a beer or two even when I had the duty as Officer of the Day. It caused me to argue with people, behave badly, and get into embarrassing situations with enlisted men. After a 4th of July party at which I had gotten very drunk and, with Tom Sweeney, been prevailed upon to dance with two "go-go dancers," who were really clumsily cross-dressed and made-up Navy corpsmen, the commanding officer complained that there had been too much alcohol consumed by officers in front of the enlisted men and an internal medicine doctor gave me a stern lecture on the evil effects of drink.

As I was clearly drunk when I composed many of my letters and tapes to her, Nancy cautioned: "please don't drink too much—it does such awful things to people!" I had been friends with the battalion psychiatrist but we had only discussed politics and culture—I assured Nancy that my talks with him were never of a clinical nature but "strictly informal." Steve and I did, however, "decide ... to keep each other sane."

Later, as my drinking worsened despite Nancy's pleas, the battalion psychiatrist suggested that I come see him. It turned out to be the first of many therapy sessions over the next 35 years. For the first time, I spoke openly about my childhood and my feelings about my parents' divorce. I met several times with the psychiatrist and found it "cathartic" and helpful in reducing the stigma I had felt toward counseling. A primary motivation, as I told Nancy, was to get myself "cleaned up and refurbished" before coming home, "so I can face you with everything intact." In my sessions with the psychiatrist, I began to feel more articulate again, "back in the groove, forming arguments and logical chains of thought"—capabilities that I had feared lost. However, I pronounced myself a "very volatile, changeable person." I felt happy while making that tape for Nancy, but something could happen to change my mood quickly.

I was able to reduce my drinking for a while after seeing the psychiatrist but there continued to be episodes of excess, including during a party when we hosted female nurses from the hospital ship—I was faithful to Nancy but otherwise acted pretty outrageously in many ways which I have since lost to the "fog of war." The "Battle for Hooch 14" was, however, preserved for posterity.

In that instance, among others, I was, from my safe position "in the rear with the gear," making light of the horrors of war being suffered by many of my fellow Marines and other American troops, not to speak of the Vietnamese on both sides. This seemed funny at the time but is perhaps not so funny now. To some extent, I felt guilty and ashamed that I had had it so easy, but I also hated this senseless war and thought it worthy of parody. In any case, with all my mixed feelings and conflicted views of myself and the war, the trashing of the hooch represented, really and truly, the end of my first tour in Vietnam. And, indeed, I was soon to return to "my area"—not just my part of the hooch I had defended during the battle but "the World," where I longed to be again with Nancy.

8

Seeking Danger

In late February 1969, with only a month left in my tour, I accompanied a friend who was serving as pay officer for his artillery unit, to Fire Support Base Russell in the mountains near the DMZ, which had been nearly overrun by NVA sappers a few nights before.[1] We joked that I would be Sam's bodyguard. Third Medical Battalion's hospital in Quang Tri had received mass casualties from Russell, and a similar assault on nearby FSB Neville. No further attack occurred while I was at Russell, but we were unexpectedly forced to overnight there when low clouds and mist prevented choppers from landing. I spent a sleepless night in a bunker in which several Marines had died, listening to outgoing artillery and small arms fire on the perimeter. In an attempt to prove that I had been there, I posed for some pictures by the aiming stakes in a 105mm howitzer pit. However, they did not come out clearly enough to present here.

The trip to FSB Russell was part of my effort, perhaps to please my father, to get some limited experience of the real war. In May, I had facetiously told Nancy that I hoped to keep busy, which might be aided by "some exciting things like getting shot at." Although I was in Vietnam during the period with the heaviest American casualties, I saw no combat and was in no real danger. We had very occasional rocket attacks at Phu Bai and Quang Tri and sometimes there were base blackouts and alerts during which, invariably, nothing happened. I commented to Nancy on the discrepancy of conditions in which American troops lived in Vietnam. Field Marines justifiably felt that those of us lucky enough to be based at Phu Bai or Quang Tri "had it made," while we thoughtlessly compared our spartan conditions to those enjoyed in Danang, such as the Stone Elephant Navy Officers Club with its thick pile carpets, plush furniture, and beautiful bar.

In Phu Bai, we did have a large spider construct a web across the entrance to our bunker and this spider often sat right in the middle of the bunker floor. I was afraid that "if we get hit, someone will be grievously bitten." Still, getting into the bunker quickly would surely take precedence.

My one-night accommodation at FSB Russell.

In fact, I was the butt of jokes for my speed in reaching the bunker. When we got rocketed on my first night in Phu Bai, my hooch-mates teased me about a "streak of white underwear" going by, but I replied that "I'll be happily the first one in every time."

Later, we had some issues with rats in our hooch. In a "battle royale," one of my hooch-mates scared an invading rat away at first by yelling at it but, when it returned, beat it to death with a 2×4. Luckily, the rest of us were at the O-club at the time. We were able to put metal screening over the rat's point of entry and the problems subsided. Rat bites were not only painful in themselves but necessitated 14 daily rabies shots in the stomach—a most unpleasant prospect.

When I told Nancy about our impending move from Phu Bai to Quang Tri, she expressed concern that we were going to be in a less secure area and urged me to be careful. The move was important because it enabled the hospital to receive casualties directly from the field instead of through the much smaller Delta Med in Dong Ha, which could then be closed down. Moreover, Quang Tri proved to be just as secure as Phu Bai, despite its closer proximity to the DMZ. Quang Tri Combat Base was sometimes jokingly referred to as "sandbag city"—with more than 500,000 sandbags to protect its residents.

I visited Delta Med at Dong Ha in June, the day after the base's ammunition dump had been hit by NVA artillery, causing dangerous shrapnel shards to be propelled over a wide area. Explosions and fires continued the day I was there and then a secret message warned of a ground attack on Quang Tri where I was planning to spend the night. So, I decided to hightail it back to Phu Bai instead. The C-130 transport on which I was to fly out of Dong Ha had an engine go out. Because of frequent NVA shelling of the Dong Ha airbase and the continuing explosions at the ammunition dump, the pilot didn't want to keep the airplane there for repairs, so we had to take off with three engines. The crew chief gave the passengers a rather ominous warning and the noise of the engines on the roll down the runway was incredible as was the almost perpendicular climb-out, but we successfully got airborne and made it back to Phu Bai without incident. On the climb-out, we could see the ammunition dump explosions on one side, a firefight complete with tracer rounds on the other side, and air strikes in progress up near the DMZ. I got to ride in the cockpit for part of the trip. The views of the mountains, ocean, and countryside were spectacular. Vietnam is a very beautiful country, even with a war raging and, as I would later see, much of its beauty survived the ravages of war.

I participated gratuitously in helicopter rides and truck convoys. Once, on a helicopter trip to visit the Navy hospital ship *Sanctuary* in the South China Sea, a round just missed us as we flew over the Cua Viet River. Our unit took occasional truck convoys to Danang to get supplies and later to Vandegrift Combat Base near Khe Sanh to deliver supplies to our Charlie Med unit there. These convoys were a kind of quasi-combat duty as we would mount 50-calibre machine guns on a few of the "six-by" trucks in case of ambush, particularly as we threaded our way over the Hai Van Pass just north of Danang or out Route 9 from Dong Ha toward Vandegrift. I wrote sarcastically to Nancy that these guns were to "protect us from the evil Communist aggressors." We were in fact never ambushed and had nothing to shoot at, much to the disappointment of my gung-ho supply chief, an apparent grunt wannabe. (Nowadays, you can take a tunnel to avoid the Hai Van Pass and speed the trip from Danang to Hue. However, you can still go over the pass and enjoy the spectacular views in both directions and the abundant tourist shops offering refreshments and souvenirs.)

While these convoys afforded opportunities to view Vietnam's scenery, the beauty was marred by numerous bomb craters and scarred mountainsides. To my mother, I wrote, "It's tragic that such beautiful country has to be ruined." Our medical facility at Vandegrift was on a high bluff overlooking the base with views of the mountains into North Vietnam and the Khe Sanh Valley five miles away. Once, I took a medevac chopper from Vandegrift to pick up a casualty at a remote firebase to the northwest. As we approached, I saw some people on the ground, who I at first thought were NVA soldiers. In fact, they were our Marines. We only landed for about a minute—"I wouldn't want to spend too much time on the ground there," I told Nancy.

During the hospital-moving convoy from Phu Bai to Quang Tri, one of our trucks slipped into a muddy ditch in an ambush-prone area and the whole column had to wait for some uneasy minutes while a wrecker pulled it out. We were then on our way without incident. During the halt, I had a staged photo taken in which I pretended to be on the radio giving a "sit-rep" (situation report) to some higher up. Even though I was certainly not a grunt, I liked to appropriate some of their terminology.

On another flight from Dong Ha back to Phu Bai, I had to pose as a "neuro-psych consult" (someone being sent to the rear to see the shrink) in order to get a seat on the C-130. I was required to wear a prominent evacuation tag identifying me as "N-P" and to hide my .45 pistol in my bag. No one would come near me on the plane. I wrote to my mother that "I was going to act the part and burst into insane laughter, but they probably would have put me in a straitjacket. Anyway, the Division shrink is a good friend of mine in case the need arises."

In August 1968 I landed very briefly at the site of the Khe Sanh Combat Base. By then, the whole complex in which a reinforced Marine regiment underwent almost constant rocket and artillery bombardment the previous January to April, had been abandoned and blown up by our side. So much for this hitherto vital piece of war real estate.

In my final months in-country, I deliberately sought a few more experiences of being shot at. I was still beset by doubts as to my courage or cowardice and felt I needed to get into a little danger before I went home. After all, my father would expect this. To get his Vietnam War experience, he and retired General Joseph Lawton "Lightning Joe" Collins, a World War II hero, visited Saigon in the early 1970s to gather evidence for the defense of Pfizer pharmaceuticals in an anti-trust case. While they may have done some work in Saigon, I suspect that my father, true to form, spent at least some of his time with the ladies on Tu Do Street.

As I grew shorter, I told Nancy that I would curtail my risk taking and begin sleeping in the bunker. With 39 days to go, I wrote her that "I don't want an offensive as a going-away present." Fortunately, Tet 1969, unlike the year before, was quiet in our area except for one major firefight southwest of Quang Tri. "It's now the 19th—as you were! (that's 'Marine speak'), the 20th of February and 'I can't go to sleep unless I have a few beers.'"

I did have one final "adventure." Several weeks before I was due to go home, I took an in-country R&R trip to visit my stepbrother Jiggs who was an Army helicopter pilot in the Mekong Delta. After a boozy overnight layover in Saigon, I reached his base at Vinh Long. I wit-

Convoy to Quang Tri: Faking the "SitRep."

nessed him being awarded an Air Medal by his commanding officer and went up with him in his Huey a few times. It was one of these rides that we pretended to strafe some Vietnamese villagers working in their rice fields. I also rode along on a night mission during which a converted C-47 transport (known as "Spooky" or "Puff the Magic Dragon") rained thousands of 7.62-millimeter rounds on a village and the Viet Cong sent tracers back up toward my helicopter.

These episodes didn't add up to much real danger to my life and health, in fact probably much less than my drinking and smoking. But they helped me to pose for my father as a real Marine Vietnam veteran and to feel at least slightly justified in wearing the Combat Action Ribbon that I was awarded.[2]

The last weeks and days of my tour dragged but finally my flight date beckoned. I had to be in Danang on April 6, 1969, for my flight back home and to Nancy.

9

Coming Home

It was, unnecessarily, an adventure getting to Danang. Unlike W.D. Ehrhart's last-minute extraction by helicopter from the field in the midst of a firefight,[1] my difficulties were self-induced. I almost missed my flight due to an alcohol-blurred trip from Quang Tri. After drinking beer in our hooch with Tom Sweeney and Andy Richards for a good part of the afternoon of April 4 (my replacement had taken over the supply office by then), the three of us took Tom's motor T jeep to Camp Evans, an army base about 25 miles south on Route One. At Camp Evans, we joined a poker game with some Army guys, one of whom, a lieutenant from the Boston area, had spent time on temporary duty in Quang Tri and lived in our hooch.

I guess Tom and Andy somehow made it back to Quang Tri after the poker game, but I overnighted (passed out?) at Camp Evans and next morning caught a flight to Danang. Upon reaching Danang, I dropped my gear at the temporary officers' quarters and went immediately to the Air Force's Gunfighters Club, one of the best clubs on the base. After a long night of further drinking and carousing there, I called "Motley 123" for a jeep taxi back to the officers' quarters, stumbling in well after midnight. I was supposed to check in for my flight to Okinawa, the first leg of my trip home, at about 6 a.m. I awoke in a fog at about 5:45 a.m. and realized my predicament, quickly dressed, and rushed to the Marine air terminal at the last possible moment. What would they have done if I missed my flight—sent me back to Quang Tri for another 13 months? Or worse, as an infantry platoon commander?

I left Vietnam on April 6, 1969—that month saw the peak of U.S. troop strength in Vietnam at 543,000. I had a short layover in Okinawa, where I reconnected with a few lieutenants who had been on my flight over to Vietnam 13 months before and were now going home at the same time. I also reconnected with the permanent staff officers who were still winning money at poker from the transients at the Camp Hansen officers' club. This time, however, it didn't matter so much whether I won or lost, because I was, as Simon and Garfunkel sang, "Homeward Bound."

In Okinawa, before the flight home.

Even this leg of the trip brought surprises. When I reached San Francisco International Airport after landing at Travis Air Force Base, I called my Philadelphia home and my stepmother informed me that my father "is no longer living here." He was with Jane, later to be his third wife, in New York City.

Only Nancy was there to meet my flight in Philadelphia but that was great enough. I don't remember all the details of our reunion scene at the airport, but I know it was emotional. I was so relieved and so happy to be with Nancy again. We had decided to be "unofficially engaged" before I left for Vietnam, but we were now going to make it official.

We spent a few days with my stepmother and my half-sister Nan. I didn't see my father until a week or so later, in New York. In February, I had written to Warren, hoping for "a reconvening of the old group at Trader Vic's, Maxwell's Plum (now of movie fame), Elaine's, etc." But I worried that "these places are all passé by now." Whether that was true or not, sadly the reunion with Warren, John and the group did not occur during that trip to New York. Instead, I was coming to terms with my father's new situation and meeting Jane, whom I liked immediately. I don't think we talked too much—or argued—about the war.

I had a bit more than a month's leave before I had to report to my next and final duty station, good old Camp Lejeune. I spent most of this time in Madison, Wisconsin, with Nancy, meeting her friends, many of whom were involved in antiwar activities and the Union of Radical Political

Economists, and learning about the new social and political radicalism in America. I attended some classes—I particularly liked the lectures of Harvey Goldberg, a "New Left" historian, because that is what I thought I was going to become when I made it to graduate school the next year.

In those days, of course, there were no endless recitations of "thank-you for your service" but rather often hostility to or, at best, a silent shunning of Vietnam veterans. When I visited Nancy in Madison after I returned home but was still on active duty, I used to fly in uniform to get the military standby fare but ducked into the men's room at the airport to change into civilian clothes so as to avoid being confronted by angry anti-war students in town. This worked to some extent, but my short Marine haircut probably gave me away. I always seemed somehow to be betwixt and between.

Just as with the time of my leaving for the war and my time being there, I will always associate certain songs with the time of my coming home: the Zombies' "Time of the Season" (appropriately, a time "when love runs high"[2]), Simon and Garfunkel's "The Boxer,"[3] the Fifth Dimension's hyper-optimistic (somewhat strange for the time) "Aquarius/Let the Sunshine In"[4] and Glen Campbell's Vietnam love song "Galveston."[5] We also heard some great live music, including Janis Joplin with her Kozmic Blues Band at the Dane County Coliseum in Madison, Charley Musselwhite and others at Marsh Shapiro's Nitty Gritty, and the Super-Cosmic Joy Scout Jamboree, featuring Muddy Waters, Otis Spann, Paul Butterfield, and Mike Bloomfield at Chicago's Auditorium Theatre, some songs from which were later included on the album *Fathers and Sons*. The Chicago police stopped that concert early for some unknown but no doubt spurious reason—not before Waters got to sing several of his classics, including "I'm Ready," "The Same Thing," and "Long Distance Call."

I had first seen the Paul Butterfield Blues Band, who famously backed Bob Dylan when he went electric at the Newport Folk Festival in 1965, at Jordan Hall in Boston in January 1967. Unaccountably, Nancy was not with me for that concert. However, in February 2019, with Nancy in the same hall at a concert of the Handel & Haydn Society, listening to Aislinn Nosky's virtuosic performance of Vivaldi's "La Tempesta di Mare" violin concerto, I thought of Mike Bloomfield's blistering guitar work on Willie Dixon's "Mellow Down Easy" that January night 52 years before.

We drank stingers at The Portobello, where Nancy's roommate Pat (a dear friend ever since and our daughter's godmother) worked as a cocktail waitress. When the Madison police used tear gas to break up a demonstration near Nancy's apartment, we were forced to take refuge in Mr. Giblin's, their neighborhood bar, where we were able to watch Bill Russell and the Boston Celtics win the NBA championship from Wilt Chamberlain and the Los Angeles Lakers in game seven, as thousands of "World Champion Lakers" balloons remained stuck in the rafters of the LA Forum.

On my way from Madison back to Philadelphia and thence on to Camp Lejeune, I totaled my red Volkswagen beetle on the Ohio Turnpike near Toledo. (It was probably just like the one W.D. Ehrhart purchased "with blood money" the day after his return from Vietnam and drove 18,000 miles in its first ten weeks.[6]) I had bought mine when I began my active duty in June 1967 and, apparently, the tires were worn. I lost control while passing a semi in a windy rainstorm. After flipping the car end-over-end I landed right side up in the medial strip with the windshield wipers still going but no windshield. Apart from a few bruises, I was unhurt. I was wearing a lap seat belt (shoulder belts were not yet in use), which probably saved my life. Another driver stopped and waited with me until the state police showed up. He offered me a cigarette, which I declined. This was the closest I ever came to smoking a cigarette again, except in one of my latter-day anxiety dreams where I have again become a smoker.

The police took me to a hospital emergency room, but I was released with no need for treatment. I had to spend one night in a motel in Bellevue, Ohio, and met some guys in a nearby bar who did, in some form, thank me for my service. Three years later, during a family camping trip in Pennsylvania, my brother-in-law Bruce and I went into a bar to buy some

With Nancy in Madison: April 1969.

beer. On the TV, Spiro Agnew was accepting the Republican nomination for a second term as Vice President. I was almost 27 years old. When the bartender had the temerity to card me, Bruce shouted that I "was a fucking Marine in Vietnam!" W.D. Ehrhart had a more dramatic experience when some regulars in a bar in his Pennsylvania hometown started trouble over Ehrhart's long hair and were met with a righteous and near-violent demand that they recognize his service and his well-earned right to wear his hair as he pleased and hold the opinions he chose.[7] In his eponymous 2018 poem, Ehrhart's response to the by-then tired phrase of thanks to veterans was

> "You're welcome," let it go at that,
> when what I'd really like to say is,
> "Thank you for my fucking service
> in that fucking war I've dragged
> from day to day for fifty fucking years
> like a fucking corpse that won't stay dead."[8]

The day after my accident in Ohio I flew to Philadelphia from Cleveland and made my way to Camp Lejeune in a rental car, which I soon replaced with a shiny new Chevy Camaro. I had another 13 months to go in my Marine Corps active duty.

Part II: Between My Tours

10

Detachment

It was the summer of Woodstock, the moon landing, Stonewall, and Charles Manson. I wish we had gone to Woodstock but, unlike many who were there but couldn't remember that they had been, I didn't forget not going. I just re-watched the movie to remind myself. A guest I regularly sit with at my church's meal program told me that he hitch-hiked to Woodstock from Cape Cod and remembers seeing Santana, among others, although he left before Jimi Hendrix's iconic performance of "The Star-Spangled Banner." I definitely remember that Nancy and I attended the Atlantic City Pop Festival, two weeks before Woodstock, mainly to hear Jefferson Airplane and Creedence Clearwater Revival. I recall the Airplane being pretty stoned and feeling very self-conscious in my low white sneakers and short Marine haircut.

For a good part of the period 1969 to 1997, true to Nancy's letter to me during my first tour, I didn't think or care very much about Vietnam. I had had it with that Godforsaken country and its people, and I wasn't paying much attention to their plight after 1975. My reconnection with Vietnam happened almost by chance and that chance stirred up in me a growing desire to return and do something positive there.

I spent the remainder of my Marine Corps active duty at Camp Lejeune, North Carolina. Luckily, there was insufficient time to accommodate another tour in Vietnam and my assignment to Force Troops rather than 2nd Marine Division made it highly unlikely that I would catch a Mediterranean cruise or a stint at Guantanamo Bay, Cuba, which junior officers in the Division often did. I certainly didn't want another long separation from Nancy.

Since I had stopped smoking while in Vietnam, I had gained weight. So, I started running, first in my Marine combat boots for a few miles along the base roads at Camp Lejeune before drowning myself with gin and tonics and whatever else at the Officers Club. These desultory jaunts ultimately led to a long and sometimes obsessive running career, which included 18 Boston Marathons.

In 1969, Nancy had a summer job in Washington, working as a research assistant for Joseph Pechman, an influential economist at the Brookings Institution. I spent every weekend with her, first in her small apartment in Georgetown and later when she was house-sitting for my Uncle Dick and Aunt Suzy. On hot afternoons we sat by their pool in Chevy Chase drinking wine coolers with Spirit ("I Got a Line on You"), Creedence Clearwater Revival ("Bad Moon Rising"!), and Blood, Sweat and Tears ("And When I Die") blaring from the outside speakers. Dick and Suzy were at Chatham, on Cape Cod, where Suzy was working on a book about 17th-century British proto-feminist playwright Aphra Behn. Suzy used to describe her writing time as mostly spent "glaring out the window."

That summer, Nancy and I saw Haskell Wexler's innovative but strange film *Medium Cool*, about the power of TV reporting and two people inadvertently caught up in the violence at the Democratic National Convention in Chicago. It was the weird summer in which, according to Joan Didion, "Everything was unmentionable but nothing was unimaginable.... *I remember that no one was surprised*" by the Manson murders.[2] These horrible killings were coincidentally linked in several ways to the wonderful music being made in Laurel Canyon between 1965 and 1975. The Tate-Polanski house on Cielo Drive was just off Laurel Canyon Boulevard and very near those of David Crosby and other musicians. Terry Melcher, producer of several of the Byrds' albums, was the prior tenant of 10050 Cielo Drive, and his refusal to record Charles Manson's songs seems to have been a reason that the house was targeted. Johnny Echols, a member of the band LOVE who also lived in Laurel Canyon, was horrified to discover that his friend Bobby Beausoleil had committed another Manson-ordered murder.[3]

Didion asserted that the Sixties ended "abruptly" when word spread on August 9 of the killings on Cielo Drive. (Had Quentin Tarantino's counter-factual ending in *Once Upon a Time ... in Hollywood* really occurred, Didion would no doubt have reached the same conclusion.) But, in fact, Woodstock—perhaps the best exemplar of the Sixties—happened only a week later. The Sixties did seem to end more resoundingly with the Hell's Angels, hired as "security," murdering a man for allegedly knocking over one of their motorcycles during a Rolling Stones free concert at Altamont Raceway on December 6. This was less than a month before the calendar would have brought the decade to a close in any case.

With the help of a supply of Ritalin, prescribed for me by a doctor friend in 3rd Medical Battalion, I was able to stay in D.C. until past midnight on Sundays during that summer and still make it back to Lejeune in time for work Monday mornings. I wrote to Nancy that amid a seemingly constant confusion of contradictory thoughts and motivations, "perhaps the only identifiable long-term thread in my life has been my developing affection for you." In July, we announced our engagement at a party for my Hammett grandparents' 50th wedding anniversary.

In the fall semester, Nancy and my sister Peggy, who had transferred from Wellesley College to the University of Wisconsin to complete her undergraduate work, shared an apartment in "Miff-land," a neighborhood that was a center of radical agitation and disruption in Madison. I visited from Camp Lejeune as often as I could. We enjoyed the Beatles' and Stones' new albums *Abbey Road* (including "Come Together") and *Let It Bleed* and regular visits from "Dave the Hippie," the neighborhood drug dealer who had a sample case like the Fuller Brush Man. Peggy, her boyfriend, Nancy, and I went to see the movie of Arlo Guthrie's *Alice's Restaurant,* which seemed even more hilarious under the influence of Dave's dope.

In Washington, Nancy and I went to the November 1969 march against the war after she had a fitting for her wedding gown. I was still on active duty but did not wear my uniform to the march. We got married in February 1970 and moved to Camp Lejeune. We lived in an off-base apartment and she kept up with radical politics through *The Militant* and the writings of members of the Union of Radical Political Economists and other leftist groups. Out of curiosity, she also attended several lunches of the Marine Officers' Wives Club, where she saw, and humorously reported to me afterward, that there was just as rigid a rank hierarchy among the wives as among their husbands. Obviously, there was no Officers' Husbands Club.

Nancy and I saw Robert Altman's darkly hilarious antiwar film *M*A*S*H,* set during the Korean War but clearly Vietnam-inflected. I followed the outcomes of Nixon's "secret plan to end the war," which really amounted to more escalation and suffering by the Vietnamese, Cambodians, and Laotians while U.S. troop levels began to be drawn down. I cut out and saved a letter to the editor of *Quicksilver Times,* a Washington underground paper, that quantified "WHAT ONE YEAR'S VIETNAM WAR BUDGET WOULD BUY" in nine items, each of them huge. They included one million complete four-year scholarships, one year's groceries for 10,000,000 hungry people, and one million units of housing. I don't know if these numbers were all accurate, but I doubt that they were off by orders of magnitude. This letter, which I did cut out for some reason, should have mobilized me to take stronger action against the war. Alas, I did not.[4]

Soon after taking up my new duty assignment at Camp Lejeune, I found a peace sticker that was as innocuous as possible—a dove holding an American flag, with no slogan—to put on my Camaro. Even so, I was worried that the MPs at the base gate might notice and report me to higher authority. I was against the war but still not that courageous in my statements of opinion where there may have been some risk involved. This reluctance may have been a carryover from my fraught relationship with and cave-in to my father over the war in 1966. Sometimes, understandably, Nancy called me out for my timidity.

As in Vietnam, I was a battalion supply officer in charge of about twenty enlisted Marines. I left most of the actual work to them while I occasionally napped on the couch in my office and daydreamed about my life after release from the Corps. The men sometimes got into difficulties—bar fights in town, domestic troubles, usurious loans for clothing or cars—and I tried to help them as much as I could. Like my group in Vietnam, several had been given a choice by a judge: join the Marine Corps or go to jail. Unlike most of my friends from Chestnut Hill and Harvard, they had little opportunity or capability of employing trickery or artifice to avoid military service.

I was released from active duty in June 1970, shortly after the Kent State shootings. Riot-ready trucks and troops were being prepared at Camp Lejeune for quick dispatch in case of demonstrations in Washington or elsewhere. My release orders closed with the following (no doubt, boilerplate) statement from my last commanding officer: "It is my warm hope that your future is filled with many years of good health and happiness. Your professional skill and devotion to duty have contributed substantially to the success we have achieved."

Nancy and I stopped in Washington to see her parents and siblings. During that visit, we got to see James Taylor perform at The Cellar Door in Georgetown. We loved Taylor's album *Sweet Baby James*—especially "Fire and Rain" and the title tune, which became a favorite lullaby for our daughter and her own daughters.[5]

Nancy and I spent the summer camping in Europe. It was her first time abroad. We retraced some of the steps of my 1966 trip to France and England, relying extensively on *Europe on Five Dollars a Day*. Our Renault rental car broke down repeatedly and it rained every day we were in England, but we still had a (generally) good time. We gazed lovingly at the Impressionists at the Jeu de Paume in Paris and the Turners at the Tate in London. We toured the Heineken brewery in Amsterdam and drank from big steins at the Hofbräuhaus in Munich. We went hiking in Evolène in the Swiss Alps with Nancy's friend Pat and her boyfriend. We awoke to gulls squawking over our tent on the Isle of Skye as the sun rose at 3 a.m. after setting only a few hours earlier. We thought of a lullaby both our mothers had sung to us. It told of "Bonnie Prince Charlie" the star-crossed Stuart "pretender" to the British throne fleeing after his disastrous defeat at the Battle of Culloden in 1746:

> Speed, bonnie boat, like a bird on the wing,
> Onward! the sailors cry;
> Carry the lad that's born to be king
> Over the sea to Skye.

We returned to live in Cambridge in the fall. Nancy worked for a Harvard professor who was helping Pakistanis implement the "Green Revolution" in agriculture. I began my PhD program in American history at nearby Brandeis University. Nancy teased me about my approach to historical analysis and writing that always seemed to take the form of "on the one hand, but on the other"—always seemed to stress uncertainty and ambiguity over clear, bright lines of interpretation. At one point during graduate school, I sought to explain this approach in a somewhat tortured (and unpublished) essay called "The Psychology and Politics of History." This "links 'liberal confusion' and ideological imprecision with authoritarian familial relationships [in my case, with my father], and with a consequent persisting fear of confronting or rejecting any figures of authority or power."

In 1970, I drew on my already developing memories to compose "a short poem for you [Nancy] on my new electric typewriter":

> I found a box of souvenirs
> In my top drawer today
> I got a bunch of old records
> That I can't seem to play
> I got a poem for you
> That I can't make rhyme
> But all I want to say
> Is you were with me all the time.

Nancy found a Consciousness Raising Group, where the survival of marriage was under serious discussion, and we joined the North Cambridge Food Co-op, whose main issue was which wholesaler at the Chelsea market was more politically correct in his sourcing of produce. WCAS, Cambridge's little daytime progressive folk/rock station, introduced me to Jackson Browne, Mary McCaslin, Jesse Winchester, John Martyn, Kate and Anna McGarrigle, John Prine, and Bruce Springsteen. Danny Schechter "your news dissector," had crossed the river from Boston's WBCN. We heard about Bob Dylan's "Rolling Thunder Revue" on WCAS and were able to secure almost the last two tickets to its Harvard Square Theatre performance. As we were headed home afterwards, we spotted Scarlet Rivera, the statuesque violinist in the Revue ensemble—her performance on "Hurricane" was passionately dazzling. Rivera was bound, we assumed, for some exclusive after-party. We tried to follow her in our old VW bug but lost her in the streets behind Harvard's Memorial Hall. Oh well, it was still a great show.

My father's second wife Ann died in 1972. When he moved to New York to live with his woman friend Jane, he had left his daughter Nan, aged six, to a chaotic and terrifying life with a mother who was mentally ill, abusing alcohol and drugs, and acting out in extreme and unpredictable ways. Ann sometimes telephoned me incoherently in the middle of the night. Once, she called from a hospital emergency room where she had been taken by the police. Nancy and I talked about how we might try to rescue Nan from this horrendous situation and bring her to live with us in Cambridge. I flew to Philadelphia to see what I could do. My father was furious at this intervention. Once again, I caved in to him and we ended up doing nothing. I have ever since felt deeply guilty about this and Nan, no doubt, has felt lingering anger. The two of us have talked about these feelings over the years and I hope reached as much resolution as is possible.

Nancy's and my only gesture was, for several summers after Nan's mother died, to take her on family camping trips. These trips introduced Nan to Nancy's five siblings. Nancy's youngest brother David and Nan were the same age. My sister Janet and her soon-to-be husband Bruce joined one of these trips. We camped in state parks in Virginia, West Virginia, and Pennsylvania, with historical side visits to Monticello, Harper's Ferry, and Gettysburg and final dinners at Emerson's "unlimited" steak and beer place in D.C. It was car camping at its finest with plenty of beer drinking, starchy, fatty, and sugar-y food, fart jokes, cigar smoking, and silly games like "fris-tree," which, as I vaguely recall, involved getting a frisbee stuck in a tree and trying to dislodge it with thrown shoes and other objects. Nancy and her siblings insist that it rained every day on all of these trips, our tents leaked, and we had to take our sleeping bags to laundromats in town to dry them out. I firmly believe it only rained during the first.

Once, my father visited Nancy and me in Cambridge. I should have mentioned his irresponsible abandonment of his daughter, but I'm sure I did not. However, we did have a big argument about the war. I told him I resented his pressure on me to join and remain in the Marine Corps. He shouted that I was a "shitbird," just about the worst thing to call a Marine.

I had a fleeting involvement with Vietnam Veterans Against the War, but I was never much for demonstrations and I did not join VVAW's Operation RAW, a 1970 march from Morristown, New Jersey, to Valley Forge, Pennsylvania, punctuated with guerrilla theater enactments of American soldiers' atrocities against Vietnamese villagers. Nor did I join John Kerry and hundreds of other veterans to throw my medals, which were in fact just campaign ribbons, over the fence in front of the Capitol building, the culminating action of VVAW's Operation Dewey Canyon III.[6] Within a few years, VVAW was hijacked by various Trotskyite and Maoist factions in a classic internecine struggle of the early 1970s Left, and finally ruined by government prosecutions and endless internal strife.[7]

I was supposed to serve five years in the Marine Corps' inactive reserve but after the first year I received a letter informing me that I had been twice passed over for promotion to captain. This was not unexpected. The letter terminated my Marine Corps service and came with a certificate of Honorable Discharge. In some sense it was surprising that my service was deemed honorable, since I had been considered a poor performer and even a troublemaker at times. From 1952 to 1974, the armed forces used Separation Program Numbers (SPN or "spins") to denote sometimes negative assessments of those receiving honorable discharges. For example, SPN 46A was for "unsuitability, apathy, defective attitudes, and inability to expend effort constructively."[8] This seems, at least in part, descriptive of my Marine Corps service. However, I can find no evidence on my discharge papers that any SPN was assigned to me.

The North Vietnamese entered Saigon and united their country at the end of April 1975. But I was at work on my doctoral dissertation in American history and Vietnam had pretty much faded from my consciousness. I won a prize for a graduate school essay that carried publication in a leading American history journal. Despite an academic job crisis, I was offered a tenure-track position at Colgate University in rural upstate New York. Nancy and I visited the campus and found that there were no real professional opportunities for her there. We agreed that a career as a faculty wife was not acceptable, so I turned down the position.

Probably because the war had occasioned so much domestic discord and because we ended up losing, most Americans seemed to blot it from their memories in the second half of the 1970s. This apparent amnesia or willful forgetting, whatever it was, is a major theme of the interviews with veterans in Myra MacPherson's book *Long Time Passing: Vietnam and the Haunted Generation*. In one of the first great memoirs of the Vietnam War, published in 1977, Philip Caputo remembered a Marine friend who fell in the war:

> As I write this, eleven years after your death, the country for which you died wishes to forget the war in which you died. Its very name is a curse. There are no monuments to its heroes, no statues in small-town squares and city parks, no plaques, nor public wreaths, nor memorials.[9]

Of course, those who served in Vietnam and their families and loved ones did not forget but formal recognition of their service and sacrifice did not really begin until the early 1980s. In October 1981, a Vietnam War Memorial was dedicated in South Boston, Massachusetts, a tight-knit community with one of the highest American death rates in the war. In November

1982, the National Vietnam Veterans Memorial opened in Washington. It was funded entirely by private donations. Efforts to recover the remains of missing Americans had to wait until relations between the U.S. and Vietnam improved in the 1990s.

Although I knew nothing about it, this was also a terrible time for the Vietnamese people—the "Subsidy Period" with near starvation for many and severe hardship for almost all, cruel re-education camps for former South Vietnamese soldiers and officials, and the flight of thousands who feared reprisals or could not bear the policies of the communist government. Vietnam's travails were the combined result of the government's economic policies and a U.S.-led trade boycott.

In 1978, Nancy obtained a master's degree in management from the Sloan School of Business at MIT and got a good job with a consulting firm in the Boston area. The next year, after a brief and unsuccessful career as an academic historian—after turning down the Colgate job and finishing my degree, I was able only to land a position at a Massachusetts state college, which I hated—I took a mid-level analyst's job with Abt Associates, another research and consulting organization in Cambridge. The same day I accepted the job at Abt, Nancy and I closed on the house in Watertown in which we still live. Two years later, our daughter Abigail arrived. Another way in which my father had wanted me to follow in his footsteps was by providing a "male heir." I failed to do that. On the other hand, despite being somewhat terrified about raising a child based on my own experience with my father, Nancy and I somehow succeeded in producing a strong, spirited, and accomplished daughter who carries on the Hammett name.

I celebrated my 40th birthday in August 1985 with a dancing party of my favorite songs from the already rapidly receding old days of the 1960s and 1970s. One of the most resonant tunes Nancy and I danced to at my birthday party was Fleetwood Mac's "Landslide," with its unintended allusion to my 1966 "Avalanche" poem and its melancholy realization that "I'm getting older too." Nevertheless, I ran my personal best marathon two months after I turned 40.

When I was in Washington on a business trip, my brother-in-law Paul Haaga took me to a meeting of the group led by Jan Scruggs, Bobby Muller, and others that was advocating for and planning the Vietnam Veterans Memorial. The design by Maya Lin was extremely controversial at first—criticized by some veterans and their advocates as an obscene "scar" that devalued the 58,000 American fallen and sought to discredit the cause for which they sacrificed their lives. To address these concerns, a more traditional sculpture of soldiers and an American flag were added near the angle of the "Wall." After its opening in 1982, the Vietnam Veterans

Memorial quickly became, and still remains, the most visited memorial in Washington and, variously, a place for pilgrimage, remembrance, grieving, healing, and perhaps at least some reconciliation.

Myra MacPherson perceptively notes that the Memorial "captures that confusion, that ambiguity … the coexistence of both nobility of service *and* the inevitable misguidedness" of the war. For some, the message could be even more neutral but nonetheless compelling. According to John Binder, the father of a wounded Vietnam veteran, the Memorial "Doesn't say whether the war was right or wrong.… It just says, 'Here is the price we paid.'"[10] Inevitably, both before and after its appearance, the Wall became entangled with the relentless debates over the War. Kristin Hass asserts that the thousands of "things" of every description left at the Wall "articulate a struggle on the part of ordinary Americans to be a part of a conversation about how the war should be remembered." Moreover, these gifts left at the Wall—flags, ribbons and medals, dog tags, letters, poems, photographs, paintings, flowers, wreaths, sculpture, clothing, jewelry, cigarette lighters, shot glasses, fishing rods, and teddy bears, among many, many others—reflect anger that the nation's debt of gratitude and honor to the lost "was not paid after Vietnam."[11]

I went to the Memorial soon after it opened and the experience moved me deeply, as has every one of my numerous visits since then, most recently with a reunion of my Marine Basic School class in 2015. Visiting the Memorial rekindled in me visceral feelings about the War that for years I must have suppressed or disembodied. Seeing the size of the Wall and finding on it and touching the names of Marines I had known and served with brought home to me the enormity of my country's loss and evoked the inevitable question—"for what?" At the time, I did not consider what the Memorial omitted to acknowledge: the millions of Vietnamese, not to speak of the thousands of Cambodians and Laotians, who also died in the war.[12] These feelings were slower to evolve in me.

11

Returning to Vietnam
for the First Time

It was September 1997, eight months before the death of my father, who had had much to do with my first trip to Vietnam. Of course, I had never been to Hanoi, so I was full of mixed emotions as my Vietnam Airlines flight from Hong Kong landed at Noi Bai Airport. As I came down the steps from the plane to the tarmac and across to the tiny airport building, I again, as I wrote in my journal of the trip, "experienced the spontaneous Vietnam sweat" that I remembered well from my first landing in Vietnam in 1968—"there was no incoming, however." Over the Thang Long Bridge with its banners proclaiming Hanoi "The City for Peace" I found a bustling city with millions of motorbikes (but not yet too many cars), all seemingly trying to get to the same place at the same time on the same narrow streets. In my journal, I asked, "Where is everyone going?" and pronounced Vietnam "a very busy country [with probably] more shops per capita than anywhere on earth.... The scene is endlessly fascinating wherever you go—the crowds, the activity, the conversation, the sheer busy-ness of it all."

Having been dropped off by a taxi on the other side of Cat Linh Street from my hotel, I wondered how I would get across. There I stood with my suitcase watching the ceaseless throng of motorbikes until a kind soul tapped me on the shoulder and urged me to "just go." So, I learned to cross the street in Hanoi, a skill that many tourists and, in fact, my wife never fully mastered. That first night in Hanoi, I wrote "I feel kind of shell-shocked (bad choice of words, I guess!). Here I am back in the 'Nam after 29 years. I feel like a dumb tourist."

I had begun to work on AIDS projects at Abt Associates in 1985—first on AIDS policies in U.S. prisons and jails and then on HIV prevention programs for people who use drugs. This new focus of my work at Abt brought about my re-acquaintance with Vietnam in September 1997. I had the opportunity to help present a training session for Chinese government officials on HIV prevention among people who use drugs. I decided to visit Vietnam as a tourist for a week afterwards. Former Marine infantry platoon commander Philip Caputo wrote of a common feeling among veterans: "In spite of everything, we felt a strange attachment to Vietnam and, even stranger, a longing to return ... [that] ... arose ... from a recognition of how deeply we had been changed" by our experience of the war.[1] My experience of the war was, of course, very different from Caputo's—I had not been a combat Marine—but, as I was beginning to learn, Vietnam had nonetheless changed me in profound ways as well.

Like my first Marine summer camp at Quantico, but much more pleasantly, my first week back in Vietnam in September 1997 was a hectic blur. I had my first taste of Vietnamese coffee and chả cá, a classic Hanoi fish specialty. I saw some important sites in Hanoi including the Hoa Lo prison—originally the Maison Centrale in French colonial days and later the "Hanoi Hilton" where the POWs were held during the American War. I purchased a pirated copy of Graham Greene's *The Quiet American* from a street vendor outside. At first, I tried to participate in the expected bargaining over prices but soon stopped and paid what was asked, as it seemed absurd from my position of relatively extreme wealth to quibble over such trivial amounts of money. At the Army Museum, I viewed the extensive exhibits on Vietnam's victories over the French and the Americans. At one point, I overheard an Australian couple remark that the accounts seemed "a bit biased." Yes, I realized, the victors usually get to write the history. (This isn't always the case, as demonstrated by the persistence of the "Lost Cause" narrative of the Civil War.)

I also visited the Temple of Literature, where mandarins took their degrees back as far as the 15th century and latter-day students came to touch for good luck on upcoming exams the tortoise steles listing the mandarins and their accomplishments. Outside the Temple of Literature, I bought from another street vendor a photocopy of Bảo Ninh's antiwar novel *The Sorrow of War*, a bleakly realistic portrayal of the American War as experienced by an NVA foot soldier.[2] Many years later, there appeared another searing antiwar novel by a Vietnamese writer, Nguyễn Phan Quế Mai. In this tale, based on the experiences of her own family, Quế Mai's main character "realized that war was monstrous. If it didn't kill those it touched, it took away a piece of their souls, so they could never be whole again."[3]

I enjoyed my first big bottles of Bia Hà Nội (Hanoi Beer) on a terrace overlooking Hoan Kiem Lake, the spiritual center of the city. I then traveled to Hue and, as the Vietnam Airlines turboprop approached the airport, I noticed that the patterns of the fields remained the same as in 1968. However, I wrote in my journal, there were some areas near the airfield that looked like they couldn't be reclaimed for agriculture—just burned and scorched these 30 years later—the people in the fields with their conical hats and water buffalo—all that's missing is the omnipresent sound of the helicopters' rotor blades, the artillery and bombs—no more of the outgoing or incoming—no sandbags—no flares or small arms fire on the perimeter. Peace has come to Vietnam. I'm glad to be here to see and hear it.

The small Phu Bai airport building was the same one that I remembered from 1968. I walked across the parking lot and found the former location of the 3rd Medical Battalion hospital and compound where I served the first five months of my wartime tour. I took a picture of the Hue Citadel from the same spot as I had when I passed on a truck convoy in 1968. Only this time there were children playing soccer where before there had been stripped trees, shell craters, and war rubble.

Sitting on my balcony at the little Thai Binh Hotel in the evening

Hue Citadel from truck convoy, 1968.

Hue Citadel with children playing soccer, 1997.

warmth drinking a local Huda Beer ("brewed with Danish technology"), I wrote in my journal:

> The most important thing, I guess, about Vietnam—whether the people are poor or not, better off or not, is that they're at PEACE—no bombs or napalm are falling. The people are laughing and living without fear of imminent death. The dogs are barking and howling at the Mid-Autumn Festival drumming.

Still, as I went to bed that night, I felt that the drumming "in the distance sounds a little like artillery."

I had dinner at Lac Thien restaurant, near the Citadel, run by a family of deaf people. A "succession of visitors" came to my table, including 16-year-old Tùng who gave me his address and a small photo, and Lâm, a little younger, who made me a drawing and a good luck message on a Hue note card. Lâm also showed me a book of contributions from a Hue street kids art project. I added my message of thanks for the warm welcome and said that the last time I saw Hue, it was destroyed by the war, but it had since risen again to be a beautiful city with wonderful people.

The "DMZ Tour" from Hue, which I shared with an amusing British couple, passed by the site of the field hospital in Quang Tri, where my 3rd Medical Battalion had moved from Phu Bai in August 1968. Approaching this place for the first time since April 1969 brought nothing like the anxiety felt by W.D. Ehrhart as he entered Hue for the first time since the battle: "As the bus I'm riding in gets closer to Hue, my heart begins to pound and my palms are sweating. What will it be like? How will I react?"[4] Ehrhart returned to the very building in Hue where he and a fellow Marine had been wounded on February 5, 1968. Reflecting on the meaning of their service and survival, Ehrhart wrote:

> Who would've thought
> the day that RPG exploded
> we'd live to see this day,
> this house, this city, this Vietnam?
> Who would have thought
> we'd ever want to come back
> or be happy because we'd lost?
> This is the very building, Ken.
> This is where we almost died
> for nothing that mattered,
> but didn't.[5]

Of my return to the site of the 3rd Medical Battalion hospital I wrote, rather more prosaically, that

> now there are houses along the road and [it is] open behind [them] where our compound was—Didn't spot [the] old French blockhouses that were on our perimeter but [the] tree line in back looked vaguely familiar. Very funny how you can live in a place for 8 months and not recognize it. The base itself is totally gone.

The tour wound out the now paved Route 9 from Dong Ha to Khe Sanh. Many of the hills still revealed large bomb craters and defoliation from Agent Orange. Indeed, the ravages to Vietnamese land and people wrought by this highly toxic chemical, applied indiscriminately by the U.S. during the war and then continuing to leach into the ground from large storage facilities after we departed, have been long-term and intergenerational.

There was not much at the site of the besieged[6] Marine combat base but an overgrown area that I was told was the site of the airstrip. A few old white phosphorous shells were still lying around. At Khe Sanh, I noted in my journal, there was also an abundance of "the tell-tale red clay mud of the DMZ area—I have a good dose of it on my shoes. I always remember seeing the Marines coming in from the bush with that red clay mud caking their jungle boots."

A few local people were selling war "artifacts" that they claimed to have found using metal detectors—dog tags, rank insignia, USMC eagle, globe, and anchor pins, religious medals, Zippo lighters, mess kit utensils, purported Viet Cong and NVA buttons and insignia. I bought a few real-looking U.S. dog tags bearing Marine Corps service numbers. Later,

I found the owner of one of these dog tags through an Internet search and had a brief telephone conversation with him. He told me that he had served in the 4th Marines and had suffered from PTSD for a long time after the war. I had thought it would be interesting to meet him but quickly gave up that idea and regretted very much my thoughtlessness in bringing his trauma back to him. He didn't ask me to, but I mailed his dog tag back to this former Marine with a simple "Semper Fi" written on the envelope.

My last day in Hue, I took a boat trip on the Perfume River and visited the Thien Mu Pagoda, which displays the car driven by the monk in 1963 to the Saigon intersection where he immolated himself to protest the Diệm regime's persecution of Vietnam's Buddhists. At the pagoda, I was invited by one of the current monks to have tea and cake with him in his room. We talked quietly and amiably. He asked me what I had done during the war and how I felt about it. I tried to explain. He wanted to know what I thought of Vietnam now. I said that I already loved it. The monk made me a beautiful calligraphy drawing with the Chinese characters for angel and good fortune and both of our names at the bottom. This moment captured for me the new peaceful relations between America and Vietnam.

I had some anodyne conversation with my father about my return trip to Vietnam. He always referred to Vietnam as "out there," as if it was in outer space, in contrast to "the World," as our troops generally called the U.S. during the war. No doubt, I focused on how much I liked the beer. I did not tell him about my conversation with the monk in Hue. I probably did not mention to him that my experience being back in Vietnam had

At the site of Khe Sanh air strip, 1997.

deepened my feelings not only for what the U.S. had done to the country but also what I had done to disrespect and mistreat the Vietnamese people during my wartime tour. I had believed that the American war was wrong. Over time, I also came to understand and feel personally guilty for my own racist attitudes towards the Vietnamese and my own contribution to the carnage and destruction of the war. So, slowly percolating in me over the years was a desire to do something positive in this country and for these people we had so wronged. Some American veterans had already gone back to take up this work of reconciliation. Chuck Searcy helped to launch an organization to find and remove unexploded ordinance in Quang Tri province, where I had served. Thousands of Vietnamese children and adults have been maimed or killed by the land mines, artillery shells, and bombs that littered the countryside. Other veterans had begun returning to Vietnam to help build schools, libraries, and health clinics. Still others worked on Agent Orange mitigation.

12

The Cross-Border Project

In 1997, the HIV epidemics in northern Vietnam and southern China were growing, as opium smokers turned to heroin injection along drug trans-shipment routes linking the poppy growing and heroin producing "Golden Triangle" of Thailand, Burma, and Laos with Hong Kong and the wider world. The transition to drug injection in the Vietnam-China border area brought the sharing of contaminated injection equipment and a sharp increase in HIV infection and AIDS.

At the training session in Kunming, China my colleague Don Des Jarlais and I met an official of Vietnam's National AIDS Committee and we began to discuss with him and some of the Chinese participants a possible HIV prevention project for people who inject drugs in the Vietnam-China border area. This would become my opportunity to return to work in Vietnam. It was also my great opportunity to work closely with Don Des Jarlais, one of the world's leading experts in HIV prevention among people who use drugs. Don and I and our initial Vietnamese and Chinese collaborators wanted to implement and evaluate the effectiveness of interventions, such as provision of sterile needles and syringes, to reduce HIV infection among people who inject drugs on both sides of the border.

Getting the project off the ground was extremely complicated. Even though they had become major trading partners, China and Vietnam had a fraught and often bloody relationship going back thousands of years. This project raised the very sensitive possibility of one country blaming the other for exporting HIV across its border. In addition, needle and syringe programs were quite controversial in both countries. They fall into a category known as "harm reduction," which calls for less attention to the arguably quixotic goal of eliminating drug use and more to reducing the risks and harms associated with its inevitable persistence. In the late 1990s and early 2000s, few if any such programs existed in Vietnam and the government was very skeptical of them based on the view that they would only encourage drug use. Finally, the U.S. had diplomatic relations with both countries, but American funding and technical collaborations were still in their early stages, especially in Vietnam. The Centers for Disease Control and Prevention had established an office in Hanoi, but the U.S. Agency for International Development (USAID) was not yet present.

The Cross-Border project achieved significant success over eight years. Risk behaviors (sharing of injection equipment), HIV prevalence (the percentage of the target population infected with HIV at a given time), and HIV incidence (the annual rate of new cases of HIV among previously uninfected drug injectors) were all substantially reduced.

In launching and implementing the Cross-Border Project, I had the good fortune to meet and work with several Vietnamese champions of enlightened approaches to HIV prevention. Professor Pham Manh Hùng, Vice Chair of the Communist Party's Central Propaganda Department, came to a talk I gave on the Cross-Border Project at the Ford Foundation, which was one of its principal funders. Prof. Hùng was impressed with the project's achievements and became a champion of harm reduction and other effective HIV prevention strategies. His support contributed to the acceptance and proliferation of such interventions in Vietnam.

As director of the National AIDS Committee (NAC), Professor Chung Á had to approve Vietnam's participation in the Cross-Border Project. He had recently overseen a successful pilot test of a needle/syringe program in Hanoi, but the Cross-Border project required a much larger and lengthier commitment. Chung Á gave his enthusiastic support and designated Dr. Đoàn Ngữ as the NAC's point person for our collaboration.

The Cross-Border project and several other HIV/AIDS projects that I worked on for Abt Associates between 2002 and 2008 gave me the opportunity to visit Vietnam multiple times each year. All the while, I was meeting new colleagues and making new friends in Vietnam. I was coming more and more to understand and appreciate the country, its people, its scenery, and its food.

Dr. Đoàn Ngữ was my first true Vietnamese colleague and became a very good friend. Born in 1960, he was a medical doctor and trained as a pediatrician. During the American War, his parents evacuated him from Hanoi to Lang Son to escape the bombing. Their Hanoi home was just off Kham Thien street in a neighborhood leveled with significant loss of life in the U.S.'s Christmas bombing of 1972.

Dr. Ngữ helped smooth the way through multiple bureaucratic tangles to obtain the approvals needed from the government to implement the Cross-Border project. He was also instrumental in winning and maintaining the cooperation of the provincial health departments with whom the project partnered on the ground.

In 2000, I traveled with him to visit prospective project sites in Cao Bang and Lang Son Provinces. On that trip and many more thereafter, we were lucky to have the services of Mr. Hưng, a "champion driver." On the five-hour drive from Hanoi to Cao Bang, he drove incredibly fast and, as I wrote in my journal, we had "innumerable near misses with trucks, busses, people on motorbikes, pedestrians, bicycles, dogs, water buffalo, donkeys, ducks, pigs, [and] piglets." Horns honked constantly and I observed that "everyone seems fearless, heedless of danger."

The scenery was increasingly beautiful as we traversed mountain passes named "windy" and "heaven" in Vietnamese, with mist on one side and clear sky on the other, rocky outcroppings, terraced rice fields and green tea growing on the steep slopes. We stopped for local fruit at the top of "windy" pass but declined the offers of bee and lizard wine. In Cao Bang, we had good meetings with local health officials and the Vice Chair of a commune People's Committee, who expressed enthusiasm for the proposed project. We also had the opportunity to attend the 50th anniversary celebration of a major victory of the Việt Minh over the French, complete with Cao Bang's first fireworks display since 1975. From Cao Bang to Lang Son, we passed through more

> beautiful mountain scenery, spectacular passes, drop-offs, sudden quick showers, then sun again. Incredibly rough road for stretches—steep grades, hairpin turns, loose gravel, ruts, potholes and the usual assortment of motorbikes, trucks, busses, children playing in the road, chickens, dogs, water buffalo, cows, one rabbit—Nobody got a scratch and we didn't fall over the edge. What a drive!

Dr. Ngữ and I shared many more long trips over rough roads and mountain passes to visit the selected project sites in Lang Son and Ha Giang, where we met with provincial health officials, police, peer educators (current or former drug injectors who delivered HIV prevention education information, sterile injection equipment and condoms in the community), and community leaders, and oversaw the behavioral surveys and HIV testing of people who use drugs that were the basis of our evaluation of the Cross-Border Project's interventions. During these site visits, Dr. Ngữ patiently translated for me the oral reports of peer educators and our meetings and interactions with provincial and local government officials.

On our trips, Dr. Ngữ always pointed out for me the scenic and cultural sites and described the local customs and foods. He introduced me to the sautéed bees and duck phở of Lang Son and the ấu tẩu (rice and pork gruel) of Ha Giang, which we would always seek out when we arrived there late at night after the long drive from Hanoi. On one of these trips, our car got stuck in the mud and we had to push it out by hand. On another, we had to take a boat across a flooded-out portion of the road and continue to Ha Giang in another car.

Throughout this work, Dr. Ngữ revealed his love of the history, variegated beauty, and cultural diversity of his country. After the day's work was done, we attended many banquets with government officials, peer educators, and other project collaborators, sang many songs, and sometimes drank too much "local liquor." Dr. Ngữ's dedication to the work and his wry sense of humor always helped us along.

Dr. Ngữ invited me to his home near Kham Thien, which he had inherited from his parents, and I got to know his family. We enjoyed many meals together. His daughter Linh shared with me her recipe for rice porridge (cháo)) and his son Hưng told me about his chess tournaments—he became an age-group champion. I was amused by the family's Premier League rivalry—Dr. Ngữ and Hưng rooted for Manchester United while Linh was a devotee of Chelsea—which reminded me of my own family's bitter Red Sox–Yankees divisions.

Dr. Ngữ visited us in Watertown, Massachusetts, while he was on a training fellowship in New York City and we were able to introduce him to some of the history of Boston, walk through Harvard Yard, and treat him to some New England seafood. I also took him to a Red Sox game at Fenway Park, which he seemed to enjoy although he did not fully understand the rules. For good luck, Dr. Ngữ had done the traditional rubbing of John Harvard's statuary foot by University Hall, but this didn't work out too well for him. During a flight connection on his way back to Vietnam, Dr. Ngữ lost his wallet at LAX. Since he had lost his drivers' license, I was pressed into service to drive part of the way back from Ha Giang to Hanoi when I was in Vietnam a few weeks later. It was one of my very few experiences driving a car in Vietnam, which was exhilarating and hair-raising at the same time. Dr. Ngữ casually napped in the back seat and later complimented my driving.

Nancy never joined me on my trips to Vietnam between 2002 and 2008, but our daughter Abigail did make one trip with me in the summer of 2003. It was a gift for her graduation from the University of Pennsylvania. She immediately loved Vietnam and would come back to visit us five times, including every Christmas, when we later lived in Hanoi.

During Abigail's first visit, we spent a few days in Hanoi seeing the usual tourist sites and shopping for gifts for a seemingly endless list of her friends. She is an inveterate shopper and, despite temperatures in the upper 90s with excruciatingly high humidity, insisted on visiting and re-visiting virtually every silk shop on Hang Gai Street in Hanoi's Old Quarter before settling on the perfect gift for each of her friends. I was completely wilted by then, but Abigail was very happy with her purchases. Leaving Hanoi, we headed for an overnight boat trip on Halong Bay, including kayaking into karst-surrounded lagoons, swimming in the bathtub-hot water, and eating delicious seafood meals. From Halong, we went on to Lang Son for a visit to the Cross-Border Project's sites there, and Abigail got to sample some local delicacies, including sautéed bee larvae and adult bees, and to join a traditional Vietnamese after-work banquet with abundant local rice wine.

During my work travels I did several more "DMZ tours" with my new Vietnamese colleagues, including Dr. Ngữ. In 2006, with the help of some older residents of a village that by then occupied the site of the 3rd Medical Battalion field hospital in Quang Tri, we found its exact location. Like the area by the Citadel in Hue, it was now a children's soccer field. Khe Sanh was being developed as a tourist site with a small museum. The guest book contained many entries posing various versions of the question: "Will we never learn?"

In October 2008, after a year in which I travelled to Vietnam ten times, Abt Associates prevailed in the re-competition for a U.S. government-funded HIV/AIDS policy project. I had been proposed to lead the project. Nancy had recently left her position as executive director of an environmental NGO and agreed to move with me to Hanoi, sight unseen.

Part III: My Second Tour

13

Living in Vietnam

In March 1968, I was not at all happy to be going to Vietnam to participate in a war that I believed was wrong. Forty years later, I felt excited to be moving to Hanoi and having the chance to live and work in Vietnam. My excitement derived in good part from a desire to atone for my sins against the Vietnamese people during my wartime tour. I was also putting to rest my regret for having submitted to my father by remaining in the Marine Corps and going to the war. On the other hand, if I had not submitted to my father, I would have had no such personal sins for which to atone and no compelling reason to go back to live in Vietnam. It is strange how bad things can sometimes lead to good. In addition, I must acknowledge that this was a good move for my career. It would be an engaging, nicely compensated job in a pleasant setting with rich opportunities to do interesting research and publish some good journal articles.

I left the U.S. in October 2008 in the midst of a financial crisis and an election campaign in which Barack Obama appeared likely to become the nation's first African American president. I arrived in Hanoi during an historic flood that inundated several of the city's neighborhoods. Some of our project staff were unable to get home and had to sleep in the office for almost a week.

Although I had by then visited Hanoi many times for other projects, this was my first time actually living there or indeed anywhere abroad since my first Vietnam tour during the war. It was my first experience of the "expat" life. For the first month I lived in a hotel next door to our office. In that hotel room, I watched the election returns on CNN and tears of joy came to my eyes as Barack Obama was declared the victor. Joined by his beautiful family, he addressed the huge crowd of his supporters, and the nation, in Chicago's Grant Park with a powerful message of hope.

Obama's defeated opponent was Senator John McCain, a former naval aviator who had been shot down on a bombing run over Hanoi in 1967. His parachute had settled in Truc Bach Lake, not far from my new home. McCain, the son and grandson of admirals, was the most famous of the

American POWs imprisoned at the "Hanoi Hilton." He was an undoubted war hero, despite Donald Trump's shameful preference for "those who were not captured." After the war, despite his brutal treatment at the hands of his captors, McCain was one of the leaders in the effort to establish friendship and diplomatic relations between the United States and Vietnam. The anti-aircraft gunners who brought down McCain's fighter in 1967 are commemorated in a marker by the shore of Truc Bach Lake. Upon McCain's death in August 2018 many flowers were placed at the monument in his honor by both Vietnamese and American people. I was happy to see this display of reconciliation, friendship, and respect between our countries.

Barack Obama was inaugurated a few days before Tết (Vietnamese for the Lunar New Year), 2009. He mentioned Khe Sanh in his address—one in a list of hallowed places where American blood had been spilled in war. This was by way of remembrance of and tribute to the men who served and suffered at Khe Sanh, like Bruce Springsteen's in "Born in the U.S.A.,"[1] rather than endorsement of the misguided policy that caused them to be there. I was living in Hanoi for almost all of President Obama's first term. I was thrilled to see his photo go up in the lobbies of U.S. government offices in Hanoi. I was proud to be an American and it seemed to me that real change had come to the U.S. and Vietnam.[2]

I came to love many of Hanoi's oddly contradictory qualities—its architectural charm and quiet spaces as well as its walkability, vibrant street life, noise, smells, and relentless bustle. Nancy was new to Vietnam when she arrived in Hanoi in January 2009, and understandably a bit apprehensive. Everything was so different from home. It was her first experience of living overseas. A few days after Nancy's arrival, we took a long walk around town, ending up on a bench at the head of Dien Bien Phu Street, just inches from the chaos of vehicular and pedestrian traffic. But we sat there for a long time watching the Hanoi world go by. Nancy grew to like the place, hanging out at Saint Honore, a French café on Xuan Dieu, getting hot stone massages, viewing and discussing classic Vietnamese movies at the Hanoi Cinematheque, visiting pagodas and communal houses, and learning about Vietnamese culture and spirituality.

How Hanoi had changed since 1984, when William Broyles became the first Marine combat veteran to visit Vietnam after the war and write about that experience: "to visit Hanoi is like coming upon an ancient city…. Only the hiss of thousands of bicycle wheels on the pavement penetrated the silence."[3] The changes even since my first visit in 1997 were almost as dramatic: to the millions of motorbikes had been added thousands of larger motor vehicles and the previous low-rise city now had many tall modern apartment buildings and even some skyscrapers. However, it remained as true as it had been for John Balaban in 1989 that "Walking through Hanoi is like walking through history"—the narrow streets of the Old Quarter with their medieval market names and the broader major streets commemorating a thousand years of heroes who fought a string of foreign invaders.[4]

Hanoi's Old Quarter always had streets devoted to different crafts or products, such as silk, copper, bamboo, shoes, and musical instruments. These still exist and are now home to multitudes of shops all selling the same types of items. Hawkers and street vendors abound. The specialized offerings have been updated to include more modern wares such as eyeglasses, electrical supplies, plumbing, luggage, stationery and office supplies, holiday decorations (including Christmas and Halloween, as well as Tết), mannequins, and every imaginable type of clothing. "Underwear Street," a narrow alley off Hang Dao catering mostly to women shopping from their motorbikes, was always one of my daughter Abigail's favorite Hanoi destinations.

Amid all the shops in the Old Quarter are beautiful pagodas and shrines, as well as many restaurants and street food stalls, souvenir shops, art galleries (some featuring the original work of accomplished local artists and some offering pretty good copies of European masterworks), and boutique hotels. The Old Quarter is almost always crowded and busy, with Vietnamese people and foreigners enjoying the shopping, food, and chaos. I sometimes found it a bit too crowded but always somehow exhilarating. It offers perhaps the best vignette of the vibrance of the new Vietnam.

We lived in Tay Ho (or West Lake) District, named for the largest of Hanoi's many lakes. We rented a typically tall (five floors) but narrow (due to the shortage of land) Hanoi house on a lane off Xuan Dieu Street, just a few doors in from the lakeshore. Nancy helped write a guidebook of walking tours around West Lake for the Friends of Vietnam Heritage.

Phương Châu was Abt Associates' first Vietnamese employee who launched our Hanoi office in 2005. She helped Nancy and me to find our house in Tay Ho and to get acclimated to Hanoi in countless ways. Phương introduced us to the prayers and special foods constituting the cultural rituals of moving into a new house or new office. She recommended for Nancy the best fortune tellers and massage places and provided us with bunches of medicinal herbs that helped cure our winter colds. At work, Phương always made sure that we were on the right side of government and police regulations for foreigners living in Hanoi. She was also expert in navigating the licensing requirements for foreign organizations, helping to ensure our continued ability to do our work.

Vân Phùng was our housekeeper in Tay Ho. She came highly recommended and we were lucky to have her with us the entire time we lived in

Hanoi. Like most Americans, Nancy and I had only limited experience with household employees. We tried to pay her fairly—actually above the normal scale—because she has two children and a husband who doesn't make very much money. Vân did all of the work to keep our house and our clothes clean, dealt with the landlord and the utility companies, and cooked us three delicious dinners a week to boot. Her help was a luxury that we missed greatly when we left Hanoi. In addition to being a house-keeper for two families, Vân maintained two on-line businesses, selling lipstick she made from organic ingredients and cuts of meat she sourced from wholesale butchers. For me, Vân exemplifies Vietnamese diligence, imagination, and initiative.

Tay Ho was, until early in the 21st century, a district primarily of small villages, flower gardens, nurseries, and lotus ponds. Some of these survive. The traditional communal house (dinh) still marks each "village," although these are now interlinked urban neighborhoods. Tay Ho nurs-eries remain the chief source of traditional kumquat trees for Tết and the lotus ponds still fill with beautiful red flowers every summer. But thou-sands of new homes, apartment buildings, high-rise hotels, businesses, and restaurants and hundreds of expatriate residents have transformed the area. Nancy and I loved living in this neighborhood with its diverse blend of Vietnamese people and foreigners, which also retained many qualities of a traditional Vietnamese urban village.

At group lunches and book club meetings, Nancy also saw the "Ugly American" side of expatriate life. Many foreigners come to live in rela-tively poor countries as rich, highly privileged people, taking little or no real interest in the culture or people of the host country except as exotic

West Lake from our house; in the distance, new skyscraper under construction.

curiosities, household staff, or sexual objects. Indeed, the expat gatherings were often dominated by complaints about Vietnam, the difficulty of finding good "help" and the corruption and mendacity of the Vietnamese government. When Nancy pointed out that the U.S. government had done a certain amount of lying to our people about the American War, she was met with astonished silence. After this, she stopped showing up to expat group events.

In the tradition of wartime sexual exploitation of Vietnamese women by American soldiers, many American and other Western white men—particularly older men who have for whatever reason been unable to find suitable Western partners or achieve satisfying relationships with them—come to Asian countries like Vietnam to find younger women, whom they fetishize as exotically beautiful and to whom they can offer economic security. Some American and other Western men have abandoned their families to take up with much younger Vietnamese women.

Since our project worked all over the country, I had the opportunity to see and appreciate more and more the beauty and diversity of Vietnam's culture and scenery: remote mountainous regions; dense jungles; terraced fields of rice and tea; beautiful pagodas and temples; the villages of some of the country's 53 ethnic minority groups around Sapa and Mai Chau; a seacoast of more than 2,000 miles studded with beautiful beaches and bays; rice fields of vivid green yielding three crops per year in the south and two in the north; and the Mekong Delta with its multitude of intersecting rivers and canals, floating markets, and waterborne life.

Nancy and I had many visits from family and friends. Family visitors included my stepbrother Jiggs (on his first trip to Vietnam since his time as a helicopter pilot in the Mekong Delta during the war), and my sisters Peggy, Janet, and Jill, with their husbands Rudy, Bruce, and Dick. We enjoyed very much playing tour guides, showing off the sights, sounds, and tastes of Hanoi and other Vietnamese destinations. My sister Jill later wrote me that her first impressions of Hanoi were

> total amazement and a desire to understand and learn more. Going around the corner, sitting on plastic milk crates for pop-up breakfast phở was really new and different for me…. Loops of tangled wires hanging from every pole. The shrines and altars laden with whoopie pies, beers, and cigarettes prompted so many questions.

Without reason or understanding, I had disliked and mistreated the Vietnamese people during my wartime tour. I had also assumed that Vietnamese culture was negligible. When I returned for my second tour, I already knew and liked many Vietnamese colleagues from the projects I had begun working on in 1997. These friendships and professional relationships only expanded and deepened from there. My fondness for the Vietnamese was also influenced by many kind and hard-working people I met in our neighborhood, in shops, cafes, and restaurants, and on the lanes and streets of Hanoi and other cities and towns.

Most Vietnamese people that I encountered were extremely friendly toward me and other Americans. More than three-quarters of the people in Vietnam were born since the American War ended in 1975. These demographics help to explain the positive attitudes of many Vietnamese people toward American culture and their warmth and welcoming behavior towards Americans.

At home in the U.S. those who have spent time in Vietnam invariably get the question, "Are the Vietnamese people hostile to Americans?" The answer is emphatically the contrary. In an email to me as the Covid-19 pandemic exploded in the U.S. in the spring of 2020, Diệp, a university student and daughter of one of our staff members in Hanoi, wrote that "I always have a strong [belief] in Americans and the USA. Your country [has] dealt with many even harder obstacles before and overcame them successfully." Diệp is very interested in American history, especially our Founding Fathers, and I recommended to her several biographies of Washington and Jefferson. Hồ Chí Minh taught that it was the U.S. government and not the American people who fought the war against Vietnam.[5] He also famously cited the American Declaration of Independence in his proclamation of the Democratic Republic of Vietnam in 1945. All over Vietnam are places selling large stone statuary. Invariably, those on offer include both busts of Hồ Chí Minh and replicas of the Statue of Liberty, often right next to one another. This may seem incongruous, but it is not.

Some of our Tay Ho neighbors had small sewing workshops in their houses, looking out onto the lane. These seemed to be in operation seven days a week. As is common in many Hanoi neighborhoods, there was a morning market on our lane, starting very early, with a wide variety of food and other goods for sale. Some of the vendors lived in the neighborhood and set up shop right in front of their homes. Others came in with their goods by bicycle or motorbike from other Hanoi neighborhoods or the countryside. We often bought fruit, vegetables, and eggs from these market vendors. Some storefronts were built right into houses. At a family-run convenience store on Lane 31, I bought Bia Hà Nội, Cosy Marie biscuits, Vietnamese 3-in-1 instant coffee, and smooth custardy Vietnamese yogurt. The family was often having their meals at a table right in the shop. I also got to know the lady and her husband who sold bread on the lane. Many mornings I bought their bánh mì (Vietnam's French bread made with rice flour) with pork pâté, a French influence.

Some mornings, particularly in the cool weather months, I brought my own bowl to buy delicious cháo sườn—rice porridge with pork rib meat, ginger, and herbs—from another lady in Lane 31. There were also several beef phở stalls nearby. Many of the same customers were often present at these places every day; we got to hear a lot of neighborhood gossip, as much as we could understand. Sellers of housewares, ceramics, and clothing were also part of the street market. These vendors all spent long hours selling in all kinds of weather. Sometimes they would have to scatter if the police showed up—as they were largely unlicensed and would be called upon to bribe the police in order to stay in business.

On the road by the lake at the end of our lane, I met Mr. Long, a local driver with an old Mazda sedan that sometimes seemed on its last legs. It broke down once on a steamy summer day when Mr. Long was driving Nancy downtown. Mr. Long is a very cheerful guy who seems to work around the clock, seven days a week to support his family. He proudly reported on the accomplishments of his two sons, one in university and one working in Danang. Mr. Long is always available to do late-night airport drop-offs and pickups. He speaks fairly good English although occasionally we miscommunicated. His old Mazda finally died, and Mr. Long had for a while to join the populous ranks of the xe ôm (motorbike taxi) drivers until he was able to afford a new car. He now drives freelance, as well as for Grab, the Southeast Asian equivalent of Uber and Lyft.

The Vietnamese are generally kind and gracious, both to each other and to foreigners. Women friends and colleagues often walk arm in arm on the street and young men with their arms draped over each other's shoulders. Young people frequently greet foreigners on the street with a cheerful "hello" or "xin chào" and "where are you from?" Students often approach foreigners to practice their English. Some observers, Vietnamese and foreigners, believe that the people in the South are friendlier and more open than those in the North. This was not my experience. I found Northerners to be equally warm and friendly.

At the same time, to foreign eyes, Vietnamese people can sometimes seem pushy and rude, especially to each other. They cut in line and cut in traffic and yell peremptorily for "em ơi!" (wait staff) in restaurants. Actually, "em ơi," "anh ơi," and "chị ơi" are also warm greetings for friends and colleagues of different age groups.

During their long wars and the subsequent hard economic times, the Vietnamese demonstrated remarkable determination and endurance in the face of everyday difficulty and existential threat. In the recent more prosperous and forgiving times, they still display these qualities.

It may be a relatively trivial matter, but I always noticed the resilience of the Vietnamese in dealing with the weather. Hanoi in the summer is subject to frequent heavy rains with occasional street flooding. When a storm breaks, the thousands of motorbike riders simply pull off to the side of the road, put on their plastic ponchos, and just keep going on with their journeys, no matter how heavy the rain. Often two or three riders will be huddled under one poncho with their legs drawn up to avoid being splashed when going through big puddles. Life goes on. The weather is what it is. The people just seem to accept it without complaining.[6]

The same is true of the heat and the congestion of the urban environment. Parked motorbikes often block sidewalks but, during times of congestion, sidewalks become part of the streets, allowing for more movement of traffic. Everybody lives so close together and, in the hot months, they spill right out onto the streets with food stalls and shops crammed together and virtually no personal space. Street vendors sit placidly waving their bamboo fans. Even on scorching days, women riding their motorbikes cover themselves completely with back-to-front full-length garments, long gloves, and masks to protect their skin from the sun. I often spotted an old man moving very slowly and perhaps painfully with a cane, faithfully performing his daily exercise along Ong Ich Khiem and Le Hong Phong streets, even on the most brutally hot summer afternoons.

The father of Vân Nghiêm, a member of our project staff, was sent by the government to work in the Soviet Union during its time as a strong ally and provider of major financial assistance to Vietnam. He was a machinist who was away in Russia for almost all of Vân's early childhood. He returned with a disabling injury. Vân's mother was a primary school teacher who supplemented her income by giving extra classes in her home in the evenings and on weekends. Unable to continue working after his return from Russia, Vân's father turned to raising birds and orchids at their home on Doi Can. Despite their difficulties, they built a strong and happy family.

My Vietnamese teacher Báu's five years studying and working in Russia are mainly memorable to her for the bitter cold weather. When she returned to Vietnam, Báu took up a university position in which she taught Russian for several years. When the Soviet Union fell and the second language of choice changed, she switched to teaching English to Vietnamese people and Vietnamese to English speakers. Báu says that when she really does retire, she may join her daughter Quỳnh in the U.S. But retirement is something that many people in Vietnam never seem to do completely, perhaps because they can't afford it.

Báu did her best to teach me Vietnamese, but I never came close to mastering the language. It helps that Vietnamese uses the Roman alphabet (minus the F, J, W, and Z) but I didn't practice enough, partly because our project staff were all fluent in English and it wasn't efficient for me to try to communicate with them in my halting Vietnamese. I did learn a lot of practical words—directions for taxi drivers, food items for ordering in restaurants, the age-appropriate pronouns, numbers, times of day, and some important exclamations like "no vấn đề!"—hybrid Vietnamese-English for "no problem!"—and "ối giời ơi!," the equivalent of "Oh my God!"—OMG in social media parlance and applicable to things on the full spectrum from wonderful to awful. Had I thought of it, "ối giời ơi!" would have been my perfect response to witnessing the birth of my granddaughter Iggy.

Despite Báu's best efforts, however, I was never able even to form simple Vietnamese sentences. When I had to give opening speeches at project events, I did occasionally try to speak the first few sentences in Vietnamese but that was only by memorizing them. And memorizing their pronunciation. Pronunciation in Vietnamese is extremely precise, based on six tones—in the South five tones are used but the same written diacritical marks are used in all regional Vietnamese dialects. Even the slightest mistake can make the word mean something completely different from that intended—and often something obscene. Such mistakes resulted in surprise outbursts of laughter during several of my attempted opening speeches.

Mr. Vinh is a tour guide from Hue who took me and various of my colleagues and guests on "DMZ tours." Mr. Vinh had quite a war history of his own. He was a sergeant in the Army of the Republic of Vietnam (ARVN, or South Vietnamese Army), assigned as a translator to several U.S. Army units. He was awarded a U.S. Army Commendation Medal for his exemplary service. In 1975, as the NVA made their final push to take over the South and unite the country, Mr. Vinh found himself in Danang on the eve of that city's fall. Fearful of his treatment at the hands of the advancing northerners, he destroyed all the documentation of his service in the ARVN and with U.S. units, including his medal and citation.

Mr. Vinh was indeed captured by the NVA and spent several years in a re-education camp. His two brothers both had it worse—they were in the camps for about seven years but then were able to emigrate to the U.S. Mr. Vinh himself tried to emigrate but was ineligible for the program because he had not been an officer in the ARVN. So, he moved back to Hue and, when diplomatic relations were established with the U.S., began to teach English. He taught all of the staff at La Residence, a beautiful hotel on the banks of the Perfume River, at which we enjoyed many stays.

He also began conducting his battlefield tours for the increasing number of U.S. veterans returning to Vietnam and other tourists from all over the world. Mr. Vinh is very knowledgeable about the war's history. His tours stop at the well-known sites: Khe Sanh; the Rockpile; the

Da Krong River Bridge where the Ho Chi Minh Trail crossed Route 9; the former DMZ; and the museum run by an organization that removes unexploded ordnance, a terrible scourge of this area and its people. Mr. Vinh's tours also stop at lesser known places: the site of Ai Tu, an American base near Con Thien[7]; a U.S. Marine helicopter revetment now embedded in the expanded City of Dong Ha, Quang Tri's provincial capital, that arose on the site of the American airbase; a Catholic Church that was the scene of heavy fighting and virtually destroyed during the NVA's Easter Offensive of 1972; and the "Horrible Highway," the stretch of Route 1 south of Quang Tri City where fleeing civilians and ARVN soldiers were, according to Mr. Vinh and many commentators, slaughtered by the NVA after it overran the city. According to Judith Coburn, an American reporter who was there, most of these civilian casualties actually resulted from U.S. naval gunfire.[8] Mr. Vinh takes his tour groups to visit the cemetery by the highway where many of these victims were buried and where their descendants still return to pay tribute to them and maintain their graves.

During one of our tours, Mr. Vinh asked me if I could help him recover his Army Commendation Medal and citation which he had destroyed in 1975 in hopes of avoiding NVA retribution. I was able to contact the right agency of the U.S. Army, which found Mr. Vinh's decoration. They sent it to me in a handsome embossed leatherette case and I presented it to Mr. Vinh during a later trip to Hue. He was very pleased. We have remained friends and I have seen him on many of my visits to Hue. I have invited him and his wife for meals at La Residence, where he greets members of the staff to whom he taught English. Mr. Vinh has worked extremely hard to make a life for himself and his family and bring knowledge and pleasure to many tourists. He is seemingly tireless and, at the age of 72, still leads DMZ tours almost every day. I regularly see the photos Mr. Vinh posts on Facebook of him with his tourists from the U.S., Europe, and Australia. He is a true survivor.

The Vietnamese have faced many challenges throughout their history. Some have portrayed them, particularly the Communists of the North, as dour, stoic, and humorless. On the contrary, I think that the Vietnamese people's rich and often irreverent sense of humor, which I very frequently observed, must have played an important role in their surviving and overcoming these difficulties. My Vietnamese friends and colleagues seemed fully able to laugh at themselves and each other and the foibles of their government.

Our next-door neighbor on Sublane 31 was Ms. Mai, an elderly lady who lived with her children and grandchildren in a typically multi-generational Vietnamese household. I never saw her husband and assumed that he had died. Due to our relative closeness in advanced age, we used the appropriate pronouns: I called her "Chi Mai" and she called me "Anh"—but never knew my given name. We always greeted each other amiably in the lane. Sometimes, if she thought I'd gained weight, Ms. Mai would give me a gentle pat on my tummy.

14

Birds and Animals

Nancy and I kept several caged birds in our Hanoi home. These were given to us by the family of Vân Nghiêm and by Dr. Ngữ. The first one given us by Vân's family was a gorgeous "five-color" bird that we had only briefly. Unfortunately, we were not well versed in bird care and left his cage directly under the air conditioner in our bedroom on a surprisingly warm early spring night. The bird caught a severe cold and we sent him back to Vân's father to nurse back to health. Sadly, he died after a few weeks. We learned that lesson and Vân's father gave us another chance with two chim quyên (we named them "Bird" and "Ernie"), lively little yellow birds that lived healthily with us for several years.

Bird left us a bit earlier than Ernie. We had an American student intern living with us for the summer and she was apparently opposed on principle to keeping birds in cages. Perceiving that one of the chim quyên was particularly unhappy in its captivity (we had not noticed this), she probably allowed it to escape out the window one weekend when Nancy and I were away. She told us that Bird had escaped accidentally but we suspected the truth. Ernie lived with us until our departure from Hanoi in 2012, when he went back to Vân's family and lived several more years with them.

We also had a chích chòe lửa (white-rumped shama in English), a bird of remote mountainous and jungle areas of Southeast Asia, including Northwestern Vietnam.[1] Dr. Ngữ had bought him in Ha Giang and gave him to us. His name was Oscar, and he was a prolific and beautiful singer, often waking us early in the morning with his various calls, demanding to have the cover removed from his cage and be fed breakfast. He actually sang intermittently all day and into the evening. We enjoyed giving the birds their weekly baths. Oscar joined Ernie in returning to Vân's family and he, too had several more good years of singing left in him before he passed on.

Ms. Mai, our Tay Ho neighbor, had a cat who became quite interested in our pet birds. One nice evening, when we had the windows open in our second floor living room with the bird cage just inside, the cat, who had somehow climbed to this level, came right in the open window, and knocked over the cage in an effort to get to Ernie, our little yellow chim quyên. Ernie was terrified but we were able to push the cat back out the window before it did any damage. The very next day, however, the cat somehow got back into our house and was looking for the birds. The landlord's handyman, who happened to be there, chased the cat up to the fifth floor, caught it, and threw it out the window. Naturally, I was concerned that the cat might have been killed by the fall but, in fact, the next day I saw it prancing along in Ms. Mai's yard apparently none the worse for wear. More evidence of Vietnamese resilience! The cat, however, never tried to get into our house again. Ms. Mai thought the whole episode quite amusing, as apparently did her cat, who lived quite contentedly for several more years.

Many Vietnamese keep pet birds and one can hear them singing in the lanes where bird cages are hanging out on balconies above. Also, there are places on Nguyen Du street and elsewhere in Hanoi where owners gather with their birds on weekend mornings so the birds can sing to each other. Hanoi seems to have relatively few wild birds, except for small egrets in the lakes and the brightly colored miniature kingfishers that I occasionally saw by West Lake.

We had some acquaintance with other Vietnamese birds and animals. Hanoi's ceramic wall, commemorating the city's 1000th birthday, includes many panels depicting actual Vietnamese creatures and those of Vietnamese legend and superstition: elephant; monkey; stork; dove (especially because Hanoi is the "City for Peace"); phoenix; carp and other fish.

There are many dogs in Vietnam, mostly mongrel street dogs, some of which are family pets, but many others are strays. They are generally allowed to run free on the streets but are very savvy about crossing and rarely get hit. Most of these dogs are very gentle. Dog meat is eaten in specialty restaurants, mainly by men, and dogs running loose are subject to being stolen to become restaurant fare. In recent years, as the middle class has grown and disposable wealth has increased, purebred dogs have become much more popular in Hanoi. It is not uncommon to see owners parading the streets with leashed miniature poodles, corgis, labradors, and dalmatians.

The number of wild animals in Vietnam has sharply declined as deforestation, expansion of agriculture, poaching and corruption-aided animal trafficking have combined to produce an "empty forest syndrome." Vietnam has boasted a tremendous diversity of flora and fauna but many of these species are in fact extinct or nearly so.[2] Wild tigers and elephants, occasionally seen by troops during the American war, have vanished from

The elephants on Hanoi's Ceramic Wall.

the country. Monkeys of various species still exist in some mountainous areas and on certain islands, such as Cat Ba in Haiphong, where they are quite aggressive toward tourists. Cuc Phuong National Park in Ninh Binh Province has a large primate sanctuary that is popular with visitors. Guests at the nearby guest house can hear the monkeys begin their loud calling before dawn. However, the park itself has very few wild animals.

A rescue center for moon bears and sun bears, saved from cruel captivity and painful extraction of their bile for traditional medicine, has been established by an international NGO at Tam Dao near Hanoi. We took several outings with our staff and their children to this center which now has several hundred bears at carefree play in large enclosures with jungle gyms, trampolines, ponds for cooling off, and other recreational equipment. Our staff and their kids loved seeing the bears and hearing about their rescue and care.

There are still some wild creatures to be seen and heard even in the midst of Hanoi and other cities. Swarms of bats swooped down and around me as I walked home from work along the lake. Geckos are plentiful and their squeaks from behind wall-mounted air conditioners and elsewhere reminded us of their usefulness in insect control. Unfortunately, they are not able to handle some of the largest cockroaches or biggest spiders I have ever seen. I was occasionally able to swat a large roach with my flip-flop as it moved swiftly in a newly lighted room. To my terror, I once uncovered a huge spider, like the one that had established residence in our bunker in

Phu Bai in 1968, as I reached for a towel in a hotel bathroom in Long Xuyen in the Mekong Delta. Another appeared unannounced in our kitchen in Hanoi, but our housekeeper Vân calmly removed it and assured me that this was a variety that doesn't bite. I found rats drowned in our indoor swimming pool a few times, but they were small ones. The big guys were usually observed running the lanes and alleys outside.

15

Thoughts on Vietnam
Since the War

When I came back to Vietnam, I saw it through multiple lenses—some perhaps clearer than others. Think of it as that machine the eye doctor uses to test your vision with rapidly changing lenses in order to determine the correct prescription for your glasses. It is sometimes hard for me to sort these lenses out by veracity and to separate the wishful and emotionally driven from the objectively factual. When it comes to Vietnam, I feel that I am sometimes prone to a "nostalgia for the present."

I returned to Vietnam as a veteran of the American War, a historian, a public health researcher and policy analyst, an employer of Vietnamese people, and a collaborator with the Vietnamese government and civil society. I was a foreigner living in Vietnam. I was also part of a U.S. government aid initiative that was providing relatively well-paid employment to Vietnamese people and large amounts of funding to the Vietnamese government. My observations on the state of politics, governance, and economic policy in postwar and contemporary Vietnam have been influenced by my varied perspectives, not least perhaps by my position, how Vietnamese officials and others behaved towards me, and by what I, as a foreigner, was and was not allowed to see.

My first time back in Vietnam after the war, and my first trip to Hanoi, came in 1997, just two years after the United States and Vietnam established diplomatic relations. By then, the U.S. was already providing some aid to Vietnam in health and other fields. Friendship between the two countries was on the rise. Among Vietnam's probable motives for the rapprochement were the desire for American economic aid and for a new ally or at least a mediating force in its relationship with China. That relationship had been strained and often overtly hostile for more than a thousand years. This ancient enmity with China was but one of the reasons that the "domino theory" used by the U.S. government to justify its war in Vietnam made little sense. A more logical theory may have been to consider Vietnam as a counterweight to China rather than simply a gate through which the Chinese could pour to subjugate all of Southeast Asia. Admittedly, this theory may benefit from 20/20 hindsight; in a 1970 interview, Lyndon Johnson referred to it as "sheer Fulbright nonsense."[1] However, in recent years, the U.S. has cultivated its relationship with Vietnam for this very reason.

Aftermath of the War

In the years since the American War, the Vietnamese government has removed most of the evidence of American military presence. All the former U.S. bases were leveled, and many were returned to forest or had new villages planted in their places. Returning to the site of LZ Gator in Quang Ngai Province, where he had served with the 198th Light Infantry Brigade, Tim O'Brien found that the "huge and imposing and permanent" base had been "utterly and forever erased from the earth. Nothing here but ghosts and wind." A veteran who in 1985 visited Long Binh, once home to the largest U.S. base, likened it to "searching for some remnant of a lost civilization."[2]

Most of the U.S. airbases became commercial airports. However, at several of them—notably Danang and Tan Son Nhat in Ho Chi Minh City—one may see some of the original American aircraft revetments, now used for storage of supplies. Souvenir shops in Hanoi's Old Quarter and many other Vietnamese cities sell supposed American war artifacts, many of which are fake. These include Zippo cigarette lighters that many American troops carried, often with sayings such as "Yea, though I walk through the valley of the shadow of death, I will fear no evil because I'm the meanest motherfucker in the valley."[3] I had a Zippo lighter during my first tour. My father gave it to me; it was sterling silver and bore only my initials.

Some of the ill effects of the war and American depredation of the country, such as Agent Orange contamination and its health consequences, vast defoliated areas, unexploded ordnance, and thousands of bomb craters, could not be concealed. Only years later did the U.S. give up its resistance to funding the mitigation of Agent Orange contamination, which had been based on concerns about the design of studies to test the causal connections between the agent and various adverse health outcomes. During the Obama administration, the U.S. government finally made what seemed clearly the right moral and political decision to provide substantial funds for cleanup and mitigation, regardless of the design flaws or inconclusiveness of the causal studies. This aid focused on the Da Nang and Bien Hoa airbases and surrounding areas, where the largest stocks of the chemical had been abandoned and allowed to leach into the ground.

Some American bases and battle sites like Khe Sanh, where Vietnam claimed victory, were developed as tourist sites. Khe Sanh (called Ta Con in Vietnamese) now has a museum, reconstructed bunkers, artillery pieces, several helicopters, and a C-130 transport that was disassembled in Da Nang and put back together on the site of the American airstrip. A monument to NVA tank troops at the site of the Lang Vei special forces camp between Khe Sanh and the Laotian border commemorates the NVA's attack there in January 1968. This was the North's first use of tanks in the war, which caused fear and consternation among American commanders, although it did not recur until the later stages of the war after most of the U.S. troops had left.

Some sites that testify to Vietnamese bravery, fortitude, and suffering have also been preserved and opened for tourism. These include the tunnels at Cu Chi, near Saigon, which were used mainly for Viet Cong offensive action, and those at Vinh Moc, just north of the former DMZ, where an entire village lived underground for more than three years under U.S. bombing. A number of babies were born in the Vinh Moc tunnels and most of these babies grew to adults who still live in today's above-ground village. On my first visit to Vinh Moc in 1997, after spending just 30 minutes in the stifling, claustrophobic tunnels, I realized even more powerfully than ever why the U.S. could never have won the war. This conviction was reinforced each time I went back there. During the war, however, some American servicemen, took a different view of this remarkable Vietnamese endurance. After watching villagers' "passive" reaction to the burning of their homes, Marine platoon commander Philip Caputo recalled that "my pity for them rapidly turned into contempt.... Why feel compassion for people who seem to feel nothing for themselves." He later realized that he had had "no conception of the ordeal that constituted their daily lives.... They had acquired a capacity to ... suffer what we would have considered insufferable."[4]

Hanoi's anti-aircraft and missile gunners are always remembered with posters and cardboard cutouts on anniversaries of the 1972 Christmas bombing. These celebrate the numbers of U.S. B52s and fighter jets brought down by SAM missiles and anti-aircraft fire. Hanoi has several permanent monuments, one on the grounds of the Army Museum, built of wreckage from downed U.S. aircraft. In addition, tourist sites and monuments recall U.S. atrocities, such as the My Lai Massacre. A grim exhibit at Ho Chi Minh City's War Remnants Museum shows babies with birth defects and other physical deformities attributed to Agent Orange preserved in jars of formaldehyde. At the same time, reflecting improved bilateral relations, Vietnam now welcomes periodic visits by U.S. Navy warships to Danang, Haiphong, and Cam Ranh Bay, and Vietnamese people flock to tour these ships and greet U.S. sailors on shore leave.

Key dates in the history of the Communist Party and the nation are marked with street banners, many of which feature Hồ Chí Minh's picture, often with children, and quotations from his writings and speeches. Wartime propaganda posters are sold in several shops in Hanoi and are popular purchases among tourists. Some of these posters depict American leaders, usually Richard Nixon, with evil faces, American planes being shot down, heroic Vietnamese at anti-aircraft guns, and people working hard in the fields under the constant threat of bombing by the American imperialists.

However, some Vietnamese people believe that their government and the Communist Party have not been fully forthcoming about the horrible human costs of the war. These are variously estimated at two to four million dead and millions more wounded or still missing. The government's reluctance to acknowledge openly the costs of the war may help account for the country's failure to engage in the same intensive efforts as the U.S. has made to find, identify, and repatriate the remains of its missing.[5] In Vietnam as in the U.S., but in very different ways, the fate of the missing got inextricably entangled in the politics of the war and its aftermath.

The Vietnamese estimation of U.S. war losses is typically quite different from that of their own. In museums and official histories, the losses suffered by the Americans are generally exaggerated. For example, the number of B52s shot down during the Christmas bombing of 1972 is far higher in Vietnamese than in U.S. statistics.

The Vietnamese government has not been truthful about—and consequently many contemporary Vietnamese may be unaware of—the brutality of the communist regime during and after the war: the murder of more than a thousand civilians during the battle of Hue, for example, or the confinement and harsh mistreatment of thousands in re-education camps for years after April 1975. Of course, the U.S. government also systematically lied to our people about the war, as amply demonstrated by *The Pentagon Papers*. For Max Hastings, what makes the war even more of *An Epic Tragedy,* the subtitle of his 2018 history, is that neither side really deserved to win. Viet Thanh Nguyen may not subscribe to this conclusion, but he does call for an "ethics of recognition" in which both parties to a conflict acknowledge not only the flaws of their enemies but also their own, and without which true reconciliation remains elusive.[6]

On banners along the roads in from the airport, Hanoi is proclaimed "the City for Peace." In fact, Vietnam has been largely at peace since its last border clash with the Chinese in 1979 and its withdrawal from Cambodia shortly before that. However, the country continues to maintain a huge army, largely out of sight, and tensions with China, Vietnam's ancient enemy despite its support during the American War, periodically erupt over the disputed islands in the East Sea, known by the Chinese as the South China Sea.

Economy

As we sipped green tea on tiny plastic stools at a crowded street stall or navigated the tumultuous Old Quarter in search of the perfect gifts, my daughter Abigail aptly commented that "in Vietnam, there is always something interesting to look at." Indeed, Vietnam's economy—not to speak of its family life and culture—produces an endless and varied stream of fascinating scenes. I don't know if the Vietnamese are really busier than we Americans, but their busy-ness is certainly more visible and omnipresent. Perhaps less so in the countryside, but in Hanoi, the other big cities, and even smaller cities and towns, much of everyday life happens right out on the street: street food, street vendors, small shops of every kind with their goods spilling out onto the street, motorbikes parked everywhere, the clogged traffic, the pedestrians crossing everywhere and in every direction, everybody going somewhere or doing something with purpose and dispatch. But this has not always been the economic scene in Vietnam.

As the Vietnamese government continues to obscure the extent of the country's losses during the American War, it also for a long time downplayed the starvation, disease, and economic privation caused by its economic policies and by the U.S.-led trade embargo in the decade after the war ended. However, beginning in the mid–1980s, Vietnam's leaders reversed important elements of the country's economic policy. Led by Nguyễn Văn Linh, who became Communist Party General Secretary following Lê Duẩn's death in 1986, and then by his successor Đỗ Mười and Prime Minister Võ Văn Kiệt, both of whom took office in 1991, Vietnam implemented đổi mới or "renovation" of the economic system. Like China's reforms, this involved grafting a more open economy, with individual freedom to operate private businesses, make money, and exercise limited rights to own property, onto a continuing one-party political system. Even state-owned enterprises began to be required to turn a profit. As early as 1994, Bobby Muller, a wounded American veteran of the Vietnam War, was in Hanoi seeking support for his non-profit organization's effort to establish a prosthetics workshop in a children's hospital. The hospital director emphatically rejected Muller's request: "If you're not here to make a profit, I don't want you as a partner." Muller mused that "I had gotten thrown out of a meeting in Hanoi because I wasn't a *capitalist*...."[7]

A 2011 exhibit at Hanoi's National Museum of Ethnology, funded by the Ford Foundation, gave a frank and accurate account of that grim post–1975 "Subsidy Period." It graphically depicted the hardships of the Vietnamese people when everything was rationed, raising pigs in small city apartments was common, and having a bicycle or a radio was a real luxury. Writer Lê Minh Khuê described the Subsidy Period: "Something had broken down; something had fallen apart. People had no money, but money was the master. We lacked everything, even soap and rice. It was terrible."[8]

The Vietnamese economy has been growing rapidly since the 1990s. The government typically announces annual GDP growth of about 6–7 percent, although some people are suspicious of these figures. There was a period of sharp price inflation from 2008 to 2012 but this has leveled off since.

Many Vietnamese people are skilled entrepreneurs, and the economy is vibrant with small businesses. It is hard to understand how virtually every city block can support five coffee shops, five pho stalls, and five clothing stores but many blocks seem able to do so. Vietnam also boasts extensive and growing light and medium industry—clothing, shoes, electronic components, beer, automobile and motorbike assembly. Following đổi mới, many "Việt Kiều," or overseas Vietnamese, a group previously banned from the country, have returned to work or to launch successful businesses, such as Highlands Coffee.

The diligence of the Vietnamese is on display in all types of organizations, businesses, schools, shops, and fields throughout the country. As the economy opened, the entrepreneurial spirit of the Vietnamese burst forth. Vietnam's combination of individual economic assertiveness with focus on the cohesion and well-being of the larger community may seem paradoxical. However, the intersection may be that individual economic success goes to the benefit of that individual's immediate and extended families. In fact, this seems to be a clearer connection in Vietnam than in the U.S. and many other countries.

Sure signs of upscale life in the 21st century are appearing in and around Vietnamese cities: fancy cars; golf courses; pure-bred dogs with grooming salons and boarding kennels to serve them; glitzy gyms and fitness centers; yoga studios; Starbucks Coffee shops (competing with the local Highlands Coffee); and craft beer establishments. The Bana Hills near Danang, the site of Philip Caputo's platoon's first offensive operation in April 1965,[9] is now home to a gaudy mountaintop resort reached by an aerial tram. One can almost see the ascetic Hồ Chí Minh rolling over in his glass case in the Hanoi mausoleum at such sights. Residents of the increasingly vibrant and sophisticated cities often good naturedly ridicule the mores of people from "the countryside," apparently forgetting that the latter led, until quite recently, the dominant way of life in the country.

The cities are exploding—Ho Chi Minh City (the former Saigon—in fact, many Vietnamese people, Northern and Southerner alike, still use the old name) and Hanoi, both with populations of close to 10 million when unregistered residents are included—and Danang, which has surpassed Haiphong as the country's third largest city, continue their rapid growth. New office and residential towers and shopping malls are going up everywhere. It could be a real estate bubble, but the building continues unabated, even as some projects sit abandoned and half-finished for loss of financing. Some buildings are torn down or completely renovated within a few years of being built. Even historic buildings in Hanoi's Old Quarter are threatened. In Vietnamese culture, it has been said, there is more respect for the land than for the buildings on it.

Development is king and environmental concerns are often marginalized as a result. Vietnam suffers from serious problems of air and water pollution, not to speak of vulnerability to climate change, storms, and sea-level rise in the low-lying Mekong and Red River deltas. Trash and discarded construction debris are everywhere. Littering appears to be neither a public concern nor a target of law enforcement.

Some women collect cardboard, plastic bottles and bags, metals, and construction debris to sell to recyclers. Many of these women are from the countryside and spend several months at a time collecting and reselling recyclables in Hanoi, living in crowded boarding houses, and only rarely returning to their families and home villages.

Trash collection in Hanoi seems to happen by magic. You simply place your trash and garbage on the lane or curb in front of your house and one or several of the seemingly thousands of trash collectors (pushing their big wheeled bins) and recyclable scavengers (usually on bicycles) cause it to disappear within an hour or so, usually before the rats can get to it. I am sure that the trash collectors are well organized and have territories assigned by someone. In any case, they are incredibly efficient. Once in a great while, a trash collector will appear at your door asking for a small payment. Otherwise, this service appears to be free of charge.

Corruption seems widespread in Vietnam, despite frequently announced laws and campaigns to curtail or eliminate it. The forms of corruption or quasi-corruption seen in Vietnam are by no means unique to that country. In fact, these are probably even more rampant in other developing and middle-income countries. Moreover, my own country reveals its own highly insidious forms of corruption, beginning with the most recent former occupant of the White House and the pervasive and pernicious influence of money on politics and policy. So, I report what I saw but claim no moral high ground.

In Vietnam, many jobs and assignments within jobs are allegedly for sale. These include government jobs and flight attendant positions with Vietnam Airlines. Reportedly, higher school grades may be purchased. Bribes or other under-the-table payments are often needed to get the attention of or services from government agencies, such as clearance of shipments through customs. Allegedly, the police auction off assignments to the best street corners for shaking down motorists for invented traffic violations.

Part of the problem is that government salaries are so low, in turn the result of the huge informal economic sector and poor tax collection, that many officials seek ways to supplement their incomes in order to have decent lives. Teachers supplement their low salaries by offering extra sessions after regular school hours. Many parents believe these extra sessions are needed to help their children do well on the standard examinations required for graduation from primary and secondary school and acceptance at the best schools at the next level. Many teachers, like my friend and colleague Vân Nghiêm's mother, set up small classrooms in their homes to teach evening and weekend sessions.

Infusions of international funding have been a mixed blessing for Vietnam, as they have been for other low- and middle-income countries. During the war, Max Hastings writes, "American decision makers failed to recognize the economic and cultural impact of a huge army upon an Asian peasant society.... A Vietnamese secretary at USAID earned more than an ARVN colonel."[10] The salary disparity reappeared when the U.S. and other international donors began to fund programs in Vietnam in the 1990s. These programs, including the project I worked on, pay Vietnamese staff many times the salaries of people in comparable positions in the Vietnamese government or Vietnamese private organizations. This situation, while of clear temporary benefit to those employees, is not only unsustainable but may also distort and destabilize the local economy, as previously occurred during the war. However, the problem persists with little seeming recognition or remedy in view.

Party and Government

In my dealings with Vietnamese government officials, I sometimes felt like J.J. Giddes, the Los Angeles private detective whose associate tried to console him at the inexplicable end of a classic movie: "forget it Jake, it's Chinatown." Of course, I was a foreigner who did not speak the language and did not have a full understanding of Vietnamese political culture or ideology. As a result, I often found it difficult to comprehend and navigate opaque Vietnamese laws and regulations, political and government structures. The relationships and lines of authority and responsibility among different types and levels of government agencies, as well as the underlying role of the Communist Party apparatus, are all complex. They posed challenges regarding whom to approach about specific issues on policy matters and how the roles of the people we worked with were influenced or controlled by others with whom we had no interaction or potential to reach. Personal and family connections are also extremely important, and nepotism is common.

Although đổi mới brought big changes to the Vietnamese economic system, the country's governance remained largely the same. This was the structure with which I interacted in my work in Vietnam.

Vietnam is a one-party communist state; the Party and Government are organized in parallel at all levels. At the national level, the Party Congress meets every five years, and the Party Central Committee elects its powerful subunit, the Politburo. The General Secretary of the Central Committee is the Party leader and heads the Politburo. The Party has commissions addressing broad areas of policy. Each Province is divided into Districts and each district into communes (in some cities called wards) and each of these units has its own Party committee. The Party sets general direction and lays out overall principles and plans but is not directly involved in legislation or day-to-day governance. However, the Party's influence is extremely important, if largely hidden to unfamiliar eyes. Government officials may be frustrated if they try to advance policies inconsistent with Party direction.

The Government and Party are not coterminous although most government officials must be Party members. The government is also organized from national down to commune/ward levels—each with legislative and executive bodies. At the national level, there is an elected National Assembly (with very limited competition for seats permitted) and executive Ministries, as well as an Office of the Government, headed by the Prime Minister, who is elected by the National Assembly. The President, also elected by the National Assembly, is head of state and commander in chief of the armed forces and carries out many ceremonial duties such as greeting visiting dignitaries. In Vietnam's 63 Provinces and autonomous cities, the executive power is vested in a People's Committee and Departments with the same areas of responsibility as the national Ministries. A limited legislative role at Provincial level resides in a People's Council. Each district and commune/ward also has a People's Committee.

The existence of authority at multiple levels sometimes conflicts with the ostensibly very centralized governmental structure of Vietnam. National ministries theoretically have great power over policies and programs implemented on the ground and most budget allocations come from the central government, except in a few of the wealthiest cities like Ho Chi Minh City and Hanoi. In reality, however, sub-national officials can sometimes resist or tacitly fail to implement policies or programs they oppose or cannot afford ("unfunded mandates"). The old saying that higher authority stops "at the village gate" has some validity in Vietnam.

Freedom of speech and press are limited, and the government and Party have little tolerance for dissent. Newspapers and mass electronic media are still owned and operated by the government. International news media such as CNN broadcast with ten-minute delays to allow for government censorship if necessary. In some respects, however, there is more freedom in Vietnam than in China. Social media such as Google, Facebook, Twitter, Instagram, and YouTube are banned and blocked in China but available, and widely used, in Vietnam. Limited demonstrations critical of the government are sometimes allowed. Individuals with stellar reputations, exemplary service to the nation, and strong connections, such as the late General Võ Nguyên Giáp, sometimes openly voice objections to government policies.

Vietnam's governance does remain largely authoritarian. The people, even if they often express cynicism about the government, generally seem predisposed to follow its dictates. This may help to explain Vietnam's success in addressing HIV/AIDS and other public health crises such as SARS and Covid-19.[11] I hope that these successes are not entirely dependent on an authoritarian form of government, but rather have been rooted in science and respect for human rights. I was happy to read that at least part of Vietnam's successful response to Covid-19 was based on extensive and multi-modal communication of facts and data to the public.[12] However, with the emergence of the Delta variant, a major Covid-19 outbreak has occurred in Vietnam in 2021. It may be that the government's dependence on public health control measures and relative inattention to achieving high rates of vaccination will prove to have been mistaken.[13]

Because internationally funded projects brought vastly more resources than did Vietnamese government budgets, Abt Associates and other international organizations were frequently viewed as having "deep pockets" by our Vietnamese counterparts. They sometimes presented us with inflated budget requests for workshops, study tours, and other activities. Moreover, they sometimes simultaneously sought funding for the same activities or events from multiple international donors or projects. Although U.S. government regulations strictly limit "salary supplementation" for host-country government officials, some Vietnamese officials found creative ways around this by inducing us to hire consultants who would report to and divert part of their billed fees to these officials.

I would often joke that I felt lucky to understand half of what was going at any time in our project's interactions with the Vietnamese government. This extended beyond my work to everyday life in Hanoi. Bans on taxis from city streets appeared and disappeared without apparent rhyme or reason. Procedures for obtaining customs clearance on incoming packages were essentially impossible to understand. For 2010's 1000th anniversary of the founding of Hanoi, the pattern and schedule for street closures were impossible to fathom, seeming to bear no relation to when a parade was due to come by or an event was to occur. A fireworks show in Hanoi was cancelled because the government said it didn't want to divert valuable resources to such an entertainment when people in Central Vietnam were suffering the effects of a serious flood. In fact, it was later revealed that the show was called off because most of the fireworks had accidentally exploded, causing several deaths and injuries.

Health System

On the way back to Hanoi from a work trip to Son La Province, my colleagues and I stopped for dinner at a small restaurant. As I sought out the toilet in the dark region behind the kitchen, typical of such places, I slipped on the wet floor and suffered a severe hamstring pull. I did not go to a Vietnamese clinic for this injury or, indeed, for any cough or cold or any other health problem I experienced while living in Vietnam. Instead, I went to a clinic in Tay Ho that served expats. The Vietnamese health system is, in some ways, coming to resemble that of the U.S., in that those with money are able to access high quality care—often in private clinics or hospitals where they pay out of pocket—while those with limited means rely on government facilities, which are chronically understaffed and under-resourced. Visiting our staff or their family members in Vietnamese hospitals, I was troubled by how crowded they were and how patients' families had to provide their own food and nursing services.

My work involved almost daily collaboration and interaction with agencies and officials of Vietnam's health system. This system operates at the same levels as the government: country, province, district, and commune/ward. There are national specialty and general hospitals—some of which, such as Hanoi's Bach Mai, which was severely damaged in the 1972 Christmas Bombing, and the French Hospital, are excellent. Most provinces and districts also have general hospitals. Some large cities and provinces also have specialty hospitals or clinics. These vary in quality. The communes and wards have health stations which typically provide only very basic care, such as immunizations and simple medications.

With the advent of the unified communist government in 1975, health services at all levels were provided by the government and were free of charge to patients. The quality of care was often poor. The period of economic reform that began in the mid–1980s brought a movement to "socialize" health services and other enterprises that had been run entirely by the government. In this context, "socialization" has a somewhat counter-intuitive meaning—it involves reduction of free services, proliferation of user fees, establishment of social health insurance and other schemes for covering the costs of care, and expansion of private clinics and hospitals.

Civil Society

My work in Vietnam involved collaborations with numerous civil society organizations (CSOs). Early in the 21st century, CSOs of many types and with many areas of interest began to appear in the country. They do very important work in their communities. However, the communist government was suspicious and resisted their development, suspecting that such organizations would be composed of troublemakers and might promote dissidence. There is limited freedom of speech in Vietnam and the government is not friendly towards those who criticize it or point to defects in its policies. Still, many of the new organizations persisted and some thrived.

The remarkable Khuất sisters stand out as success stories in Vietnam's civil society movement. I was fortunate to work with both of them. Khuất Thị Hải Oanh and Khuất Thu Hồng are the daughters of a prominent army general who had fought with the NVA in the American War. They each founded innovative civil society organizations. Hồng's Institute for Social Development Studies (ISDS) did groundbreaking research on gender, sexuality, HIV/AIDS, migration, and gender-based violence. The ISDS strongly advocated for women's rights and the rights of marginalized populations such as people living with HIV, people with disabilities, the LGBTQ+ community, and migrant workers. Oanh's Center for Supporting Community Development Initiatives has been a leader in the reform of Vietnam's policies on substance use and was a key partner in the HIV/AIDS policy project that I managed starting in 2008. Both sisters are now recognized as leading women in Vietnamese society.

Throughout their work, the Khuất sisters have stood up for and helped empower marginalized groups and taken visible roles on several controversial issues. Vietnamese culture is not generally very open to discussions of sex. Sex education in schools is still quite limited. But Oanh and Hồng are committed to a candid and rights-based approach to sex education, as this is critical to public health, in general, as well as to the health and well-being of girls and women, in particular. They helped to develop a Vietnamese version of *Our Bodies, Our Selves*, the pathbreaking women's guide to sexual and reproductive health first published in Boston in 1970. Hồng's ISDS became the principal Vietnamese sponsor of the project. Instead of a full revision of the book, Hồng and her colleagues decided to develop training materials in Vietnamese for schools and local governments. Some modifications from the original content were made in deference to Vietnamese cultural norms and the training materials have been well received in Vietnam.

During our time in Vietnam, Nancy and I met courageous advocates in fields beyond public health and HIV/AIDS. Ngụy Khanh is an environmental activist and founder of two Vietnamese environmental NGOs. Khanh spearheaded efforts to fight hydro-electric dams on the Mekong that would destroy communities and damage the river's ecosystem. She has also championed efforts to address climate change and associated sea-level rise and flooding, which pose particularly catastrophic threats to Vietnam with its lengthy coastline and low-lying river deltas. Khanh has also advocated for programs to monitor and improve air quality in Vietnam's large cities, which suffer from serious pollution. In all of this work, for which Khanh has received international recognition and funding, including a prestigious Goldman Environmental Prize, she and her organizations have been willing to question government policy and stand up to powerful development interests that favor the status quo and promote projects that are environmentally dangerous.

At the request Khanh's NGOs, Nancy drew on her experience as an environmental consultant to offer training and policy analysis to these groups. She also helped to write comments to the government calling attention to the downstream environmental risks of huge, proposed dams funded by China on the Mekong River in Laos and Cambodia and a proposal for cleanup of Halong Bay, one of Vietnam's prime tourist sites that is affected by serious water pollution.

Nancy also gave occasional talks to groups of Vietnamese students about environmental issues, including, on one occasion, how the pollution and algae blooms in Hoan Kiem Lake may have contributed to the deteriorating health of the lake's famous and sacred turtle, whose ancestor had helped Lê Lợi defeat the Chinese and win Vietnam's independence in the 15th century.[14] "What could be done to improve the turtle's health?" she asked the students. While a few recommended finding the turtle a girlfriend, more suggested improving the water quality of the lake. This has since been done, although not before the turtle finally died, at a reputed age of several hundred years.

Vietnam now has several types of civil society organizations. There are many non-government organizations (NGOs) registered and monitored through a quasi-government entity, the Vietnam Union of Science and Technology Associations (VUSTA). These NGOs have some, but not complete, freedom to pursue their work, advocate for their policy goals, and advance the interests of their clients and stakeholders. More informal community-based organizations (CBOs) have also appeared, and these have faced more serious challenges in gaining recognition and funding. Indeed, significant barriers remain to all civil society organizations' reaching their full potential to serve their communities.

Family

Many American families are fragmented. Kids move away from their hometowns when they grow up. In many cases, only an economic downturn may induce them to return to live with their parents. Grandparents often live alone or in continuing care or nursing facilities when they age. In Vietnam, by contrast, family seems more central to everything in life.

In the time of Covid-19, Diệp, the daughter of a former colleague, wrote to me from Hanoi: "Today is Easter—the season of hope of a new life and renewed vitality. I am sad that your family are separated. I hope you will reunite as soon as possible." Actually, Nancy and I are blessed to be somewhat unusual for an American family, especially during the Covid-19 pandemic. We are living together in our house in Watertown with our daughter Abigail, her husband Theo, and our two wonderful little granddaughters Iggy and Sisi. We are more like a multigenerational Vietnamese family than the vaunted American nuclear family.

Evidence of the strength of Vietnamese families is ubiquitous. One sees very few homeless people in Vietnam. This is because families take care of their own and will not allow them to live on the street. One rarely sees parents shouting at or even more rarely spanking or striking their children. Kids seem happy and well cared for. The government's tacit policy limiting families to two children has loosened a bit and three-child families are becoming more common. After marriage, couples typically go to live with the husband's parents. And even if they don't physically live together, many grandparents perform a lot of the childcare, including watching pre-school children and carrying older kids to and from school on their motorbikes while the parents are at work.

Of course, not all Vietnamese families are intact and mutually supportive. For example, some people who use drugs are ostracized by their families. And some families were not able to heal after the war. In *The*

Sacred Willow, Mai Elliott asserts that, in most cases, "the tenacity of family bonds that, though strained [by individual decisions of which side to take in the war], were ultimately stronger than any political differences."[15] However, this was certainly not true in all cases. In a story by Nguyễn Ngọc Tư, two brothers had fought on opposite sides in the war. The one who fought for the North died. The other is tormented by their mother's persistent accusation, albeit irrational and dementia-fueled, that it was he who had killed his brother in battle.[16] A Hanoian in the 1990s recalled that the "war has separated us from our native land and from each other. That's why our music is so full of sorrow."[17]

Most Vietnamese families devote substantial energy and resources to the education of their children. Vietnam's literacy rate is 95 percent, among the highest among middle-income countries and comparable to that of most developed countries. As they grow older, children prize higher education and most parents strongly support these educational ambitions.

Paradoxically, the perceived imperatives of education can sometimes outweigh those of family togetherness. A common ambition among Vietnamese parents is to send their children to university in the U.S. or another Western country. Despite their military victories, their patriotism, and the growing prosperity of their own country, many Vietnamese people seem to view America and other Western nations as offering more educational and economic opportunities for their children. Many young Vietnamese people are receiving excellent educations in the U.S., Australia, or Europe but the downside is the problem of "brain drain." Many of these students tend to stay in the countries where they received their educations and do not come back to Vietnam to contribute to the growth, prosperity, and governance of their homeland. On the other hand, many Việt Kiều have returned to Vietnam to start businesses and reconnect with family members.

After working for Abt Associates in Hanoi for four years, Vân Nghiêm won a Vietnam Education Foundation Fellowship to attend graduate school in the U.S. Vân earned her MPH at the University of North Carolina and then a PhD in health decision sciences from the University of Texas. She is now a professor at the University of Alabama–Birmingham's School of Public Health. Vân still deeply loves Vietnam, however, and misses her home and family very much. She is aware of Vietnam's continuing health challenges as well as its age-old struggles against physical and economic invaders, especially China. I have no doubt that she will return to live and work in Vietnam one day.

Phương Châu, another of our staff members, wanted to take her son Tom to the U.S. for his last two years of high school and then university. She arranged a transfer to Abt's Washington-area office so Tom could attend the academically excellent Bethesda–Chevy Chase High School. During the summer before their move to Washington, I tutored Tom in American history. Tom and I enjoyed this, and I think he learned some history. A highlight was our discussion of the Civil War, for which I assigned Tom to read Michael Shaara's *The Killer Angels*, a famous novel about the Battle of Gettysburg. We also talked about the American War in Vietnam and Tom admitted to not knowing its history very well. He asked my advice for a paper he was writing on Hồ Chí Minh for his Hanoi high school class. After our tutoring sessions, we went to the local Al Fresco's for pizza and ice cream sundaes. Tom ended up getting an A in his U.S. history course at Bethesda–Chevy Chase, graduated from George Mason University's honors program (on a full scholarship), and now works in the financial industry.

Vietnam's reverence for the family often emphasizes traditional patriarchal values, as influenced by Confucianism. Not unlike many societies worldwide, it appears to be quite sexist in some ways. In my observations, most husbands take their responsibilities as economic providers very seriously. They love their children and spend significant time with them. Many husbands faithfully love their wives as well. However, I noticed that husbands typically do little or no housework, leaving it to their wives and daughters, even though most women also work outside the home. Men openly comment on female appearance. Some men seem to feel that it is their right to spend as much time as they want out drinking with their friends. It is also quite common and seemingly acceptable to many for husbands to cheat on their wives.

Homophobia also remains quite commonplace in Vietnam. Same-sex marriage is still prohibited, although legalization proposals have been presented and support for them is growing. There is an increasingly open LGBTQ+ community, with Pride events in the major cities and many community-based organizations of gay men advocating for and providing HIV/AIDS prevention, care, and support services.

Despite the strong vestiges of tradition and resistance to change, the Vietnamese family remains a bedrock of society. In fact, tradition and resistance to change may be drivers of the strength of Vietnamese families. Just as the country's successful response to Covid-19 may be related to its authoritarian form of government and willingness of the people to obey government orders, so too the persistence of family strength may to some extent depend on limitation of the rights of women and LGBTQ+ people and resistance to diversification of family structures. But this is not necessarily a tradeoff: it is certainly possible that the Vietnamese family can remain strong, loving, and resilient while also supporting and welcoming the rights of women, diverse sexual identities, and family configurations.

Patriotism and Celebration

On all national holidays, seemingly every house and shop on every street and lane in Hanoi prominently displays the Vietnamese flag, solid red with a large centered gold star. Every time a Vietnamese national soccer team wins a major match, the streets fill with processions of motorbikes, cars, and pedestrians with everyone chanting victory slogans, waving flags, honking horns, and beating on drums and makeshift metal items.

Some Vietnamese people I knew were quite cynical about the political system and concerned about the corruption and lack of transparency in the government and Party. Some say that "the elections mean nothing," even though token opposition candidates are now permitted to appear on ballots. Voting is mandatory but some people send substitutes to cast their votes. The Party is sometimes ridiculed for its continuing calls for a "transition to socialism" and its unintelligible ideological jargon.

Despite all this, most Vietnamese people I knew remained extremely patriotic and loyal to their country. They are proud of Vietnam and its accomplishments, often against great odds. Most know that China is an ancient enemy whose invading and occupying forces had to be repelled by the Vietnamese multiple times over a thousand years. When Vân Nghiêm and I visited the Tan Thanh border gate in Lang Son Province, she pointed to the tall, bulky buildings that the Chinese had placed directly on the border. "They are trying to demonstrate their dominance over us," she angrily commented, "but they will never succeed." The Vietnamese resist referring to the "East Sea" as the "South China Sea," even though that is the name used on most maps produced outside of Vietnam. After reviewing the manuscript of this book, Vân complained that the map of Vietnam at the beginning did not show the islands in the East Sea that are claimed by Vietnam. I added a separate map of these islands.

The Vietnamese also know that their country defeated the French and the Americans in successive wars from 1945 to 1975. Beyond these basic facts, as is probably true in most countries including the U.S., most peoples' command of the details of their history may be limited or biased. This may be partly attributable to the government-controlled teaching of history in the schools. Of course, there are ongoing battles about the teaching of history in U.S. schools as well, exemplified by the recent controversy over curricula drawing on the *New York Times'* "1619 Project" and other efforts to acknowledge and learn from the terrible things in our past that have shaped the troubles and continuing struggles of our present day.

The patriotism of the Vietnamese appears in various ways. They faithfully follow their national football (soccer) teams and their delegations to the Southeast Asia Games and other international competitions. The victories of Vietnam's Under-23 football team in their quarterfinal and semifinal knockout-stage games bought thousands into the streets of Hanoi to celebrate. Even when the team lost in heartbreaking fashion in the finals, the city turned out for a huge welcome-home rally. These scenes were duplicated in cities throughout the country. This would never happen in my home city of Boston, where parades and celebrations are only held for teams that win the championship.

National holidays include Independence Day (September 1, commemorating the declaration of the Democratic Republic of Vietnam by Hồ Chí Minh in Hanoi's Ba Dinh Square in 1945) and Reunification Day (April 30, marking the end of the American war and unification of Vietnam in 1975). These holidays are occasions for ceremonies remembering the fallen and other heroes as well as display of national flags. Although the government organizes this practice, the people participate enthusiastically.

Special celebrations may last for weeks or months and include many types of observances, such as elaborate street decorations and the unveiling of new monuments. Hanoi's 1000th birthday in 2010 drew thousands for fireworks, parades, and concerts, including a performance of Mahler's "Symphony of a Thousand" by the Vietnam National Symphony Orchestra at the newly opened convention center in My Dinh. Our project staff and many of their children attended this concert as a group. During the

A Hanoi neighborhood with flags flying (NguyenQuocThang / Shutterstock).

Hoan Kiem Lake decorated for Hanoi's 1000th birthday (photograph by Sơn Đặng).

millennial celebration, Dien Bien Phu Street and Hoan Khiem Lake featured beautiful colored lights and illuminated balloons and lanterns. I joined thousands of Vietnamese people in admiring these displays.

Hanoi's 1000th birthday was also commemorated with the opening of the restored Thang Long Citadel and construction of a 6.5-kilometer ceramic wall depicting historical and contemporary Hanoi. The Citadel is the site of the oldest part of the city, originally called Thang Long, which was the seat of successive ruling dynasties. Beginning in the 1990s and continuing to this day, extensive archaeological excavations have revealed multiple layers of building remains, wells, and water systems, and yielded troves of important roof decorations, pottery, and other artifacts. Several of the more recent buildings have been restored and galleries on the Citadel grounds display many of the artifacts. An adjacent museum also displays a stone rendering of Hanoi's famous turtle encrusted with semi-precious stones.

Visitors to the Citadel may observe ongoing excavations and large previously excavated sites that are now covered and show the positions and layouts of buildings and retain several of the original water wells. The construction of the new National Assembly building had to be modified to avoid damaging the Citadel remains or interfering with the ongoing archaeological work. The Citadel was opened to the public for the first time for Hanoi 1000. A few years later, the nearby building that housed

Hoan Kiem Lake with Turtle Tower decorated for Hanoi's 1000th birthday. The Vietcombank building; Hanoi's first skyscraper, is in the background (photograph by Sơn Đặng).

the Politburo, which carried out all the major military planning during the American War, was opened to the public. This includes the heavily reinforced underground meeting rooms where work went on during U.S. bombing, as it had at the Churchill War Rooms in London during the Blitz.

Dien Bien Phu Street decorated for Hanoi's 1000th birthday.

Thang Long: The original name of Hanoi and the Hanoi logo.

Traditional dancers.

The ceramic wall is one of my favorite Hanoi sights. It holds the admittedly somewhat obscure Guinness world record for "longest ceramic wall," stretching six kilometers along the elevated "dike road" designed to protect the main parts of the city from Red River floods. Several years and great persistence were required to raise the funds and obtain the official permissions to build the ceramic wall. The Hanoi artist and sculptor Nguyễn Thu Thủy was a driving force behind the success of the project. The wall comprises 21 sections, some sponsored by businesses and some designed by school children. Collaborators included 20 Vietnamese and 15 foreign artists, 100 local craftspeople, and 500 children.

In addition to the birds and animals already mentioned, the wall displays a wide variety of cultural styles, historical and everyday scenes from the times of the imperial dynasties and more recent times in Vietnam. Landmarks such as the iconic Long Bien Bridge, which was knocked down several times by American bombs but quickly rebuilt, are depicted in several panels. The bridge itself is visible above the wall at a few points. There are colorful depictions of flowers, abstract and geometric shapes, women fan dancing in traditional dress, longboats of ages past with oarsmen driving them forward, as well as more prosaic scenes of villages and gatherings of friends and neighbors. Hanoi's motto—Thành Phố Vì Hòa

Ancient long boat and Long Bien Bridge above the Ceramic Wall.

Bình (The City for Peace)—and the legend "Chúng Tôi Yêu Hà Nội" (We love Hanoi) appear on several panels. I walked the length of the wall soon after its completion. One of my favorite panels, most likely designed by an international school class, has a jack-o'-lantern side by side with a snowman. Halloween is growing in popularity in Vietnam, so the pumpkin is

The snow man and jack o' lantern.

potentially relevant, but it has never snowed in Hanoi as far as I know, so the snowman may be a mystery to most Hanoians. I loved living in Hanoi and enjoyed the colorful panels depicting the city's history and culture. Still, the jack-o'-lantern and snowman reminded me of my New England home, so I always made a point of looking for them whenever I passed by in a taxi or on my bicycle.

While I have made some negative observations, my thoughts on contemporary Vietnam are overwhelmingly positive. The country has made great strides for its people and in its economic and social policies since the war ended. Vietnam is thriving in many ways and its people are benefiting from the growing prosperity. Poverty rates have been dramatically reduced. The reforms instituted by the government and Party have unleashed the natural vigor and entrepreneurial spirit of the people. The people understand their country's flaws but, perhaps especially because of its long and painful struggles, they love it just the same, and maybe even more. While some problems persist, Vietnam is clearly a nation on the rise.

16

Working on HIV/AIDS Policies with Vietnamese Institutions and People

Martha Gellhorn, a passionate commentator on war and injustice and dedicated advocate for ending both, including adamant opposition to the Vietnam War, sometimes struggled with conveying that passion and zeal in her writing. Disgusted with her completed draft of a novel, she described it as "a perfectly lifeless story in which all the details are accurate and who cares."[1] Likewise, I have struggled to make the following description of the work on HIV/AIDS that my colleagues and I did during my second tour in Vietnam human-centered and personally engaging. I want to provide some details of my work. After all, this was what I spent more than three years doing in Vietnam. Our project's work was often tedious and abstract, even impersonal and disembodied, but my colleagues and I always tried to keep before our eyes the very real people and communities we were trying to help. Our staff shared Gellhorn's passion and commitment to work hard, do right, and tell the truth. I have tried to show that they not only did very good and important work but were also very real and wonderful people.

The HPI Project

The HIV/AIDS epidemic in Vietnam is similar to that in the U.S. Both are "concentrated" among certain groups, including people who use drugs, sex workers, men who have sex with men (MSM), and the sexual partners of members of these groups. Neither country has large-scale heterosexual epidemics and, as a result, overall HIV prevalence in the adult population is very low—less than 0.5 percent. By contrast, HIV prevalence in African countries with generalized heterosexual epidemics reached or

162

exceeded 25 percent. Because relatively few Vietnamese people have HIV infection and those who do are primarily in marginalized groups, stigma and discrimination against people living with HIV have been serious and persistent problems in Vietnam. This resulted in real economic, social, and psychological pain for many people, and primarily people already suffering from addiction and poverty.

During my second tour, I led a project designed to make Vietnam's HIV/AIDS policies and programs more responsive to the country's "concentrated" epidemic. No longer the disaffected drunk of my wartime tour, I believed strongly in the mission of the project. I loved and respected our staff and together we worked hard to achieve the project's goals. We faced challenges but we achieved some success. I felt good about our accomplishments.

Health Policy Initiative (HPI) Vietnam was funded by the U.S. Agency for International Development under the President's Emergency Plan for AIDS Relief (PEPFAR), a global program. The HPI was part of a substantial commitment of U.S. foreign aid to Vietnam, our former enemy, which had begun on a small scale soon after the establishment of diplomatic relations in 1995 and steadily expanded thereafter. It collaborated with Vietnamese government agencies at multiple levels, local NGOs and community-based organizations, and other USAID and PEPFAR funded projects. Our project headquarters were in Hanoi, with a smaller office in Ho Chi Minh City, and we had activities in all nine of the PEPFAR focus provinces of Vietnam.

Our staff spent a lot of time analyzing policies, drafting proposals for their improvement, creating PowerPoint presentations, and holding workshops with stakeholders where we presented the evidence for adopting improved laws and policies. We developed data. We argued with and cajoled government officials based on the data and the lived experience of people. We tried to represent and advance the rights and interests of affected and marginalized groups. We designed and pilot tested some new types of HIV prevention programs.

The Vietnamese government officials we worked with were largely smart and dedicated; they worked hard and did the best they could within a system that sometimes made it difficult for them to perform with the transparency or effectiveness they might have preferred. In Vietnam, as in any country, one might find the lazy, time-serving bureaucrat who drinks too much at lunch and essentially takes the afternoon off. But I found this to be decidedly the exception.

The HPI sought to address some key policy issues that we believed hindered Vietnam's HIV/AIDS response. In 2006, Vietnam's National Assembly adopted a Law on HIV/AIDS Prevention and Control that sounded many of the right notes of an effective and enlightened HIV/ AIDS strategy—providing effective community-based prevention and care, eliminating stigma and discrimination towards people living with HIV and treating them with compassion and respect, and protecting patients' confidentiality and human rights. However, many of the stated principles of the HIV/AIDS law had not been fully implemented, and gaps and inconsistencies persisted across the whole body of related laws and regulations.

Trần Tiến Đức was my predecessor as HPI's Chief of Party, when the project was implemented by The Futures Group. He was also a good friend and extremely gracious during what could have been an awkward transition period. "Mr. Đức" is from a prominent family. His father was Hồ Chí Minh's personal physician who also served as mayor of Hanoi. In August 1965, Mr. Đức was editor of a government newsletter and traveling by train from Hanoi to Haiphong to collect data on the performance of industrial plants, he and a friend had to jump into a ditch from the moving train to take cover from a U.S. bombing run.

Mr. Đức became a leader in the effort to develop an effective response to HIV/AIDS that was attentive to the rights and needs of marginalized groups and others affected by the epidemic. He helped to mobilize the many advocates and stakeholders whose efforts led to passage of the national HIV/AIDS law. He was at the forefront of organizing the first self-help groups among people living with HIV in Quang Ninh and Haiphong. He designed and implemented a legal services program for people living with HIV who suffered from discrimination in education, employment, and community life.

Building on his long previous career as a journalist, Mr. Đức also launched training programs for print and electronic media members covering HIV/AIDS and related issues, such as drug use and sex work. We continued these training programs during my tenure as HPI's chief of party. The training encouraged journalists to write about and endorse policy improvements based on evidence, emphasizing the harm reduction approach to HIV prevention and substance use treatment. Almost all the participants placed stories that took positive positions on harm reduction interventions.

Mr. Đức was and remains a tireless advocate for positive change in Vietnam in many policy realms. His family history may provide some protection, but his work has nonetheless required courage and persistence. Mr. Đức is also a very good singer with an eclectic repertoire. At banquets, he often led us in powerful renditions of the patriotic song "Vietnam, Hồ Chí Minh!" He also loves Elvis and offers a fine interpretation of "I Can't Stop Loving You," accompanying himself on the piano.

HPI's People

Our HPI staff worked hard but we also gathered as friends and had a lot of fun together. We had annual retreats, typically in seacoast locations such as Danang's My Khe (known as China Beach during the American War) and Quy Nhon where we planned our upcoming activities, did team building exercises, and ate huge seafood dinners by the beach.

HPI team building.

Hương was our office janitor in Hanoi. She also made delicious lunches for us almost every workday. We always had lunch as a group, a common practice in Vietnamese organizations. This proved to be an important bonding experience. Our group lunches were times for joking and teasing. One member of our team, who had overcome repeated tragedies in her life—the loss of two young children and then her husband, prematurely—was usually a leader of the teasing. She has a wonderful, infectious laugh and is always funny but never mean.

We celebrated birthdays, gathered for beer, conversation, and laughter on Fridays after work, joined in raucous karaoke sessions, and went to concerts, museums, and tourist sites together. We enjoyed a group outing to the Thanh Long Citadel soon after it opened to the public.

The HPI project staff visiting Hanoi's Thanh Long Citadel.

I was the only expatriate on HPI's staff of nineteen. The others were all Vietnamese, some of whom had worked for the Vietnam Administration for HIV/AIDS Control (VAAC) and its predecessor HIV/AIDS agencies in the government. Several were medical doctors who had also obtained masters' degrees in public health in Europe, Australia, or the U.S. All of them spoke fluent English.

Vân Nghiêm was originally trained as an electrical engineer in Vietnam but became interested in public health and was hired as an intern for a previous Abt Associates project on avian influenza. She then moved on to HPI's task on HIV prevention for sexual partners of people who inject drugs, starting as project assistant and quickly advancing to project coordinator. Vân dedicated herself to learning all the technical and logistic details of the project and soon became a confident and effective leader. Vân also worked on our HIV prevention program for serodiscordant couples,[2] where she helped design effective graphic education materials based on couples' real-life stories. To me, Vân resembled the character "Radar" O'Reilly in M*A*S*H, who has already done exactly what Colonel Blake just ordered him to do. Vân often seemed to be a step ahead of me.

Although Vân has now been living in the U.S. for a decade, I believe that someday she will return to Vietnam with her young son, who is an American citizen by birthright. I have teased her that she would someday become Vietnam's Minister of Health. I hope she does, and I am sure she would do a great job.

Dr. Kiều Thanh Bình worked with Dr. Ngữ at the National AIDS Committee, joined our Cross-Border project team, and went on to work for HPI as well. He always looked out for me both on and off the job, helping me make my way in Hanoi and assisting with navigation of government agencies and procedures. He brought to our work a valuable network of contacts both at the central level and in provincial health departments. These helped us tremendously in developing partnerships with those agencies to implement innovative HIV prevention strategies and develop data systems to inform the effective deployment of HIV/AIDS programs.

Dr. Nguyễn Tuấn Phong and Dr. Bình were often objects of the good-natured ribbing during lunch. Phong is a sweet man with an exemplary family life, but the others liked to offer him ribald tweaks—few of which I could understand but which evoked uproars of laughter. We also teased Phong as "Dr. Phở" for his daily stops on the way to work for beef phở at a stall down the street.

Dr. Bình was a fun-loving member of our staff and an enthusiastic organizer of our beer drinking and karaoke sessions. He always knew the best restaurants and other spots to gather. He was also a consummate karaoke singer, specializing in the sentimental love songs to which the Vietnamese people seem particularly partial. He sometimes brought along his son, nicknamed "Son Watterson," to our gatherings where he liked to practice his English and engage me in conversation about politics and history, both Vietnamese and American. Son Watterson was learning to play baseball in one of the few youth leagues in Hanoi. He also played tennis with his father. When I left Hanoi, I bequeathed my bicycle to Son Watterson, who has begun his university studies. Even now, quite a few years later, Dr. Bình regularly messages me to see how I'm doing, and he never fails to close by urging me to come back to Hanoi as soon as possible to join him and our other friends for beers. Indeed, I yearn for that.

I loved our project staff's kids—so much so that, to my embarrassment, I sometimes forgot an important Vietnamese cultural taboo and patted these children on the head. Many of the kids attended our Friday afternoon beer drinking sessions, where they watched videos or played games on their parents' smartphones between snatches of conversation and mouthfuls of fried rice or French fries. I have a photo of Nguyễn Lệ Thanh's daughter "Mít" helping me blow out the candles on my birthday cake. (Many Vietnamese kids I met have nicknames unrelated to their given names; hers means jackfruit.) I watched Mít grow from a two-year old when I first moved to Hanoi to a near teenager during my last brief stint there.

Blowing out the birthday candles with Mít.

In Vietnam, workplace colleagues are often considered members of extended families. On the HPI staff, for example, I had "My Three Sons" (after the old TV sitcom), who all led important project tasks: Sơn Nguyễn (who helped provinces use data to inform deployment and funding of HIV services), Sơn Phan (who coordinated our evaluation of HIV prevention interventions in two mountainous provinces), and Sơn Đặng (who succeeded Vân Nghiêm as task leader of our HIV prevention program for sexual partners of drug injectors). The staff sometimes referred to me as "Bác Ted" (Uncle Ted) or "Ông Ted" (Grandfather Ted) or even "Godfather." In Vietnam, it is not considered impolite to comment on a person's weight, appearance, or age. Often after I got a haircut, someone on the staff would say that "you look much younger."

Santa Claus was also a part of our project family. Nancy and I hosted annual Christmas parties at our house, which were highlights of our time in Vietnam. I would be in street clothes for the drinks and dinner portion and then disappear to become Santa, making my entrance down the stairs with my bag of gifts for all the kids. Nancy was in charge of purchasing the presents in the U.S., making sure that each was appropriate to the age and gender of the recipient. The kids loved this. It didn't matter to them whether there really is a Santa who comes from the North Pole to bring the gifts they had asked for and would receive if they had been good. The important thing was getting presents and having their picture taken with this "Santa," even though most of them knew he was me. Sơn Đặng's daughter "Chip" made her first trip out of the house at three weeks old to come to our Christmas party. She is now a high-spirited ten-year old. Sơn Đặng made me a montage of photos from one of the Christmas parties with a calendar for the coming year. The legend reads "From Abt's Vietnam Family: We hope it will bring you happiness and memories about us."

Dr. Ngữ, my first Vietnamese colleague and friend, later came to work for HPI in our Ho Chi Minh City office. Sadly, Dr. Ngữ, a longtime smoker like so many Vietnamese men, developed lung cancer and died in May 2011. Dr. Ngữ's wife Tô Thị Kiều Dung asked me to speak at his funeral and I managed a few opening sentences in Vietnamese. At his burial ceremony in Cu Chi, a flock of doves was freed over his grave and afterwards I helped his brother-in-law release some fish into a river near his home. Both acts symbolize the ascension of the deceased's soul to the spirit world. I returned to the cemetery with Dr. Ngữ's family to mark the first anniversary of his death in 2012, an important part of Vietnamese custom. My co-authors and I dedicated to Dr. Ngữ the paper we published on the eight-year results of the Cross-Border project.[3] I miss him very much.

During its tenure under Abt Associates' leadership from 2008 to 2012, HPI had multiple tasks, some of which I have already mentioned. We worked principally to support improved policies and related programs in three pillars of an effective response to HIV/AIDS in Vietnam: (1) Policies on substance use; (2) HIV prevention among sex workers and their clients; and (3) Empowerment of civil society organizations to play larger roles in HIV prevention, care, and treatment. We were able to make some progress in all of these areas, but we were not able to achieve full success in any of them. The work and the struggle continue.

Substance Use Policies

Some of the most affecting scenes I recall from my work in Vietnam were the many times my colleagues and I met with people who use drugs, people who were struggling to conquer their addictions and rehabilitate their lives and people who were trying to help others overcome this disease and rejoin their families and communities. We saw residents of compulsory drug detention at forced labor shelling cashews and manufacturing soccer balls and undergoing communist-inspired "moral education" and self-denunciation sessions; we met with peer outreach workers who were teaching drug injectors to protect themselves and their friends from HIV and collecting used syringes discarded in the community to safeguard children and other residents; we observed support groups delivering home-based care to people living with HIV; we attended meetings of community-based groups of female sexual partners of men who inject drugs who were reaching out to other women in similar circumstances to help them learn to protect themselves and their children from HIV.

All of these Vietnamese people impressed me with their courage and determination to improve their own lives and help others to do so. They worked against great odds and often against a system of laws and policies that considered them morally deficient and unworthy of respect or support. Perhaps their most common statement was "we face many challenges." Surely they did, but so many persevered and gave valuable service to their families, friends, and communities.

There are approximately 200,000 people who inject drugs in Vietnam and drug use is a primary driver of the HIV epidemic in the country. Therefore, the HIV/AIDS response and drug control and treatment policies are inextricably linked. In a paper published in 2008, my co-authors and I argued that Vietnam's legal and policy approach to substance use was somewhat contradictory.[4] On the one hand, the government had embraced practical harm reduction strategies for HIV prevention among people who inject drugs, specifically needle and syringe provision and later Methadone maintenance treatment. At the same time, Vietnam has long pursued a largely punitive policy towards people who use drugs.

Vietnam's acceptance of harm reduction was based on international and domestic evidence, including from the Cross-Border project that I had helped to launch, as well as the advocacy of some outspoken and courageous champions within the Government and Party. The movement for harm reduction had to overcome an early assumption that using drugs inevitably carried a death sentence from HIV/AIDS. When AIDS first appeared in Vietnam in the early 1990s, the government adopted scare tactics, erecting all over cities, towns, and villages gruesome posters of drug users as skulls atop skeletons. As harm reduction interventions became more accepted and widespread, these posters and messages gradually disappeared in favor of depictions of people exchanging used needles and dancing condoms designed to normalize safer sex. In fact, Vietnam has generally been ahead of the U.S. in official support for harm reduction. With only a brief interruption during the Obama administration, the U.S. has prohibited federal funding of needle and syringe programs on the discredited basis that they encourage drug use.

The punitive side of Vietnamese drug policy was based on the notion that drug addiction is a moral failing and a "social evil" rather than on the strong scientific evidence that it is a chronic, relapsing biological and psychological disease. Vietnam established and still maintains a network of drug detention centers (also called "06 Centers"), modeled on the post–1975 re-education camps. These compulsory detention centers are like prisons, although commitment to them is an administrative rather than criminal process. They deliver a harsh regimen of forced labor and moral education, which overwhelming evidence has shown to be not only unjust but also ineffective and wasteful of scarce resources. Relapse rates among 06 Center releasees approach 100 percent. Nevertheless, in 2012, more than 35,000 people were confined in them.

The HPI worked with government agencies, including the Vietnam Administration for HIV/AIDS Control and the Ministry of Labor, Invalids and Social Affairs (MOLISA, the agency responsible for the 06 Centers), to assess and improve drug treatment policy. I had visited many prisons and jails in the U.S. as part of my work on HIV/AIDS policies in correctional facilities and I was permitted to go to quite a few of Vietnam's 06 Centers to observe and assess policies and programs there. However, foreigners are rarely permitted to visit prisons in Vietnam, and I never was allowed to see any of them.

The HPI project helped to identify inconsistencies and anomalies in the legal and policy framework on drug control and substance use treatment and presented evidence that the detention center-based approach failed to prevent or control drug use. Other PEPFAR partners, especially FHI 360, worked closely with the Ministry of Health and provincial departments of health to pilot Methadone treatment, with marked success. These pilot programs eventually grew into a national network of government-run Methadone clinics.

Under the parallel structure and operational procedures of the Party and government in Vietnam, HPI and other projects implemented by international organizations worked mainly with Government officials and bodies. However, HPI did have some opportunities to work with Party officials and organizations on policies and programs related to drug use. Prof. Phạm Mạnh Hùng, Vice Chair of the Communist Party's Central Propaganda Department whom I met during the Cross-Border Project, remained a strong supporter of harm reduction interventions and reform of the system of drug detention centers.

Resistance to change in substance use treatment policy was especially strong in mountainous Son La Province to the northwest of Hanoi. Here, Party and government leaders for a long time blocked needle and syringe programs and Methadone treatment. HPI held several workshops for Party and government officials in Son La on HIV prevention and substance use treatment and noted some improvements in attitudes and policies, but progress in program implementation was slow.

The Hồ Chí Minh Academy is the Communist Party's School for government officials. Lisa Messersmith, who had worked for the Ford Foundation in Vietnam and was then affiliated with Harvard's Kennedy School of Government before becoming a professor at Boston University's School of Public Health, won the agreement of the Hồ Chí Minh Academy to sponsor and provide faculty to team with U.S. counterparts in a training program on HIV/AIDS policy for mid-level government officials. This training program became a component of HPI's work. The leaders and faculty of the Academy were willing to take on controversial topics such as harm reduction and the drug detention centers in ways that sometimes involved questioning or criticizing existing government policies. Indeed, the trainees were often reluctant to engage in open discussions about such policies or programs for fear of making statements of which their superiors might disapprove. Moreover, the discussion-based style of pedagogy common in the U.S. and in the West, which we were trying to employ in our workshops, runs counter to the predominant education style of Vietnam, in which teachers primarily lecture and students primarily listen. With practice in framing questions and encouragement to participants, Academy and U.S. faculty were usually able, working together, to induce frank sharing of experiences and fruitful discussion of sensitive issues. Following this training program, the Academy made a segment on HIV/ AIDS policy a regular part of its curriculum for mid-level government officials.

In 2009, the National Assembly decriminalized drug use, which was an important first step in the reform of Vietnam's substance use policy but did not directly affect administrative commitments to drug detention centers. Then, toward the end of HPI, the government began to acknowledge the ineffectiveness, if not the inhumanity, of the 06 Centers. The government also began to adopt terminology indicating a shift from the approach based on "social evils" and moral failing to recognition of addiction as a disease requiring treatment instead of punishment. A "Renovation Plan" was promulgated, which laid out timelines and milestones for a gradual transition from the compulsory drug detention centers to voluntary treatment facilities. Some interim legal changes were also made, such as requiring court orders for committing individuals to 06 Centers, replacing the previous simpler method that required only directives from a District People's Committee. To me and our staff, these were very positive and welcome developments. Progress in this transition was uneven but significant in some provinces and localities.

Khuất Thị Hải Oanh was highly effective in convincing government organizations and officials to support the change in policy from the compulsory detention of drug users to a system of voluntary treatment. Oanh's NGO, the Center for Supporting Community Development Initiatives (SCDI) chose to engage with rather than confront the government on this issue. The SCDI understands the motivations behind the detention center system, such as misunderstanding of addiction, stigmatization of drug use and people who use drugs, and lack of effective voluntary treatment. They have sought to address these by working in partnership with government agencies, mass media, international organizations, and the community at large.

Indeed, the obstacles to reform in Vietnam remain powerful. Vested interests, including public security agencies, those who profit from the forced labor of center residents, and the large numbers of center staff who might lose their jobs, have resisted the elimination of the 06 Center system. The U.S. has similar problems. The "prison-industrial complex" has promoted mass incarceration and resisted reducing incarceration rates that might lead to closure of correctional facilities and loss of jobs in many rural areas that have long depended on them.

In its final report, HPI recommended full implementation of the Renovation Plan to complete the transition from compulsory detention of people who use drugs to voluntary, community-based and evidence-based substance use treatment. Some improvements in substance use treatment have been achieved. The number of detention centers and center residents was substantially reduced from 2012 to 2016. However, the Renovation Plan is only a government policy document with no force of law and has still not been fully implemented. The 06 Centers still exist and, in recent years, as the use of amphetamine type stimulants (ATS) has sharply increased, especially in cities, the government has begun committing ATS users to them and their populations have rebounded. Several pilot voluntary treatment programs have been implemented but the full network of facilities offering multiple treatment modalities needed to replace the 06 Centers has yet to be developed.

Along with HPI's policy work, I tried to make a small direct contribution to community safety and HIV prevention. The lake road below our Hanoi project office on Xuan Dieu Street. is now paved and well used by pedestrians and motorbikes, with several bars, restaurants, and cafes. In 2008, however, this all remained in the future. The dirt road was dark and secluded and had become a popular "shooting place" for heroin injectors, who discarded their used needles and syringes along it. These are potentially contaminated and hazardous if handled, particularly in the event of an accidental needlestick. So, as our peer educators had done for many years in the Cross-Border project in Lang Son and Ha Giang Provinces, I visited the site every few days and picked up the discarded needles and syringes—sometimes as many as a hundred. I collected these in half-gallon plastic Coca-Cola bottles and sent them to a hospital for safe disposal.

During this time, HPI also advocated for the removal of a vestigial skull-and-skeleton poster near our HPI office. After numerous bureaucratic delays, the poster, which by then was showing its age, was removed as a major street construction project began. Whatever the reason, it was good to see it go. I hoped that this would symbolize a final turn to more progressive and scientific policies on substance use in Vietnam.

Policies on Sex Work

In Vietnam sex workers have often been arrested for possession of condoms as evidence of their participation in an illegal activity. However, condoms are also the primary means of HIV prevention for sex workers and their clients. My HPI colleagues and I met and interviewed many sex workers and visited many establishments where sex work is practiced. We promoted the adoption of interventions that asked police to "keep one eye open and one eye closed"—allowing the operation of illegal establishments while enforcing measures designed to improve the public health outcomes associated with those establishments, their employees, and clients.

We always tried to distinguish between those who chose to do sex work and those who were trafficked or otherwise forced into it. Once, when I visited a female peer educator who worked for the Cross-Border project in Ha Giang and who also operated a small brothel, I noticed that she had a girl working there who appeared to be about 13 years old. We immediately informed our provincial coordinator, who dismissed the peer educator and removed the young girl from the establishment. We had another peer educator in Lang Son who regularly crossed into neighboring China and rescued Vietnamese girls who had been trafficked into sex work there.

Sex work, like drug use, is a driver of Vietnam's HIV/AIDS epidemic. The HPI designed, implemented, and evaluated an innovative "100% condom use" intervention for sex workers and their clients in An Giang province in the Mekong Delta. The goal was that every commercial sex act be protected by a condom. Our staff worked long and hard to achieve the close collaborations required among public health agencies, police, and operators of commercial sex establishments. The intervention produced positive outcomes in self-reported condom use and reduced HIV prevalence. Based on the experience of An Giang, several other provinces adopted similar interventions.

The HPI also sought to influence laws and policies regarding sex work in a parallel fashion to those on drug use. We advocated, based on scientific evidence, for moving from a punitive approach that treated sex work as a "social evil" to one based on public health considerations and the principles of harm reduction. Adopting a harm reduction approach to sex work would involve such things as wide scale adoption of 100 percent condom programs and resolving persistent inconsistencies across multiple legal documents by enacting a comprehensive national Law on Sex Work. Some progress was achieved. The parallel "05 Centers" for sex workers were abolished and the government issued a circular requiring the provision of condoms in all hotels and guest houses, which are common settings for sex work. However, the government has not revised the Ordinance on Prostitution, which embodies the "social evils" and punishment focus or developed a new Law on Sex Work. In Vietnam, as in many other countries including the U.S., legal inconsistencies continue to thwart full adoption of a public health approach to sex work.

The Role of Civil Society

In partnership with Oanh's Center for Supporting Community Development Initiatives (SCDI), HPI implemented an HIV prevention program for female sexual partners of drug injectors, a group at extremely high risk for HIV infection. Several of the peer educators in that program, notably Phạm Thị Minh, became powerful spokespeople and advocates for this group of women. At national and international conferences, Minh presented her story of personal growth and change—from a heroin-addicted sex worker confined in a 06 Center to a sober and dedicated public health worker, and a wife and mother. It is certainly not impossible for women who use drugs to be loving wives and mothers as well. But that is a difficult row to hoe. Minh spoke not only for herself but also about countless other women reached by the project who changed their own lives dramatically while also helping to better their communities. I found the empowerment of the peer educators and many of the sexual partners they reached to be remarkable and inspiring. Many lives were positively transformed.

Nguyễn Phương Lan also worked at SCDI and was a major contributor to the sexual partners project. Lan then went on to win a Fulbright Fellowship to obtain her MPH at Harvard and returned to Vietnam to work on several projects to improve health care for underserved populations. Lan remains my very good friend. She is one of the people I most look forward to seeing again when I am able to return to Hanoi.

Civil society organizations (CSOs) could be major providers of effective and cost-efficient HIV/AIDS services in Vietnam and HPI sought to strengthen and empower them, including registered non-governmental organizations (NGOs) and more informal, grass-roots community-based organizations (CBOs) to assume expanded roles in the HIV/AIDS response. We worked closely with Vietnamese NGOs on several components of our project. One, which was initiated during Mr. Đức's tenure as

Chief of Party, supported a network of specialized legal clinics in six provinces to help people living with HIV and other key populations to fight stigma and discrimination by health providers, employers, and the community at large. These provincial legal clinics achieved victories in some specific cases, which were inspiring to see. Most of these cases ended in negotiated settlements whereby people who had been fired because of their HIV status were reinstated with back pay.

Unfortunately, our subsequent efforts to mainstream HIV legal services into existing government-funded legal services programs and the curricula of law schools were not so successful. Several factors may account for this. Vietnam does have a court system but, to many observers, not really an independent judiciary. For this and perhaps other more cultural reasons, Vietnam is not a particularly litigious society. People rarely file suits or take legal action to resolve disputes or seek redress of grievances. Instead, they tend to rely more on informal negotiation, and personal connections and influence.

Many community-based organizations (CBOs) also sprang up in Vietnam. Experience shows that such CBOs often have better access to affected populations than traditional health providers. In fact, many CBOs grew directly out of those populations and thus can deliver some HIV services more cost-effectively than conventional health facilities. These include peer outreach and education, case finding, linkage to testing and treatment, treatment adherence counseling, and home-based care.

The HIV prevention program for female sexual partners of people who inject drugs was an organic, community-centered and community-driven model, in which sexual partners themselves designed the prevention messages and became peer educators reaching out to other women in their communities through group sessions and individual counseling on HIV risk reduction. The program was implemented first in five districts of Hanoi and later expanded to Ho Chi Minh City and Dien Bien Province in the mountainous northwest of Vietnam. Evaluation of the intervention revealed several encouraging results. None of the peer educators themselves became infected with HIV, communications between drug injectors and their partners improved, and these couples' condom use became more consistent. The organic CBO approach developed in the sexual partners project became a model for community empowerment and engagement in Vietnam with further funding from the Global Fund and PEPFAR and official endorsement from the Vietnamese government.

Other good examples of CBOs include the support groups of people living with HIV (PLHIV) that emerged in many provinces. These PLHIV groups provide mutual support, home care for AIDS patients, and advocacy with health providers. Effective advocacy and support groups have also appeared among people who use drugs, sex workers, and men who have sex with men (MSM). These all help to combat the widespread stigma and discrimination suffered by the marginalized groups that are disproportionately affected by HIV. These groups demonstrate that they care about their communities and are willing and able to act constructively and responsibly, which in itself helps to reduce stigmatization.

The NGOs are typically better organized than CBOs and often have donor funding, so they are better able to navigate the complex government registration procedures and requirements. Most community-based organizations, by contrast, work strictly on a volunteer basis and many lack the knowledge and skills needed to win registration. The HPI worked with the United Nations Program on HIV/AIDS (UNAIDS) to develop a handbook providing step-by-step guidance for the various registration options; they also helped to train and mentor a select group of HIV-focused community-based organizations to obtain registration as cooperatives or social enterprises—businesses that divert a portion of their revenues to fund HIV service delivery. One of these, an MSM group in Ho Chi Minh City called G-Link, began by operating a coffee shop and later opened its own HIV treatment clinic. It was gratifying to see the dedication and commitment of these groups to helping their clients and achieving organizational sustainability.

The HPI conducted a thorough review of the legal and policy landscape and laid out some policy revisions that might facilitate increased government contracting with civil society organizations. We recommended simpler and "friendlier" procedures for legal registration. Some community-based organizations have benefited from a new Law on Social Enterprises to become successful providers of HIV/AIDS services. Otherwise, progress on improving the legal basis for government contracting with civil society organizations in the HIV/AIDS response, and other realms as well, has proved challenging. A revised Law on Associations has been through more than 20 drafts, but none has yet won passage. While some limited "work-arounds" have been devised, the barriers to reform of the relevant laws and policies that could produce formal systemic change remain quite daunting.

I left Vietnam in May 2012 when HPI still had a year to run. A Vietnamese Chief of Party led the project for the last year. I left feeling that our project had contributed to improvements in some but not all dimensions of Vietnam's legal and policy framework on HIV/AIDS.

As HIV antiretroviral treatment became increasingly available in Vietnam, it was funded predominantly by international donors like PEPFAR and the Global Fund. To ensure quality in HIV treatment and care, these donors preferred to support a parallel system of HIV out-patient clinics separate from the government's public health infrastructure of clinics and hospitals. These parallel systems of care brought their own challenges, especially when donors began to reduce their funding as Vietnam achieved "middle-income status" and the HIV epidemic stabilized. Treatment services, which had been funded and operated principally by donors, had to be integrated into the government health system. A successor project to HPI took up these challenges starting in 2014.

The experience of HPI, its achievements and frustrations, illustrates Vietnam's version of a tension, no doubt observable in all countries to a greater or lesser extent, between pressure for progress and resistance to change. Old ways of thinking and acting, and the political, ideological, and economic interests that support them, are powerful. Like the Vietnamese themselves during the American War, these interests are resilient and perhaps able to outlast their opponents for a long time. However, a rising class of enlightened and committed advocates for better laws, policies, programs, and services, within and outside the government and Party, raises the promise of ultimate, albeit slow and painstaking, improvement. I remain optimistic about the future of Vietnamese policies in public health and related fields. Vietnam has, after all, controlled HIV/AIDS fairly effectively and achieved even more dramatic success in controlling Covid-19. These are encouraging indicators of what the country can do working together to meet public health crises.

17

Getting to Know Vietnamese Culture

During my wartime tour, my cultural life, especially music and books, was imported from home. I had no interest in learning about or understanding Vietnamese culture. In fact, I probably doubted that the Vietnamese people even had a culture worth my interest. In my second tour, I learned more about Vietnamese culture and came to enjoy and participate in some aspects of it.

Many Vietnamese people love to sing, and singing is a common feature of social gatherings. Possibly as a carryover from the wartime, the Vietnamese seem partial to love songs with themes of separation and loss. In a *ca dao* sung poem, a lover sings:

> My love for you is deep-aching, endless.
> In the tipped dish, I grind ink for a poem:
> a poem ... three or four, saying
> *Wait for. Hope for. Remember. Love.*[1]

Hanoian couples may be singing these romantic songs to each other as they pedal swan boats in Truc Bach Lake and West Lake or keep their trysts on motorbikes along the lakeshores or on the darkened Long Bien, Thang Long, and Nhat Tan bridges.

Many Vietnamese people also love patriotic songs, and many banquets end with rousing renditions of "Vietnam, Hồ Chí Minh!" I would always join in on the chorus. Often, foreign banquet guests are encouraged to sing songs from their country as well. Not being a very good singer, I usually reached for simple staples like "I've been working on the railroad" or "Take me out to the ballgame." At a meeting one 4th of July, my colleague Don Des Jarlais and I led the group in singing Woody Guthrie's "This Land Is Your Land."

Karaoke, another form of singing, is extremely popular in Vietnam. Our HPI staff enjoyed many karaoke sessions, which were especially buoyant if they followed bia hơi at Hanoi's beer gardens, as was often the case.

Several of our staff were excellent karaoke singers and would perform love duets with great feeling and emotion—Dr. Bình and Nguyễn Thị Thanh Hiền were among the stars of this genre. Our IT man Nguyễn Anh Tuấn was also particularly good at the romantic songs and Đoàn Thị Nga did a beautiful rendition of the American love song "Unchained Melody," which had been a big hit for the Righteous Brothers in 1965. I would hazard a few songs from the English language catalog and was usually able to struggle through the Beatles' "Let It Be," James Taylor's "Sweet Baby James," or Smokey Robinson and the Miracles' "Tracks of My Tears." Luckily, one's embarrassment was contained to the immediate group, as Vietnamese karaoke venues are divided into small private rooms unlike many in the U.S. where everyone must perform for the whole establishment, friends and strangers alike.

Many Vietnamese also love to dance. On my early morning bike rides, I would often stop for a water break at a park between West Lake and Truc Bach Lake where several hundred couples would be practicing ballroom dancing to the sounds of a boom box. They did the fox trot, jitterbug, and cha-cha, among others. The dancers were mostly older couples, but some younger ones mixed in and most did all the steps with skill, aplomb, and feeling. I enjoyed watching them. In addition to dance groups, there are many outdoor morning exercise groups doing tai chi, qi dong, and aerobics, and people playing badminton in parks and on sidewalks all over Hanoi.

In addition to enjoying some Vietnamese music, I continued to love that of my own culture and to link very firmly certain songs with certain places and times. For example, I will always associate the last 30 miles of the drive to our summer place in Maine, which are on a dirt road, with Tom Petty's "Learning to Fly" ("Started out on a dirty road"[2]) and Ralph Vaughn Williams choral settings of the English folksongs "Linden Lea" and "The Dark-Eyed Sailor." As I began to think about writing this memoir, I often revisited the music of the Vietnam War era that had influenced my thinking and served as the soundtrack of my experiences.

While living in Hanoi, I did listen to some newer music. I came to associate the beautiful, tradition-inflected songs of South Yorkshire's Kate Rusby[3] with my second tour in Vietnam almost as strongly as I had associated Bob Dylan, the Beatles, Jefferson Airplane, Judy Collins, and Tom Rush with my first. It must be said, however, that Rusby's music is clearly influenced by Sandy Denny and Fairport Convention, as well as Steeleye Span and the other English folk-revival and folk-rock groups of the 1960s and 1970s.

Nancy and I were excited to hear that Bob Dylan would make his first (and so far, only) concert appearance in Vietnam in April 2011. I had first heard him in person during my Freshman Jubilee Weekend at Harvard in 1964 and later with the Rolling Thunder (perhaps coincidentally, the U.S. code name for its bombing of North Vietnam) Revue at the Harvard Square Theatre in 1975. (I loved the live music in Martin Scorsese's 2019 film *The Rolling Thunder Revue: A Bob Dylan Story* but, to my disappointment, many of the characters, including Dylan himself, came off as not so pleasant or engaging.) In Ho Chi Minh City, Dylan was to play outdoors on the campus of the Royal Melbourne Institute of Technology. We eagerly bought tickets, but later learned that only half of the 8,000 available had sold, perhaps in part because they were quite expensive by Vietnamese standards.

The concert began with a lengthy tribute to the well-known Vietnamese songwriter Trịnh Công Sơn on the 10th anniversary of his death. Sơn was noted for his antiwar songs and love songs. Vietnamese musicians performed 15 of his compositions. Quite understandably, most of the Vietnamese attendees, including the colleague who joined us for the concert, seemed more interested in Sơn's songs than in Dylan's. But quite a few Americans and other expats waited impatiently for the great man to start his set. I have to say it was bit of a disappointment. Dylan's touring band is very good but he himself was pushing 70 and his voice had changed quite dramatically. I had sometimes liked the way Dylan transformed his songs over time. I think particularly of the folk song "Baby, Let Me Follow You Down" on his first album reinvented only a few years later in a hard rock version during his tours with The Band and in the 1978 film *The Last Waltz.* However, in this Ho Chi Minh City concert Dylan's voice was so different and he changed the old songs so much that I had trouble recognizing some of them at first.

Dylan, as diffident as ever, said very little and, perhaps surprisingly, nothing about what it meant for him to play in Vietnam. I was a bit saddened by this. His songs were so mixed up with my evolving views on the war, even though he never explicitly wrote about the war in any of them and even disavowed any implicit references. Presumably, appearing in Vietnam held some significance for him but we'll never know. Still, I was glad that we went to the concert and could say that we saw Dylan play in Vietnam.

Nancy and I attended quite a few concerts of the Vietnam National Symphony Orchestra (VNSO) at the beautiful French-built Hanoi Opera House. Memorable performances included Verdi's *Requiem* during one of our daughter Abigail's visits—my mother and I had both sung as altos in this piece when I was in the sixth grade—and a Christmas concert during which the Hanoi Children's Chorus dressed in red and white seasonal outfits sang "Silent Night," "We Wish you a Merry Christmas," and a carol involving the shepherds—which they pronounced "sheep-erds."

One of the highlights of my second tour in Vietnam was joining the Hanoi International Chorus (walk-ons welcome, no audition required—important since I can't read music) to sing portions of Handel's *Messiah* with the VNSO at the Opera House in the spring of 2012. I love *Messiah* and it was quite moving for me to sing in the Opera House. Nancy and all our HPI staff attended, along with some of their children. The staff presented me with flowers afterwards, as if I'd been the star of the concert rather than just one member of a chorus of two hundred.

In September 2011, the New York Philharmonic appeared at the Opera House, so I got to hear them for the first time since attending several Carnegie Hall concerts under Leonard Bernstein with my grandparents in the 1950s. In Hanoi, the Philharmonic first played the Vietnamese and American national anthems as the audience stood. The program featured Brahms's Violin Concerto (with Frank Peter Zimmerman) and Beethoven's Seventh Symphony, both among my favorites.

My second-tour reading still focused on my own culture. Not being able to read the language severely limited my ability to get much into Vietnamese literature, but I did read in translation Bảo Ninh's *The Sorrow of War*. This antiwar novel was banned by the government for many years and even now is largely available only in pirated copies from street vendors.

During and after my second tour, I also read some poetry and prose by Vietnamese and Việt Kiều writers. Much of this literature has to do with the enduring wounds of the country's long wars among those who remained and those who left. Ocean Vuong was born in Saigon but now lives in the U.S. His poem "Self-Portrait as Exit Wounds" paints a powerful picture of the experiences and thoughts of people fleeing South Vietnam in 1975, the perils of their voyages, the squalor of the refugee camps through which they passed, and their struggles to find new homes in America.[4]

In "Separated Worlds," poet and novelist Nguyễn Phan Quế Mai writes about the thousands of Viet Cong and North Vietnamese soldiers still missing in the South:

> With each footstep I place in my country,
> how many bodies of wandering souls will I step on?
> How many oceans of tears
> of those who haven't yet found the graves of their fathers?[5]

This and other themes of loss, redemption, and resilience in time of war are movingly explored in Quế Mai's 2020 novel *The Mountains Sing*. The spiritual and cultural bases of the Vietnamese sense of family, community, and nation, which help explain their determination to prevail in war, are evident in ancient *ca dao* poetic songs. These place humanity in the overlapping space of a venn diagram of heaven and earth.[6] In one, fishermen on a river may provide a metaphoric depiction of Vietnam's ancient struggles:

> Whose boat plies the river mists
> offering so many river songs
> to move these mountains and rivers, our nation?[7]

Viet Thanh Nguyen sounds the themes of a never-ending war in two acclaimed novels and a non-fiction book. In *The Sympathizer,* a group of South Vietnamese transplanted to Orange County, California, maintain and try to act on the quixotic hope of returning to their homeland and overthrowing the Communist government[8] while *The Committed* continues the story as wartime feuds play out in a Paris drug war.[9] *Nothing Ever Dies* analyzes the cultural uses and abuses of the memories of the war. Nguyen calls passionately for "just memory," which requires "an ethical awareness of our simultaneous humanity and inhumanity, … equal access to the industries of memory,…. [And] … the ability to imagine a world where no one will be exiled from what we think of as the near and the dear to those distant realms of the far and the feared."[10]

Andrew X. Pham, who also fled South Vietnam with his family in 1975 and arrived in the U.S. in 1977, wrote of the wrenching emotions he experienced as he struggled between being a Vietnamese person AND an American when he returned for a bicycle tour of his homeland two decades later: "I am a mover of betweens. I slip among classifications like water in cupped palms, leaving bits of myself behind."[11]

Perhaps the most extreme iteration of the never-ending war from the American perspective is Spike Lee's 2020 film *Da 5 Bloods.* Lee embeds commentary on and allusions to the War, *Apocalypse Now,* the antiwar movement, the militance of Black troops in Vietnam, racism, Donald Trump, the ravages caused by Agent Orange and unexploded bombs and mines, and post-traumatic stress disorder—all in a story of four African Americans, who served together during the War, returning to contemporary Vietnam. They aim to recover a chest of gold bars now worth millions that they had buried after the crash of a CIA plane carrying it. They are also seeking to recover the remains of their beloved squad leader "Stormin' Norman" who was killed during the defense of the downed plane and had decreed that the gold bars be used to fund reparations for African Americans. The War never ended for the group.

Lee did not have the actors made up or their bodies digitally changed to look their real young ages in the wartime scenes. Three of the veterans were killed by Vietnamese bandits during the return expedition. Paul, the veteran still suffering from PTSD, refers to these bandits as "the VC."

The only happy outcomes are that Otis, the one survivor, gets to meet and embrace his now-adult Amerasian daughter, a chunk of the proceeds from the gold bars goes to Black Lives Matter organizations, and Stormin' Norman's remains are returned home with full honors.[12]

It is interesting to compare these works suggesting a "never-ending war" to what seems a prevalent view among the heavily youthful population on the streets of Vietnam, and probably also among America's younger generations, that the war is over and forgotten. The Vietnamese generations in which virtually everyone served or at least had family members, friends and neighbors in the war, knew well what it had really been like. But these war generations began to pass on and younger ones emerged as the majority of the nation's people with little or no direct experience of the war. W.D. Ehrhart observed children playing with toy replicas of U.S. fighter jets in a Hanoi toy shop in 1990:

> And the children touch them without fear,
> pick them up with their hands,
> put them into the sky
> and pretend they are flying;
> nothing but now in their eyes.[13]

To America's remaining veterans, supporters, opponents of the war, and even Vietnamese émigrés, the war's images and memories seem more durable, although its lessons have not demonstrably been understood or reflected in subsequent American foreign policy. Many Vietnamese people also know and revere their nation's past—ancestors, heroes of the revolution, strong and resilient families, memories—but they are not lost in it and they remain able to keep their eyes and their energies firmly and practically focused on the future as well.

By the time I moved to Hanoi, I had long been a devoted fan of Boston's professional sports teams, especially the Red Sox, Patriots and Celtics. Nancy and I are among the millions who claim to have been at Fenway Park for game 6 of the 1975 World Series, won by the Red Sox on Carlton Fisk's climactic home run leading off the 12th inning. Unlike most of them, however, we still have our ticket stubs to prove it. Nancy had a business trip to Washington the next morning and suggested we might leave early with the Sox behind 6–3 in the 8th. Happily, I prevailed and we stayed, although a couple seated right in front of us did leave. Did they ever dare admit that to their friends?

During trips to Vietnam in the early 2000s, I tried to follow Red Sox playoff games on Yahoo using excruciating slow, dial-up internet connections. It was the only Internet available. I remember waiting for what seemed like an hour for the screen to refresh in my Hanoi hotel room and show me that the Red Sox had defeated the Oakland A's in the 2003

American League Division Series. Of course, the Red Sox went on to lose to the Yankees in heartbreaking fashion in the League Championship Series, extending their 85-year World Series drought for still another. I was on a work trip in Urumqi, China when they finally won the World Series in 2004. That evening my Chinese colleagues assumed that "Red Sox!" was just a generic American drinking toast. During later trips, I would get automatic updates on Red Sox games on my little Siemens flip phone. When wireless internet became available, I signed up for MLB-TV and was able to catch a lot of Red Sox games live, although with the time difference, night games on the East Coast of the U.S. began at 6:00 the next morning in Hanoi. I often watched a few innings before going to work.

During trips to Vietnam in the early 2000s, I was able to see the Patriots win a few playoff games on International ESPN. However, by the time I was living in Hanoi from 2008 to 2012, ESPN in Vietnam had eliminated the NFL and NBA entirely in favor of a steady diet of soccer, car racing, and golf (not my favorites), with a smattering of darts, snooker, and extreme sports (also of little interest). While not a huge fan of soccer, I did follow and root for Vietnam's national football teams when they played in international tournaments. International ESPN did carry some seemingly random college basketball and the occasional MLB game—but almost always the hated Yankees.

To see the Super Bowl, one had to go to the American Club or to a bar that had a satellite hookup. We watched the Patriots' disappointing 2012 loss to the New York Football Giants at Tracy's, an Australian burger place on Xuan Dieu. When the game ended at about 9:30 a.m., I had to go to work.

Much to my surprise, in the mid–1980s I had returned to the Episcopal Church. Like many, I guess, having a child and entering middle age brought the realization of ultimate mortality. Our family had discovered at Christ Church Cambridge a warm and welcoming community. However, when I moved to Hanoi, I found no Anglican or Episcopal Church. Nancy and I attended the English language Mass at Cua Bac Catholic Church (with the display in front depicting the Blessed Virgin Mary in a grotto among water buffalo) on Easter and a few other Sundays but my religious practice came to center on my private reading aloud each Sunday of Morning Prayer, in the version of Thomas Cranmer's 16th-century *Book of Common Prayer*. I looked forward to this ritual, which was a continuing comfort, more out of tradition, familiarity, and repetition, I admit, than out of literal belief in the words. But, oh those beautiful words. For example, the considered language of the General Thanksgiving, where we acknowledge those mysteriously wonderful gifts "the means of grace and … the hope of glory" bestowed solely out of God's "inestimable love," and for which "we thine unworthy servants" should be "unfeignedly thankful."[14]

I have never had much of an overt prayer life outside of Sunday mornings, but I do try, by no means always successfully, to be a good Christian in my daily life and relationships with others. My desire to befriend Vietnamese people was also no doubt part of my effort to seek their forgiveness for my past mistreatment of them. Poet and veteran W.D. Ehrhart described this feeling on his return to Vietnam: "wanting to gather the heart of this place / into himself, to make it forgive him."[15]

During my second tour, meanwhile, I became more interested in Vietnamese religion and spirituality. These blend Buddhism, Confucianism (the source of the society's persistent patriarchal culture), Taoism, and Animism (the belief in spirits). A strong component of ancestor veneration draws on several of these spiritual traditions. Remembrance and respect for ancestors is an important part of Vietnamese culture and spirituality. Indeed, according to John Balaban, the "system of spiritual belief created around the family is the highest value of Vietnamese life. It permeates all social conduct."[16] Graves are lovingly tended, and offerings of fruit, liquor, cookies, cigarettes and other goodies are offered up to ancestors at pagodas on important lunar days and anniversaries of their deaths, for their use beyond the grave.

Pagodas and temples, large and small, occupy prominent lakeside sites and secluded spots in crowded neighborhoods throughout Hanoi. Pagodas are dedicated to Buddha, the Mother Goddess, or other deities, while temples are usually dedicated to earthly personages. Some are very ornate while others are simpler. Hanoi is quite flat but in hilly or mountainous parts of the country, pagodas and temples are typically placed on high ground, closer to heaven. There, visitors must climb several hundred steep, often slippery steps, typically without railings. The views can be spectacular.

Pagodas usually offer places of peace and quiet above or amid the bustle and noise of city or town. However, the major pagodas, such as Phủ Tây Hồ (dedicated to the Mother Goddess Liễu Hạnh) near our home in Hanoi, are extremely crowded with people praying and presenting offerings to their ancestors on important days of the lunar calendar, especially Tết and the 1st and 15th of each lunar month. The streets leading to the pagodas experience major traffic jams during these days and the stalls selling fruit, cookies, and other offerings for the ancestors are crowded with customers. We liked to take our guests on a walk from our house along West Lake to Phủ Tây Hồ and then back by Dang Thai Mai street that features the small but beautiful Chùa Phổ Lin temple with resident monks and a long series of illustrations depicting various good and bad behaviors and their consequences. Some of the results of misbehavior are quite scary.

One week before Tết is the day of the Kitchen God ceremony, which grows out of a long, complicated legend explained to us and a puzzled group of foreigners by a Vietnamese expert at an annual event held by the Friends of Vietnam Heritage.[17] The legend concerns a love triangle in which "two men and a woman" die tragically but are posthumously appointed by the Jade Emperor as a tripartite deity, "Táo Quân," responsible for the care of people's houses and property. On the 23rd day of lunar December, Vietnamese households send off the Táo Quân or Kitchen God to heaven to report to the Jade Emperor on the state of their homes on earth and to pray for good fortune in the year ahead. The ceremony includes eating special foods such as young sticky rice from the new harvest, placing three votive caps for the three deities on the home altar, and releasing golden carp into a lake or river, which will help the Kitchen God ascend to heaven.

The Friends of Vietnam Heritage's Kitchen God event culminated in our release of fish into West Lake from the back terrace of the Hanoi Club, adjacent to the driving range where some members were hitting golf balls into big nets out in the lake. Our goldfish were also dropped into the lake and happily swam away. Following the fish release, we had a meal of traditional Tết foods, including colored sticky rice and bánh chưng, square rice cakes with pork filling wrapped in taro leaves. According to legend, in the second millennium BCE, Lang Liêu, the poorest son of a king of the 6th Hùng Dynasty, won succession to the throne by inventing this cake combining simple peasant foods.

During the weeks before Tết, people (usually the wives) clean and decorate their houses and prepare the traditional foods. Families also bring home their Tết trees, in the North usually kumquats and in the South peach blossom trees. Sure signs of the approach of Tết are the many motorbikes carrying Tết trees home. The HPI staff gave Nancy and me a beautiful kumquat tree, which was delivered to our house from a nursery shortly before Tết and then returned to the ground there afterwards, so as to be ready for the next year's celebration.

Shortly before and during Tết and other important lunar days, people are burning fake paper money and paper replicas of clothing, laptop computers, and other useful items in the streets and lanes in front of their houses and at the pagodas and temples. It is believed that burning these paper replicas allows the real items to ascend to their ancestors for their use in the spirit world. At burials, some favorite things of the deceased are typically placed in the grave with the casket. Sometimes, these are items that may have helped lead to the person's death. For example, one of our staff member's husband died at the early age of 50 from a stroke, probably induced in part by his heavy smoking. Nevertheless, cigarettes and a cigarette lighter went into his grave. He would doubtless welcome these in his celestial destination. There is an eerie parallel between this Vietnamese practice and the frequent offerings of cans of beer and packs of cigarettes by visitors to their loved ones whose names are on the Vietnam Memorial's Wall in Washington. The theological bases may be different, but both seem to bespeak an effort to maintain closer connections between the living and the dead.[18]

I attended several funerals of staff members, their parents and spouses. An important part of the pre-burial ceremony is paying respects to the deceased. Monks may or may not participate, chanting over the body, depending on the wishes of the family. Groups of people are arranged by organizational affiliation and advance toward the usually open casket, place burning joss (incense) sticks in the urn in front, then

Our Tết Kumquat tree.

walk all the way around the casket and greet the family members on the other side. An elaborate series of back-and-forth steps is required to carry out this observance and, after a few mistakes, I achieved some competence with it. After this ceremony, the casket is typically loaded onto a decorated wagon—the equivalent of a hearse—filled with flowers and motorized or drawn by hand, which will follow a brass and drum band all or part of the way to the cemetery, depending on the distance. The family mourners wear white cloth bands around their heads and walk behind the wagon, while the others may follow in a hired bus.

There is a worsening shortage of cemetery space in the cities, so many burials now take place in large new cemeteries quite far away. Also because of the growing shortage of real estate, the traditional custom of first burying the body just outside the cemetery and then exhuming it and moving it into the cemetery a few years later has become much less frequent. Cremation is also increasingly common.

I also had the opportunity to attend several Vietnamese wedding celebrations. The spiritual or religious portions of weddings—if, in fact, they are included—occur in private with the immediate families. A visit of the husband's family to the bride's family home, including a special tea ceremony, is an important part of this ritual. The private ceremony is followed by a party, usually for lunch, held in a hall or under a canopy erected on the street in front of a restaurant. One can tell the astrologically "lucky" wedding days by the number of these canopies and the number of couples having their elaborate wedding photos taken in front of the Opera House and the Metropole Hotel, in the Botanical Gardens, and other favorite locations. The brides often bring makeup artists to ensure their perfect appearance for the camera, and elaborate romantic poses are struck. An important part of the wedding party is the guests leaving their gifts— envelopes of money. For families that are less affluent, these gifts may in fact be needed to help pay for the meal and other wedding expenses.

As in other religions and cultures, two important elements of Vietnamese spirituality—practicality and superstition—seem easily to coexist among believers. A.N. Wilson described a hymn-singing Breton procession to the ocean bearing a statue of Mary, to pray for the success of the upcoming fishing season. This he terms a simultaneously "profound veneration for virginal purity and a very strong desire for lobsters" or, more generally, a "jarring blend of excruciating superstition and commercial self-interest."[19]

In *The Protestant Ethic and the Spirit of Capitalism*, Max Weber asserted that religious faithfulness may deservedly lead to financial and business success. Many Christians actually believe this but hypocritically avoid any overt instrumental focus in their spiritual lives. Still, in my own

Anglican tradition, the Prayer of St. Chrysostom, read toward the end of Morning Prayer, slips up by asking God to "Fulfill ... the desires and petitions of thy servants, as may be best for us."[20] Vietnamese people, by contrast, are generally more open and honest about praying for the things they really want, such as more money, a good job, success in business, and good grades on school examinations. They also pray for friends, families, ancestors, good marriages, healthy children and other less material desires.

At the same time, owing to the influence of Animism, superstition enters much of Vietnamese life. Nor is this limited to Vietnam: in fact, all religion and spirituality partakes of superstition to a greater or lesser extent. In Vietnam, many people frequent fortune tellers and some seek second opinions if a first fortune teller does not give the hoped-for prediction. Wedding partners and wedding days are often chosen with regard to compatible astrological birth years and lucky dates in the lunar calendar. Elaborate rituals with altars, chanting, sprinkling of water on the floor, and eating special foods (red sticky rice and boiled chicken) are held when moving into a new house or office. This is to bring good luck and avoid troubles from evil spirits. My colleagues led these ceremonies and I participated when we opened our HPI office and when I moved into my house. It is also considered extremely important that the first person entering an office or home after Tết be carefully selected based on having a favorable age and year of birth. If someone else is the first to enter, this could bring bad luck to the organization or family.

Ghosts and their powers are widely believed in. One of our staff told me that two people had died from dog bites in a neighboring house and this had brought bad luck to subsequent residents. Finally, monks were summoned to dispatch the ghosts troubling the house. Staff of the Dien Bien Provincial AIDS Committee told me that they had to leave the office by 5:00 p.m. every day or they might be beset by the many ghosts left over from the battle of Dien Bien Phu in 1954. It could have been an excuse to avoid working late but it seemed they really believed it.

18

Bún Chả và Bia Hơi

During my second tour, I came to love Vietnamese food and drink and the Vietnamese ways to consume them. I loved to sit in a neighborhood street food stall savoring a steaming bowl of beef phở or a helping of bún chả in its sweet-and-sour sauce. Perhaps even more, I loved being with my friends at bia hơi. These are the best places not only to eat and drink but also to enjoy Vietnamese conviviality, hospitality, and zest for life, so precious after all the death and misery of the past.

I came to love the Vietnamese methods of eating. Food is typically served family style, which enhances the communal sharing of the meal and seemingly of the conversation as well. In restaurants and at their homes, Vietnamese women often help serve the dishes to others at the table, typically selecting the best morsels to place in a guest's rice bowl. They often cut up larger food items with scissors. (At home now, we often take scissors to our granddaughter Iggy's noodles, chicken, shrimp, and vegetables.) After a while, I got to feel almost more comfortable eating with chopsticks than with knife and fork. I picked up my rice bowl to eat, drank from my soup bowl, dipped my food in fish sauce, mixed in a few red chiles or a bit of chile sauce, rested my chopsticks across my small rice bowl or propped them on the edge of a serving dish, and in restaurants called authoritatively for "em ơi!" Sometimes, my Vietnamese friends commented that I ate just like a Vietnamese person. I was proud of that.

Where to start with the delights of Vietnamese food? Breakfast? Phở bò, the classic and perhaps best-known Vietnamese dish—beef and rice noodle soup with a variety of herbs such as cilantro, cinnamon, ginger, and star anise. For me and many others, I think, phở is the ultimate comfort food. Its quality depends heavily on the broth, which requires just the right bones and just the right number of hours of simmering in the pot. I liked phở tái chín with its combination of rare and well-cooked beef. Phở also comes with chicken (and, in Lang Son, with duck), which are both good, but I preferred the beef version. Squeeze in some fresh lime juice and add a few drops of chile sauce around the edges. After finishing the beef and noodles, tip the bowl to drink the rest of the savory broth. My other breakfast favorites were cháo sườn (rice porridge with bits of pork rib meat), bánh mì patê (bread with pork patê) or bánh mì trứng (fried egg sandwich), all available right in our lane in Tay Ho.

Our office lunches, prepared by Hương, featured a number of dishes that I particularly liked, including thịt kho dừa (pork with coconut), cá kho (stewed fish), canh cua (crab soup), chả mực (squid paste cakes), chả lá lốt (ground pork rolled in lolot leaves), and bún bò nam bộ (beef noodle salad). However, my all-time favorite lunch dish was bún chả, which Hương sometimes made for us but we more often went out for. It is chargrilled bacon-like strips and small ground pork patties in a broth based on fish sauce with fresh herbs, pickled green papaya and carrots, and served with rice noodles and a bowl of additional fresh herbs, and often accompanied by nem (fried spring rolls). Bún chả is the Hanoi specialty that President Obama chose for his meal with Anthony Bourdain at a typical spot on Le Van Huu Street, afterwards renamed Bún Chả Obama. As the President emerged from the restaurant, he bantered with the crowd of ordinary Hanoians, one of whom shouted out "How do you like Vietnam?" This is a typical Vietnamese question to foreigners and normally receives a positive response, as it did from Obama, especially after enjoying some great Vietnamese food.

Phở tái chín at Pho Hoc on Xuan Dieu street in Hanoi.

I enjoyed bún chả at many places in Hanoi, including the oldest and best known at #1 Hang Manh in the Old Quarter, several in my neighborhood, and one in a lane off Lac Long Quan, where our HPI staff used to have group lunches. According to Sơn Phan of our staff, this place uses charcoal from some very special kind of wood, which resulted in the best bún chả. On a visit to Hanoi much later, my son-in-law Theo became so enamored of bún chả that he typically ordered two portions—"hai bún chả, một Coca" ("two bún chả and one Coca Cola")—for lunch.

Another Hanoi specialty is chả cá, pieces of white fish fried in oil at the table over a sterno-heated skillet with herbs, and eaten with rice

Bún chả on Lane 31 near our house in Hanoi

noodles, peanuts, and fish sauce (nước mắm)—or, if you prefer, a strong sauce of fermented shrimp. The original chả cá restaurant is on the eponymous street in the Old Quarter. I was taken there by a Vietnamese colleague on my first visit to Hanoi in 1997. During my second tour, I tended to frequent Cha Ca Anh Vu on Giang Vo Street near the Ministry of Health. Our project staff had numerous group lunches there, followed by dessert of nếp cẩm (pudding of black sticky rice and yogurt), sữa chua dê (goat yogurt), or caramen (crème caramel) at a stall around the corner. More recently, a chain called Cha Ca King (Vua Cha Ca) has opened, which also features a delicious fish head soup.

Other tasty lunches include phở xào, phở's ingredients stir-fried minus the broth. The most famous place for phở xào is on Bat Dan street in the Old Quarter. My friend Dr. Ngữ first took me there. Mì xào—also delicious—is the same but with egg noodles. Bít tết, thin beef steak with a fried egg, French fries, and pâté, served on a sizzling platter and eaten with fresh bread was also a well-liked lunch for me and the HPI staff.

Another great lunch place in Hanoi is Hoang Mai at 25 Ngu Xa near Truc Bach Lake. This is but one of several restaurants along this street that specialize in phở cuốn—beef and fresh herbs rolled in skins made of the same rice flour used in phở noodles. The bustling Hoang Mai, with two locations directly across the street from each other, also offers phở chiên phồng (phở xào with deep fried savory "donuts") and ngô chiên (fried corn). You get all of this and a Bia Hà Nội for a few dollars per person. The restaurant 25 Ngu Xa was my daughter Abigail's favorite lunch spot and we also enjoyed taking our guests there for a typical taste of Hanoi.

Besides phở, bún chả, and chả cá, Vietnam is noted for its other specialty restaurants—many serving only one type of dish. Often these are clustered along the same street. Lẩu is hotpot—particularly good in the North's cool months—and there are streets with numerous specialty lẩu restaurants—lẩu ếch (frog); lẩu hải sản (seafood), lẩu nấm (mushroom), and so forth. Several hotpot restaurants have conveyor belts that bring all the possible meats, seafood, vegetables, mushrooms, and other ingredients around to your table so you can customize your lẩu.

Phở cuốn and Phở chiên phồng, *inter alia*, as at Hoang Mai, 25 Ngu Xa, Hanoi.

There are also restaurants specializing in snakes, seafood, and birds. Most of the snake restaurants are in Long Bien District, across the Red River from downtown Hanoi. There you can make your selection from cages of live snakes. I skipped the selection but did eat some of the snake, which was prepared in different ways and was quite good. Similarly, in seafood restaurants, you may select your fresh fish and shellfish from tanks or basins out front. Fish is typically cooked and served whole with fresh herbs. Some people, usually men, particularly like the meat that must be patiently extracted from the fish's head. We had an HPI group dinner at a bird restaurant by West Lake. Being a bird lover, I was a bit reluctant but did indulge in the bồ câu quay (roasted pigeon) and others of the various large and small birds on offer.

Once, on a sightseeing trip to Ha Giang's Dong Van Plateau, after a long day of spectacular but terrifying driving on narrow mountain roads with huge drops and no guard rails, we went to dinner in a small simple restaurant in the town of Meo Vac. We ordered chicken and the proprietor said that it was available but there would be a bit of a delay. This turned out to involve their going out and purchasing a live chicken, which they slaughtered within our earshot in the kitchen. Here, luckily, we did not follow the common Vietnamese custom of wandering into the kitchens of modest small-town restaurants to assess the operation and ingredients and watch their food being prepared. We ate that chicken, probably the so-called gà đồi ("walking" or free-range chicken—not as tough as the retired "fighting" chickens) with measured relish, trying to forget its dying screams that we had just heard.

The most common dessert in Vietnam is fresh fruit, of which a wonderful array is available almost year-round: mango, banana, pineapple, coconut, papaya, watermelon, longan, lychee, jackfruit, custard apples, mangosteen, dragon fruit—even the foul smelling but quite tasty durian. Dragon fruit is beautiful but, to me, somewhat bland (the new variety with purple flesh has a bit more flavor than the traditional white-fleshed kind), whereas the bananas (particularly the tiny ones) and watermelon are much sweeter and more flavorful than the tasteless versions we typically get in the U.S. Longan, also know as "dragon eye" is one of the most common and beloved of Vietnamese fruits. To "Việt Kiều" like Eric Nguyen's character Hương living in New Orleans, the texture, aroma, and taste of the dragon-eye may be among their most precious memories of home.[1]

The ultimate Vietnamese dessert is chè, a sweet soup served at street stalls and restaurants, which typically combines several fruits with beans, tapioca, coconut cream, jelly, and crushed ice. Chè is delicious and refreshing on a hot night or, indeed, anytime.

For Christmas, birthday, housewarming, and going away parties at our house, Vân, our wonderful housekeeper, would prepare several Vietnamese foods, usually fresh spring rolls with pork and shrimp, and banana flower salad with chicken. Vân also made dinner for us several days a week. She was adept at many international types of food, but her Vietnamese dishes were the best: deep fried pork spring rolls (nem), pork ribs, mi xào with beef, morning glory (a spinach like vegetable grown in lakes) sautéed with garlic, and fried rice with seafood.

Since I lived in Hanoi, I was more familiar with Hanoi food than dishes common in other parts of the country. Even there, however, I barely scratched the surface. So many restaurants and so many street stalls serving such a variety of things—noodles in all their variety—phở, bún, miến, mi, vermicelli with all kinds of meat and seafood—including crab, snails, fish, duck (vit), ngan (Muscovy duck, sometimes referred to as "vit's brother"), pork, beef, and chicken; spring rolls; eggs (from all types of birds, some fertilized); bánh mì (sandwiches with meat, vegetables, and herbs); skewers of grilled meat; sweet potato slices; corn on the cob.

Beyond Hanoi, Vietnam has an abundance of regional cuisines and dishes, some of which I had the chance to sample on work and pleasure trips throughout the country. In general, the food in Vietnam has regional tastes: in the North, it is savory; in the South, sweet; and in the Central provinces, spicier. People from the North don't generally like the sweet taste of the food in the South ("too much sugar!") and there are whole neighborhoods in Ho Chi Minh City of people from Haiphong and other places in the North that have their own shops and markets with Northern food—like people on the Lower East Side of New York City and other immigrant communities in the U.S., they prefer the familiar tastes of home while living far away.

Some local and regional specialties that I liked were grilled goat (dê) in Vinh; fish soup in Can Tho, Long Xuyen and elsewhere in the Mekong Delta; in Danang, chicken with noodles (mỳ Quảng) and rice porridge with seafood (cháo hải sản); in Ho Chi Minh City, phở bò with the sweet taste, large basil leaves and bean sprouts; bánh xèo (pancakes with pork, shrimp, and bean sprouts); cơm tấm (broken rice, often served with grilled marinated pork chops); in Hue, considered by many to have the best food in Vietnam: bún bò Huế (spicy beef soup with thick round noodles), nem lui (sausages of ground pork and beef with sugar and fish sauce formed around lemongrass stalks); bánh bèo (small round steamed rice cakes with shrimp and pork cracklings), bánh khoai (crunchy rice flour crepes filled with shrimp and pork belly); in Lang Son, sautéed bee larvae and adult bees, and phở vit (duck pho); in Ha Giang, ấu tẩu (rice gruel with pork), only served late at night, supposedly able to cure headache and all manner of other complaints, and very welcome after the five-hour drive over rough roads from Hanoi.

The Việt Minh defeated the French in 1954, ending almost 75 years of oppressive colonial rule in Vietnam. While very few and mostly old

Vietnamese people still speak French, French influence remains, perhaps most strongly in food and drink. The French taught the Vietnamese to make great bread, although the Vietnamese use rice flour because wheat is not grown in Vietnam, and to grow and drink coffee, although here, too, the Vietnamese developed their own types of coffee and style of coffee drinking. Many Vietnamese words come from the French and, not surprisingly, many of these are food terms: cà rốt (carotte), sô cô la (chocolat), cà phê (café), and pho mát (fromage [cheese]). The continuing French influence is also evident in several high-end restaurants, such as Hanoi's Green Tangerine and La Badiane as well as Le Parfum at Hue's La Residence Hotel, which feature French-Vietnamese fusion cuisine, in some cases taking local street food dishes to the level of gourmet dining.

Vietnamese food is increasingly popular in the U.S., but Americans only get a small slice of it. This is because almost all Vietnamese migrants to the U.S. in the aftermath of the War came from the South and thus almost all Vietnamese restaurants in the U.S. serve Southern style Vietnamese food, with its attendant sweet taste. More recently, with some more Northerners moving to the U.S., a small number of Northern Vietnamese restaurants have appeared, such as San Francisco's Turtle Tower, named after the iconic monument in Hanoi's Hoan Kiem Lake. These serve decent bún chả, chả cá, and Northern style phở bò—but it's still not the same as being in Hanoi. And, while it has its interest, the Tenderloin doesn't quite match Hanoi's Old Quarter for atmosphere.

The Vietnamese people love their own food the most but have come to like some western foods, such as the ubiquitous pizza, French fries, and burgers. In the past, some Western foods, such as cheese, were not generally liked, although this may be changing. Nancy and I learned one food lesson, a bit embarrassingly. We invited some Vietnamese friends for a traditional Easter dinner of roast lamb (like my mother always served), only to find that Vietnamese people don't like its strong flavor. We had a lot of leftovers from that meal.

I can only think of a very few Vietnamese foods that I don't like or that don't agree with me. One is eel (lươn), because of its, to me, unpleasant consistency. Another is dog meat (thịt chó), principally for reasons of personal or cultural preference. I just can't imagine eating dog meat. I never did so, at least knowingly. Vietnamese men, in particular, eat dog meat, supposedly as a male bonding ritual. To their credit, few women do. Dog is served only in specialty restaurants, often clustered on the outskirts of cities. Tobias Wolff's *In Pharaoh's Army,* based on his experiences as an advisor to an ARVN unit in the American war, includes a sad story about his pet dog. His ARVN colleagues wanted to give him a party the night before his departure and partway through the banquet he realized that the main dish was his pet dog.[2] This illustrates how perfectly appropriate and even respectful a ritual offering of dog meat is to many Vietnamese people. However, it does seem to have declined in popularity, perhaps as a result of the recent increase in pure-bred dogs as pets. Vietnamese mongrel street dogs seem to have benefited from this development as well.

There is a third Vietnamese food that I don't like—based on hard experience. During lunch on a work trip to Sapa in the mountains northwest of Hanoi, I was offered "pork stomach"—I hesitated for a moment but then ate some of it. I paid dearly for this mistake with a case of food poisoning during an "uncomfortable" overnight on the train back to Hanoi. However, this was the only time that I have ever gotten sick from Vietnamese food. It remains inadvisable to drink the tap water although recently it was announced that the water in an outlying district of Hanoi was now potable.

For Western food, we sometimes headed to the good Italian restaurants apparently established to serve the large Italian expat community working at a Vespa motorbike plant. However, Don's Tay Ho was, far and away, our favorite. Don's was right on West Lake and a three-minute walk from our house. I had dinner at Don's the second night of its "soft opening" in October 2010 and thereafter Nancy and I spent a lot of time there. We became friends with Montreal-born Donald Berger, the part owner and patron. Don's served wonderful Vietnamese, Western, and fusion food. He had Canadian oysters flown in and, although they were quite pricey, I couldn't resist them sometimes, particularly on a hot afternoon with an icy glass of sauvignon blanc at Don's rooftop bar overlooking the lake. Don also had an extensive collection of music videos, many of them historically important and of my generation, that were usually to be seen and heard in the downstairs and rooftop bars. Don's also featured Alberta ribeye steaks, wood-grilled to perfection. Nancy and I usually had our Thanksgiving and Christmas dinners—with all the trimmings—at Don's.

The Vietnamese people love their coffee—evidenced by the thousands of cafes in every city and town—and so do I. It is strong and rich and slightly chocolate scented, mostly from Robusta beans, unlike the Arabica grown in Central and South America, the source of much of the coffee consumed in the U.S. Before coming to Vietnam, I always drank my coffee (except espresso) with milk and sugar, so I immediately liked the Vietnamese coffee with sweetened condensed milk (cà phê sữa or cà phê nâu [in the North]), either hot (nóng) or iced (dá). I particularly like the cà phê sữa đá in Ho Chi Minh City because they fill the whole glass with crushed ice whereas in the North, they don't give you as much ice. You need the extra ice on those hot days. "Weasel coffee" is a popular tourist purchase in Hanoi. Now considered mostly fake, it is supposedly produced by weasels or similar animals eating, digesting, and defecating coffee beans. I have never tried it. I preferred 3-in-1 (coffee, milk, and sugar) instant coffee by Vinacafe. I always brought several packages home with me to the U.S. and sometimes replenished my supply at HMart or another of the proliferating Asian markets.

The Vietnamese people also love their tea—a much more long-standing affection than coffee. While black tea (Trà Lipton, for example) and various herbal teas are popular, the tea of choice for most is green tea. The best green tea supposedly comes from Thai Nguyen Province, northwest of Hanoi. A green tea drinking group ritual is observed in restaurants, cafes, and at the tiny plastic tables and stools of street stalls. To clean the small cups, a bit of tea is poured into each, swished around, poured into the next cup, and then dumped out once all the cups have been rinsed. The tea is then poured for all. Often, in local restaurants, diners move from the table at which they ate to a nearby table for tea and fruit to conclude the meal.

Thankfully, my alcohol and drug dependence had eased since my first tour. No doubt, my increased happiness contributed to this. And, indeed, I was happy to be in Vietnam this time around. While I hadn't had a cigarette in 40 years, I still sometimes enjoyed the smell as Vietnamese men smoked strong tobacco through water pipes at tea stalls and cafes.

I did very much enjoy Vietnamese beer when I returned—the regional lager beers: Bia Hà Nội, in its large returnable bottles, although it is said by some to contain formaldehyde—and Habeco's high-end lager, Trúc Bạch; Bia Sài Gòn (especially Sài Gòn Đỏ with the red label); Hue's Huda; and Danang's Larue. The craft beer movement was still to come during my second tour, arriving in Hanoi and Ho Chi Minh City in about 2016.

Bia hơi is the best place to drink beer in Hanoi. These outdoor beer gardens are an important Hanoi institution found throughout the city. Strangely, there is no bia hơi in Ho Chi Minh City—it is the South's loss. Bia hơi serves pitchers of very cold, very fresh, low-alcohol draft beer. Our HPI staff usually went to Bia hơi on Fridays after work. I often rode with one of my colleagues on the back of his motorbike to our favorite Bia hơi at 19C Ngoc Ha, behind the Ho Chi Minh Museum. Near this spot, in the then "village" of Ngoc Ha, an American B-52 was shot down by a SAM missile and crashed during Nixon's Christmas bombing of 1972.[3] Rumor has it that this bia hơi place is owned by the police—never mind, there is no established drinking age in Vietnam. At bia hơi, the beer is cold, the conversation is loud and spirited, and the fellowship is warm. Groups at the tables engage in the traditional shouted salute when raising their glasses: "một, hai, ba [1–2–3], dzô!"

Some of my best memories are of being with my friends and colleagues at 19C Ngoc Ha on hot afternoons, cooled by the large fans, sometimes interrupted by heavy thunderstorms causing the folding roofs to be closed over us, slipping on the wet floor on the way to "William Cuong" (the WC), and eating the fresh peanuts, fried squid (mực chiên), tofu, pork leg, buffalo jerky, baby beef, morning glory, cabbage with soy sauce and hard-boiled egg (another of my daughter Abigail's favorites), and fried rice; bantering, laughing, and teasing with my Vietnamese colleagues and friends and their kids. We usually sat at the same tables every time, pulling together more as more people arrived. I have photos taken raising the distinctive cloudy blue-ribbed bia hơi glasses with the same friends—Sơn Đặng and Binh—at the same table, six years apart. My colleague Lộc and her husband Quân gave me a set of bia hơi glasses that I now use at home in Watertown and at our summer place in Maine to remind me of those good times and good friends.

The Vietnamese often host banquets with work colleagues and visitors at which there are many toasts, such as "chúc sức khỏe" (good health), and large amounts of local rice wine are consumed. Other toasts involve urgings to everyone to drink "trăm phần tram" (100 percent or "bottoms-up"). The rice wine (rượu) may be purchased from the restaurant but is more often homemade and brought by one or more of the participants in reused plastic water bottles. The stuff is quite powerful and so, to avoid drinking too much of it, I would sometimes stash a bottle of water next to my chair from which I would try unobtrusively to fill my tiny glass between toasts.

With Dr. Binh (left) and Sơn Đặng (right) at Bia hơi 19C Ngoc Ha, May 2012.

And again: September 2018.

However, if you were caught doing this, as sometimes happened, you were made to drink more of the real stuff. Also, sometimes the wine was made with plums or some other fruit, which made it red or purple rather than clear, so the water ploy could not be used on these occasions.

If Bia hơi 19C Ngoc Ha was my favorite drinking place in Vietnam, Don's rooftop bar was a close second. Here, I was usually by myself, less often with Nancy because she fled Hanoi's summer heat for Boston and so missed the best months for the rooftop bar. Here, I could read my book, drink a cold draft beer, and look out across West Lake with its unauthorized fishermen, occasional boats collecting trash, its morning glory plantings, and the heat haze on the surrounding roads and buildings. Directly across the lake is the Sheraton Hotel, where President George W. Bush stayed on his one brief visit to Hanoi. Rather than sample the local food as President Obama later did, Bush brought all his food with him—he was the loser in that.

On Don's rooftop at night, you could enjoy live music and watch the headlights crawl along the road four miles away at the far end of West Lake and the heavy traffic on the closer Xuan Dieu, possibly turning onto Quang An heading for Tay Ho pagoda, especially on the major dates of the lunar calendar. In the cooler months, Nancy and I liked Don's first-floor bar, where we enjoyed many conversations with the patron, other customers, and the welcoming Vietnamese staff, often while watching Don's vintage music videos.

This time around, my tour in Vietnam seemed to fly by. In the blink of an eye, it was over. I left so many dishes and types of food on the table. This is one of the main reasons I still hope to go back. So much great food, so little time!

19

Crossing the Street
and Breathing the Air

For me, crossing the street, riding my bike, and breathing the air were the risks of living in Hanoi—pretty trivial in relation to the joys. Nancy forbade me to get a motorbike, although I really wanted one. I did ride on the backs of my colleagues' motorbikes—sometimes helmetless on the way to bia hơi on Friday afternoons—or with xe ôm (motorbike taxi) drivers back from shopping trips downtown, wearing the helmets they provided.

Following my initial instruction on crossing the street from that stranger on Cat Linh Street in 1997, I pretty quickly got the hang of it. Just step off, move slowly but steadily and the traffic goes around you; you may stop briefly but the cardinal rule is: you must NEVER BACK UP. The cars and motorbikes do not expect you to back up, so if you do you will almost surely get hit. In fact, this happened to a visiting American professor, who was seriously injured.

I actually liked riding my bike in the Hanoi traffic, being surrounded while stopped at traffic lights by chatting Vietnamese, who sometimes greeted me and asked where I was from. I usually answered, "Tay Ho," and they would laugh. Most mornings I rode my bike to the gym at the Hanoi Club, negotiating the early rush hour traffic on Yen Phu and Yen Hoa, down by the Thang Loi Hotel built by Cuba for its ally Vietnam in the 1970s and where Catherine Deneuve stayed while starring in the film *Indochine*. Most Sunday mornings, I would leave my house at about 5:30 a.m. to avoid heavy traffic and do a 17-mile loop around West Lake—with a brief water stop to watch the ballroom dancers in the park named for Lý Tự Trọng, a teen-aged martyr of the revolution—then around Ba Dinh Square past Hồ Chí Minh's Mausoleum; down Le Duan past the railroad station to Lenin Park, making the sometimes terrifying left turn onto Dai Co Viet; up Pho Hue to a circuit of Hoan Kiem Lake; and all the way back along the dike road and the Hanoi 1000 ceramic wall to Tay Ho.

In the last few weeks of my second tour, I did some rides with the rising sun over the iconic Long Bien Bridge and out along the Red River and over the Thang Long Bridge, which used to be the primary route to and from Noi Bai Airport before the opening of the closer-in Nhat Tan Bridge. On my bike rides, I wore a mask to minimize my exposure to the pollution.

In reality, neither of my Vietnam tours posed serious risks to my safety. As I was a supply officer, "in the rear with gear," I was rarely if ever in any danger during my wartime tour. Risks on my second tour, where they existed—such as crossing the street or riding my bicycle—were much more mundane than those theoretically present in a war zone.

Although it seems absurdly unnecessary and wasteful of funds, the U.S. government mandates a "post differential" (the civilian equivalent of hazardous duty pay) for the expatriate employees of its contractors in Vietnam. Some duty stations may indeed be seriously challenging, inconvenient, or even dangerous. However, as I've described, Vietnam is a wonderful place to live with many and varied attractions and few notable drawbacks. Predictably, it is a very popular assignment for U.S. government staff and expats working for U.S. government contractors.

There are some frustrations working with the Vietnamese government and bureaucracy, and corruption sometimes impinges on an expat's life. But these are very minor irritants in the grand scheme of things. Hanoi, and indeed all of Vietnam, is extremely safe and almost entirely free of violent crime. There is the occasional pickpocket or scam vendor. I had a cheap camera stolen on my first visit to Hanoi in 1997, and once fell victim to the rapid currency-switching ploy (similar to the trick used by Ryan O'Neal's character in *Paper Moon*) of a lady selling postcards by Truc Bach Lake.

I also succumbed a few times to "cheating taxis," some with fake emblems of real taxi companies, whose meters start low and slow but soon begin to crank up very quickly. After I called out one of these drivers and refused to pay his inflated fare, I discovered that he had lifted my mobile phone from a carelessly unzipped jacket pocket. The government now seems to have virtually eliminated the cheating taxis.

Vietnam has very little armed robbery, assault, or murder. Domestic violence is reportedly on the increase and there has been some rise in crimes involving knives. However, while Vietnam does maintain a very large army, gun ownership by civilians is forbidden and, unlike in the U.S., there is no cultural glorification of or fascination with firearms. One might reasonably conclude that these factors help to explain the sharp difference in murder rates between the two countries: Vietnam's population is 96 million and it had 1.5 murders per 100,000 people in 2016, while the U.S., with a population of 326 million, had 5.4 murders per 100,000, a rate almost 3½ times higher. Although official statistics are unavailable, news reporting makes clear that Vietnam has very few homicides or other deaths associated with guns.

The traffic in Hanoi is terrible at almost all times. Tắc đường (traffic jams) are common and a usual excuse for lateness to meetings. Most of the streets are simply too narrow to accommodate the thousands of motorbikes and the more recently exploding thousands of cars. Drivers sound their horns almost continuously. This is not out of aggression but simply to let others know that "I'm here." Within the moving swarms of motorbikes, there is constant chatting among the people in addition to the constant honking. Despite the craziness on the roads, the cutting in and out and cutting off of other drivers—behavior that would be sure to draw outright anger or even violence in Boston or L.A.—I observed no road rage in Vietnam.

In fact, the traffic is so insane and so often snarled that one can't drive very fast most of the time, especially in cars but even on motorbikes or bicycles. This is not the case in rural areas, where people drive very fast and often recklessly, passing on curves and in the face of rapidly oncoming traffic. I saw several grisly accidents in small towns. The worst tend to involve motorbikes and trucks, with the motorbike driver typically getting by far the worst of it.

Serious and fatal traffic accidents are quite unusual in the cities. Occasionally, you will see a couple of motorbikes get tangled up and fall

Hanoi traffic jam (MinhHue / Shutterstock).

over. The drivers or bystanders usually just help each other up and they move on, unless the machine can no longer be driven. The paucity of serious accidents in the city should not be attributed to the carefulness of drivers, but rather more to the generally slow pace necessitated by traffic congestion.

There is nothing that cannot and will not be carried on a motorbike and virtually nothing that cannot be done while riding on a motorbike. There is a wonderful book of photographs called *Bikes of Burden* showing the incredible variety of motorbike cargoes, some of them potentially very dangerous were they to fall: large panes of plate glass, propane gas cylinders, plastic water jugs, hundreds of rolls of toilet paper, many dozens of eggs, cases of Bia Hà Nội, Tết trees, all kinds of animals and birds from the largest pig to the smallest parakeet or pet dog on the lap or at the feet of the driver, and wicker cages full of chickens, ducks, and sometimes even dogs, possibly bound for a thịt chó restaurant. Some drivers appear almost buried in huge sacks of scrap paper, bunches of balloons, or bags of vegetables.

One wonders how they can keep their balance, but I rarely saw anyone fall or spill their cargo. This is even more the case with those who cannot afford motorbikes and load enormous amounts of cargo onto their bicycles and manage to stay upright navigating Hanoi traffic. These are primarily vendors bringing vegetables and fruit from wholesale to retail

"Groceries" (© Hans Kemp, *Bikes of Burden* [Hong Kong: Visionary World Ltd., 2003]).

markets or directly from the countryside or taking their stocks of pottery and ceramics to sell in street markets. There are also legions of vendors who buy flowers from the wholesale market on Au Co early in the morning and fan out on their bicycles to sell them throughout the city.

In 2007, the Vietnamese government issued a law requiring adult drivers of motorbikes to wear helmets, reportedly because the World Bank threatened to cut off all loans and other financial assistance if this wasn't done. Children under five years old were exempted because of the perceived risk of scoliosis from heavy helmets—surely less serious than that of head injury in an accident. In fact, there seem to be no requirements as to the weight or specifications of the helmet worn. Many of them clearly do not provide even reasonable protection. Common helmets are replicas of baseball caps, many with Hello Kitty and similar logos (especially for women and girls), round pith helmets of the type worn by some Viet Cong and NVA soldiers during the American War, and replicas of U.S. Army or German Wehrmacht helmets. Chin straps are rarely fastened. In Hanoi, moreover, probably at least half of motorbike drivers or passengers stop wearing helmets after dark. People in Ho Chi Minh City seem to be more law abiding at all times. Police no longer rigorously enforce the helmet law in Hanoi. Increasingly, even during daylight hours, drivers are without helmets. Sometimes, a small group of hotshot young men will go zigzagging through the traffic at high speed without helmets, even doing the occasional wheelie where space permits. Nobody seems to mind.

Text messaging or talking on mobile phones while driving is not forbidden in Vietnam and seems indeed to be the rule. As in most countries, many Vietnamese people are addicted to their phones and can't seem to be out of contact for even a few seconds. It is not uncommon to see a motorbike with three or four people or a load of cargo on it, with everyone talking, texting, or checking social media sites while weaving through the traffic.

I no longer smoked during my second tour. In fact, I had stopped near the end of my first, due to a severe and persistent cough caused by the combination of smoking and the dusty environment at Quang Tri Combat Base. By the time of my second tour, the air pollution in Hanoi had become quite bad. The millions of motorbikes and charcoal cookers and the addition of thousands of cars caused the air quality sometimes to sink to the levels of Beijing. This caused many expatriates, including me, to develop the affectionately named "Hanoi frog in the throat." This condition sometimes worsened to a cough that might last for several weeks or, for me in one case, for several months

In fact, despite its unhealthful air, the distinctive smell of Hanoi can be very seductive, as my daughter Abigail points out. It begins to hit you almost as you leave the airport terminal and intensifies as you enter the city. Its hot and humid air (most of the year) suffused with the odors of charcoal fires, fish sauce, phở broth cooking, garbage, and subtle hints of raw sewage. It is a bit like the smell of New Orleans, but with some different foods involved and lacking the French Quarter's pervasive olfactory component of vomit.

Hanoi can be quite cold in the winter, although not what a New Englander considers really cold. Even as the weather cools to the 50s and 60s in November and December, many Vietnamese people bundle up in down jackets, wool hats, and mittens as they ride their motorbikes. Most Vietnamese buildings have no central heating, although some room air conditioning units have heating elements and separate space heaters are often used. Schools typically close if the temperature is below 10 degrees Celsius (50 degrees Fahrenheit). On cold days, people wear their coats in the office and at meetings. The air often remains humid and dank in the winter but may be less polluted.

To mitigate the air pollution's effects, I began to wear a mask not just while on a motorbike or on my bicycle but whenever I was outside, which helped somewhat. Like the Vietnamese, I soldiered through it. It was really but a minor irritant, as were the other risks, in my very pleasurable life in Hanoi. Later, the plaid Gucci knockoff mask that I brought home from Hanoi came in very handy during the coronavirus pandemic. Wearing it almost made me imagine that I was back in Hanoi. Indeed, sometimes I wished I was.

20

A Second Homecoming

There was a very nice going away party on the rooftop of our office building on Xuan Dieu, several bia hơi and karaoke sessions, at one of which I reprised "Leaving on a Jet Plane"—this time for my journey of mixed feelings from Vietnam to the U.S. instead of my decidedly sad and anxious trip in the other direction in March 1968. Another musical highlight of my last week was a Vietnam National Symphony Orchestra performance of Dvořák's "New World" Symphony at the Hanoi Opera House. The second movement's lovely American folk melody "Goin' Home" was timely and my reaction to it was quite emotionally conflicted.

Going home from my second tour in Vietnam at the end of May 2012 could not have been more different from my first departure. I had come to love Vietnam, the country and its people and particularly my colleagues and friends. Of course, as I said to everyone, it is always nice to go home and I had Nancy (who had left earlier in the month to avoid the onset of Hanoi's summer heat), the Red Sox (who were placing their hopes in Bobby Valentine after their epic September collapse in 2011—how did that work out for us?), our summer place in Maine, and my church community to return to. But I also had some uncertainty about what I would do next in my life. I was 67 years old and considering retirement but, like many at that age, wondered how I would fill my time if I didn't have to get up and go to work every day. As it turned out, I didn't retire and would, in fact, spend a good deal more time in Vietnam before I was through. But all of this was an unknown as I contemplated leaving Hanoi.

The last few weeks were busy. I was still leading the HPI project, and we were actively advocating several important policy initiatives: revisions to the Ordinance on Prostitution to give it a more public health than punitive focus; and improvements in legal registration procedures for civil society organizations and expansion of their ability to obtain government funding for provision of HIV/AIDS services. In fact, I was participating in workshops and meetings on these issues right up to the day of my departure.

I gave our Vietnamese birds Ernie and Oscar back to Vân Nghiêm's family. Her father came with his motorbike and loaded the cages on the back. I was sad to see them go.

I did a last bike ride over the Long Bien Bridge just as the hot May sun was coming up. I paid a last (I thought) visit to Don's rooftop bar and posted a photo on Facebook of "My last night in Hanoi. The view over West Lake and Xuan Dieu."

At the going away party, our HPI staff presented me with a lovely book of photos of our times together in which each of them, and some of their children, had written goodbye messages. Many of these were about my role as Santa Claus at our Christmas parties. Another gift from the staff was an oil portrait of Nancy, Abigail, and me based on a photo taken at one of those Christmas parties. A particularly interesting gift was a large mounted lump of coal from Mr. Thành Đồng who, before he took up a career in public health, had worked as a coal miner in his native Quang Ninh Province.

In addition to the gifts, we took home many artifacts and mementoes of Vietnam. Several of these we purchased at Mark Rapoport's 54 Traditions Gallery on Hang Bun Street. Mark is a physician from New York who was the City's deputy health commissioner during the first years of the AIDS epidemic and then came to Vietnam originally to work on an NIH research project regarding birth defects associated with Agent Orange. When the funding for that project ended, Mark, who had become fascinated with Vietnamese arts and crafts, and a Vietnamese partner opened 54 Traditions gallery. It is devoted to antique and contemporary work of Vietnam's 54 ethnic groups. From 54 Traditions, Nancy and I selected three water puppets (we and our guests had enjoyed many traditional water puppet shows at the theater by Hoan Kiem Lake and the National Museum of Ethnology, also devoted to the country's ethnic groups)—a duck, water buffalo, and fisherman with rod and line. We also acquired an ornate seated Buddha, an ornamental wedding shirt front from Ha Giang Province, a glazed ceramic bowl from the 12th–14th century, and a shamanic "wand" in the form of a tiger, with bits of dragon and dog mixed in. We also brought home some traditional Tết decorations—replica branches with flowers—that we had used in our house in Hanoi, and several propaganda posters from the American War period and after. The poster shops helpfully provide translations of the captions: for example, "Planting bamboos at the dike edge to anti-flood and serve the life." So, we now have several displays of Vietnamese artifacts at our house in Watertown to remind us of our happy times in Hanoi.

I was informed that I would receive the Vietnam Ministry of Health's Medal for Protecting the People's Health. Even though virtually every expat director of a health project receives this award, it's a nice recognition and I have the medal and framed certificate to document it.

After a final bia hơi session, our local driver Mr. Long took me to the airport and several of the staff came to see me off. My flights took me first to Seoul Incheon then to San Francisco and finally to Newark, where Nancy met me—as she had in Philadelphia when I came home from my first tour. This time, instead of learning about the breakup of my father's second marriage, as in April 1969, we were going to join the celebration of my niece Johanna's wedding to Jake at a summer camp not far from Max Yasgur's farm, the site of 1969's Woodstock music festival. What goes around comes around.

Part IV: After My Second Tour

21

Basic School Reunion[1]

When I came home from my second tour in Vietnam, I had hopes but no certainty that I could continue my connections with the country. As it turned out, I would maintain my relationships not only with contemporary Vietnam and its HIV/AIDS response but also with my personal history in the American War.

I was a bit apprehensive as I headed down I-95 from Washington to Fredericksburg, Virginia, in May 2015 to attend a reunion of my Marine Corps Basic School class. I had not kept up with any of my classmates and did not know what to expect from them, particularly in light of my views about the war. I almost didn't go to the reunion, but it turned out to be a fascinating and moving experience that I wouldn't want to have missed.

I confessed to my old Basic School platoon commander Captain McMaster that I had been a "real fuck-up." He disputed this saying that, if so, "you never would have made it through the program." In point of fact, as I've said, I basically faked my way through it. Nevertheless, I accepted and actually continue to wear the Marine Corps pin that McMaster gave me at the reunion. I would never have predicted this in my early days as a former Marine but, perhaps a bit like Lewis Puller, I could come to both "love and despise … the Marine Corps."[2]

At the reunion I learned that, contrary to my assumption, I was not the only member of Basic School Class 1–68 to have been against the war. I had several conversations with classmates who took what I expected to be the stock Marine Corps line that "it wasn't our job to have opinions about the war but just to do our duty as ordered." However, I met several others who were against the war at the time and even more who sooner or later came to see it as a terrible mistake.

Dave Purvis told me the story of the night during his Vietnam tour that turned him against the war. He was a dismounted amtrac (amphibious tractor) officer with an infantry unit north of the Cua Viet River, pursuing NVA units withdrawing toward the DMZ. Purvis had pre-registered 81mm mortar strikes on an open area in front of his unit's position and used a new night vision device to locate NVA troops and repeatedly hit them with 50 caliber machine guns and the pre-registered mortars. Many NVA troops were killed and wounded. Purvis was assigned to go out the next morning to do the body count and look for anything on the bodies that might contribute to intelligence. Instead, he found love letters, pictures of wives, children, and sweethearts. The plight of one severely wounded NVA soldier, who Purvis and a corpsman kept alive by using a Bic pen to perform an emergency tracheotomy, particularly affected him.

Purvis realized in a "moment of epiphany" that these NVA soldiers were just like him with the same relationships, hopes, and fears. All of a sudden, they became for him human beings rather than enemy ciphers. Purvis recalled thinking just then: "I did this; I killed and wounded these guys; what the fuck are we doing here?" After this, Purvis told me, he tried to spend as much of his time as possible doing community action work in Vietnamese villages. Later, while stationed at the Naval Academy he sought and received permission to attend the November 1969 march against the war. "As long as you don't wear your uniform," cautioned his commanding officer. After his release from active duty, Purvis had a long career as a social worker.

Jay Jacobson was an infantry platoon commander in the war, despite his long-standing opposition to it. After he got out of the Marine Corps, he worked on the staff of Rep. Allard Lowenstein of New York, one of Eugene McCarthy's and then Robert Kennedy's key supporters, and had long stints as an attorney and a high school history teacher.

David Crain, who became a broadcaster on public television in New York, told me that he was against the war the whole time he was in the Marine Corps. In fact, a superior officer had dubbed him the "Abby Hoffman of the Corps." This was an amusing surprise because Crain had always seemed to me to be among the most "gung-ho" members of our Basic School platoon. At the reunion, he told me that this resulted simply from his desire to be the best, regardless of his views. Crain is writing a book with a revisionist stance, in which he dwells on the differences between North and South Vietnam and the long history of the stronger North invading and abusing the weaker South. Still, he acknowledges that the U.S. had no real national interest at stake in that North-South conflict. His current position is one of ambivalence toward the American War.

Jon Feltner, one of a group of Dartmouth classmates who were in NROTC, opted for Marine commissions, and remain Boston area friends, is one of a surprisingly large number of my Basic School classmates who have been back to visit Vietnam since the war. During a long walk along the Rappahannock River during the reunion, Feltner told me how he had come to see the war as a misconceived waste of lives and resources. He was twice wounded as a platoon commander, and, during a visit to Vietnam in 2010, sought out Mai Xa Chanh (West), the village near Dai Do where he was wounded on March 1, 1968. While there, he met a man who had been an NVA soldier in that same battle. They joined together in a ceremony to remember and honor their fallen compatriots in this tragic war and to celebrate the subsequent friendship between our two countries.

During my time in Vietnam, I too met a number of North Vietnamese and Viet Cong veterans—we typically hugged and toasted U.S.-Vietnamese friendship. Based on his meetings with North Vietnamese veterans in 1984, William Broyles noted a striking difference between them and many American veterans of the war: "They did not look into their selves and see angst or guilt or confusion.... For them the war was long, bitter, terrible—and over. The past is past, they kept telling me.... [T]he most enduring reward of victory may well be a clear conscience."[3]

Nancy and I have hosted several dinners with the Dartmouth group—including Jon Feltner, Beirne Lovely (a weapons platoon commander with 1st Battalion, 9th Marines at Khe Sanh with whom I had a few beers several times in Quang Tri after he came out of the field), and Drew Ley (a Marine fighter pilot)—as well as Al Kyle (a 1st Marine Division communications officer who went to Duke) and Bern Bradstreet (a Harvard classmate and another Marine aviator). Beirne's unit, 1/9, had also been my father's in World War II. It became known in Vietnam as the "Walking Dead" because it had the highest casualty rate of any American unit in the war. Rodger Jacobs, who was wounded while serving with 1/9 in 1967, claims that Hồ Chí Minh assigned special troops to "wipe out" the unit after it had inflicted heavy losses on the NVA.[4]

Beirne Lovely invited me to join his table at the annual Boston commemoration of the Marine Corps birthday. He also gave me a Boston Semper Fi Society hoodie emblazoned with the Eagle, Globe and Anchor. I wear it all the time and, oddly after all these years and despite my feelings about the war and my checkered career in the Corps, I feel almost proud to be identified as a former Marine. Once I was entering Fenway Park wearing a jacket with my Marine Corps pin attached. A security guy at the gate, who had been a Marine in Iraq, asked me what unit I had been in: "3rd Marine Division in Vietnam," I answered.

22

Vietnam Battlefield Tour

In September 2016 I joined nine other Marine Vietnam veterans, most of whom were in my Basic School class, for a tour of some of our wartime scenes. Doug O'Connor started the tour telling me that he didn't really remember where he'd been during the war but seemed to recall a lot of places and experiences as we went along. When we got to Khe Sanh, Doug wrote this in the museum guest book: "I was here before. The writing on the wall [the photo captions described below] is not what any who were here recall. It was a time I hope never returns for the people of Vietnam—or for mine." Dave Randall and I also signed Doug's entry.

We started the tour in the Danang area and visited Hill 55, the site of a Marine artillery base, headed north through the Hai Van Pass (over which I had ridden supply convoys) to Phu Bai and Hue City, the scene of the bloody battle during the Tet offensive, then up toward the former DMZ, with visits to Quang Tri, Dong Ha, the Cua Viet River area, and the site of the Con Thien and Gio Linh Marine bases, which suffered heavy shelling in late 1967, and the battle of Dai Do in May 1968. From Dong Ha, as on my previous DMZ tours, we headed west on Route 9 into the mountains past the sites of Marine artillery and combat bases, Camp Carroll, the Rockpile, and Vandegrift Combat Base. While we were on the bus and at various sites, members of the group told the stories of their participation in the actions there. During the drive out Route 9, I had the chance to tell my only "war story," that of having been stranded for the night at Fire Support Base Russell, a few days after it was nearly overrun by the NVA. I received a (perhaps sarcastic) round of applause.

At Khe Sanh, a herd of goats was grazing placidly near the reassembled U.S. C-130 on the site of the airfield. It was a vastly different scene from those photographed by David Douglas Duncan in February 1968 as these aircraft landed and took off under fire from NVA gunners. One was hit and burned while on the airstrip.

Near the location of the combat base is the substantial town of Khe Sanh, population 30,000, built entirely since the war. From Khe Sanh, we

C-130 landing at Khe Sanh, February 1968. The photograph appeared in David Douglas Duncan, *I Protest! Khe Sanh, Vietnam* (Signet Broadside: New American Library, 1968) (© David Douglas Duncan Photography Collection, Harry Ransom Center, University of Texas at Austin).

Reassembled C-130 on the site of Khe Sanh airstrip, 2018.

visited Hill 881 North, assaulted by Marines three times in 1967–1968 with heavy casualties but occupied for a total of just four days. The NVA had built a network of tunnels under the hill. On 881 North we found a cell phone tower and water buffalo feeding. Finally, we drove down the former Ho Chi Minh Trail, now a national highway, from the Dakrong River

Bridge on Route 9 through spectacular mountain scenery into the Ashau Valley, also the site of multiple bloody battles including the Marines' Operation Dewey Canyon and the infamous Hamburger Hill, fought by the Army's 101st Airborne Division, both in 1969. From Aloui in the Ashau Valley we returned to Hue through the beautiful mountain passes of National Highway 49.

In Hue, our group stayed at La Residence, a hotel built up from the former French governor's residence, on the Perfume River across from the Citadel that had been the focal point of the 1968 battle.

The psychological scars of Hue and Vietnam have yet to heal fully. A February 2019 article in the *New York Times* questions the identity of a severely wounded Marine being evacuated from the battle of Hue on top of a tank, as depicted in a famous newspaper photograph of the time. The controversy surrounds whether the Marine in the picture was James Blaine, who died of his wounds, or Alvin Grantham, who survived. For some, whether the pictured Marine had lived or died reflected their assessment of the war—as if it was something wrong that should have died with this Marine in Hue or something noble that should have lived on.[1]

In a sense, this is similar to the controversy that erupted over Maya Lin's design of the Vietnam Memorial in Washington—between those who would have preferred a monument celebrating the 58,000 Americans who gave their lives in a worthwhile cause to a subterranean black "scar" listing all the names of the fallen and seeming to imply that they had died for nothing. However, the overwhelmingly positive and often highly emotional response to the Wall from veterans, the families of the fallen, and all other types of citizens and visitors—both by their presence and by the thousands of gifts they leave there—attests to its quiet power and beauty, as well as its success in truly honoring the dead, regardless of the rightness or wrongness of the war. It seems fitting that the song Ken Burns chose for his 2017 film's segment on the Vietnam Memorial was Simon and Garfunkel's "Bridge Over Troubled Water"[2] and, for the closing of the series' final episode, the Beatles' "Let it Be."[3]

This tour of Vietnam battlefields provided some insights into the minds and hearts of my Marine compatriots both then and now. My strongest impression was of "mixed feelings." The group as a whole and individuals within it displayed sometimes conflicting attitudes, predispositions, opinions, and conclusions about the war and about the Vietnamese people.

Pride in having been and always being Marines was evident, exemplified by the habitual "Semper Fi" greetings. Bob Koury shared an open letter he had written in 2004 to Marines serving in Iraq and Afghanistan in which he said that Marines were a "long line of brothers [he might have said sisters, too!]; we're with you all no matter what." Indeed, there is much

The passage of time: the pool at La Residence looking across the Perfume River to the Vietnamese flag flying over the Citadel, for the control of which so many tragically died more than 50 years before.

to celebrate in the heroism, dedication to duty, and sacrifice of individual Marines in Vietnam and throughout American history. That is why I decided to wear the pin given me by Captain McMaster and the hoodie given me by Beirne Lovely.

Marines have always had to overcome adversity. The cynically termed "Marine way" often meant higher ups failing to provide needed supplies and equipment and units having to hump the hills with barely enough time to dig in and enjoy C rations before nightfall. By contrast, Army units like the First Air Cavalry in Operation Pegasus relieving Khe Sanh were helicoptered in, assumed positions pre-prepared by engineers, and were promptly delivered hot meals. Bob Koury told of how a Marine unit wandered into a friendly minefield just below Hill 881 North in January 1968 and sustained heavy casualties, because no one had bothered to notify the unit of the minefield's existence or location. Marines always seem to get the "shitty end of the stick," but they always seem to persevere, which is a justifiable point of pride.

The tour group displayed some continued fascination with weapons and their destructive capabilities. Even those who expressed opposition to the war sometimes spoke enthusiastically about the effectiveness of our various weapons in the war. As the guide was telling us about the ongoing restoration of a Cham spiritual site at My Son south of Danang, one of our group said that "we still have some B-52s if they get too far along"; and being informed that overgrown vegetation was blocking tourists' views from the top of Marble Mountain in Danang, he offered that "maybe we have some Agent Orange left." I must say these quips, even if intended as harmless jokes, took me aback.

Our group also told some horrific stories. Some NVA and Viet Cong prisoners were being held in a fenced enclosure within the MACV compound in Hue as the battle raged all around. Somehow a fire started and these prisoners all died. Accounts differ as to exactly how they died. One member of our tour group recalled that as the fire engulfed the prisoners, the key to unlock the gate of the enclosure could not be located. Several prisoners were in flames and attempting to scale the fence. This Marine officer said that he ordered the prisoners shot before they burned to death.[4] Another former Marine, who was a member of the same unit and also at the scene, insists that no prisoners were shot but in fact all did burn to death. The "fog of war" can produce sharply differing recollections. Whatever the actual cause of death, the incident was ghastly.

For the Marine who remembers ordering that the prisoners be shot, the decision must have been an emotionally laden one. However, he described it, with a curiously flat affect, as simply "not a good day at the office." He also reported that Marines had propped up the bodies of dead NVA soldiers and placed cigarettes in their mouths. "It was a different time," he said. Such are the wages of war or *The Sorrow of War,* as the title of thfe famous novel by NVA veteran Bảo Ninh puts it.

Some members of our group continued to demonize and dehumanize the other side. One frequently referred to the NVA and Viet Cong as "the bad guys." Another described the NVA being blasted out of buildings in Hue, coming out "like ants and shooting at us." The group was virtually unanimous in its praise of the courage and determination of our enemies. Some were also quick to attribute to them atrocities, such as the murder of civilians in Hue and morally questionable tactics such as building troop bunkers under hospitals and cultural sites, such as the Cham temple site we visited near Danang. However, they did not acknowledge that we Americans did many things that were just as bad, if not worse. Indeed, probably thousands of innocent civilians were killed in Hue by American small arms fire, artillery, and air strikes. While most of these deaths were probably inadvertent, these people were no less dead at American hands. Thousands more Vietnamese all over the country died pursuant to "kill anything that moves" directives in "free-fire zones" and other places. The My Lai Massacre and the thousands of often indiscriminate killings carried out by the Phoenix Program were coldly deliberate.[5]

I perceived in our tour group a palpable sense of loss and regret. At every site, we remembered our classmates and friends who had died or been wounded there: Joe Laslie and Carl Gibson killed in action, and Jon Feltner wounded, at Dai Do; Tom Pierson, felled by incoming while shooting baskets on an improvised court at Camp Carroll. We paid tribute to Jim Muir, killed near Con Thien, and Dave Purvis asked: "Why did he have to die here? He should have gone home, married his beautiful girlfriend, and had a bunch of kids." Paul Robertson, almost half of whose platoon was killed or wounded in a mortar attack just north of Con Thien, told the group while we were visiting the site of the base that, to him, it is "a place of sadness, maybe a little pride, but mostly sadness.... Not much good happened to Marines here." Indeed, not much good happened to anyone there.

Ultimately, I think, most of the group came to believe, either before, during or after their time in Vietnam, that the war had been a mistake. A few appeared to be still of the discredited view that the U.S. had been forced to fight the war "with one hand tied behind our back." But by and large, my colleagues and comrades seemed to recognize the waste, futility, and misguidedness of the war. Paul Robertson said that Nixon's Christmas bombing of Hanoi in 1972 may have been necessary to get the Paris peace agreement but he had his doubts about it—"how much more blood had to flow?" Bob Koury acknowledged that he and most Americans had no knowledge or understanding of Vietnamese culture, spirituality, or the importance to the people of their families and the graves of their ancestors.

He recalled how we uprooted whole villages and forcibly removed the residents to resettlement areas and refugee camps and then wondered why they were so traumatized and angry.

The guest book at the Khe Sanh museum contains many expressions of disgust and despair at the loss of life there and our patent failure to learn the lessons that should have been so compelling and unavoidable. One entry by an Army Vietnam veteran decried the U.S.'s hypocrisy in spouting democratic values while engaging in imperialist adventures. Next to this, however, a Marine veteran had responded: "Fuck you. Joe Black, USMC." The museum gives a very pro–Vietnamese version of Khe Sanh, with some of David Douglas Duncan's famous photographs published in *Life Magazine* and in his book titled *I Protest!*, above captions added by the Vietnamese such as "U.S. Marines stuffing themselves in bunkers for fear of their own shadows." These, as indeed the photos, captions, and other displays in museums and war-related sites all over Vietnam, force the American tourist to become, in the words of Viet Thanh Nguyen, "a semiotician, aware of how photographs do not simply capture the truth, but are framed by their framers."[6]

Bob Koury said he was "revolted" by the museum but acknowledged that, after all, the victors do get to tell their version of the story. One of the wives was still angry that antiwar "traitors" had undermined our war effort and said that it is easy to criticize in hindsight the decisions made by our leaders.

I think Doug O'Connor's entry in the Khe Sanh guest book, endorsed by me and Dave Randall, captures the mixed feelings of our group—some resentment that our efforts and actions are not accurately portrayed in the Vietnamese version of the history and pride in what we did as Marines, but an ultimate realization of the war's futility. This verdict was solidified by seeing how relatively prosperous Vietnam is now and how friendly and welcoming the Vietnamese people are towards Americans, facts that seemed to surprise most of the group. But this begs the question again and again: "What was all this death, destruction and suffering for?"

It also intensifies the outrage and frustration that we have still not learned the lessons of Vietnam. We continue to think we can blunder into countries, ignoring or seeking to reverse centuries of history and culture. As an American who exiled himself to Canada in resistance to the war told Myra MacPherson, "Uncle Sam is always there with the eraser at the blackboard of history—so that America can start another lesson."[7] And so the past rolls on into the present. I couldn't resist this backhanded allusion to Fitzgerald,[8] who sometimes seems to have all the answers and the most eloquent way of expressing them.[9] To remind myself of this, I re-read *The Great Gatsby* every year on my first trip to our summer place in Maine.[10]

23

Last Hurrah in Hanoi

A month after the 2016 Presidential election, as I was feeling distraught over the outcome, a surprising opportunity arose for me to return once more to Vietnam. The Chief of Party for an Abt Associates project had decided to leave a year and half before its end and the company was seeking someone to lead the project for that last period. I jumped at the chance to get away physically from the toxic political atmosphere of the U.S. for a while. In a way, I felt like John Converse in Robert Stone's *Dog Soldiers* who, caught up in a maelstrom of troubles after causing a brick of pure heroin to be smuggled from Saigon to Berkeley, lamented that "If I could just get back over to Nam, I'd probably be all right. You can hole up forever over there."[1]

When I came home from my second tour in Vietnam in 2012, I was contemplating retirement—but I didn't retire. I stayed on at Abt Associates working on a variety of corporate and technical projects, a few of which took me to Malawi and Jordan for brief trips to provide technical assistance for USAID-funded health programs. I also returned to Vietnam once or twice a year for consulting assignments on current Abt projects and an international project aimed at ending the HIV epidemic among people who inject drugs in the port city of Haiphong.

Of course, I realized that my return to Vietnam would only be temporary and, in any case, it would be impossible really to leave behind U.S. politics what with the ever-present CNN, the online *New York Times*, and various social media. Still, I was drawn strongly by the chance to live in Vietnam again, even for a short time. Nancy, who had not been back to Vietnam since 2012, agreed to this "last hurrah." So, in June 2017, I set off for Hanoi with Nancy to follow in October.

I found a nice house (with a small indoor pool on the ground floor—great for cooling off after gym workouts) in the same Tay Ho neighborhood we had lived in before, but just on the other side of Xuan Dieu's Lane 31. Again, we heard the roosters crowing very early every morning. We rehired Vân, our housekeeper. I frequented many of the same market vendors in the lane, especially the cháo lady, the bread lady, and the corner convenience store. The sound of the butcher lady chopping meat on the lane below our bedroom window was another early morning fixture. Next to her was a vendor of delicious small bananas. While the phở stall in lane 31 was gone, the one at the head of the lane was still there, as was the bún chả place (also serving delicious noodles with fish), now opposite the district's Methadone clinic. We reconnected with Mr. Long, our local driver, and Ms. Mai, our former next-door neighbor. However, Ms. Mai's cat, who had terrorized our pet birds, was gone. A number of new restaurants had opened, and Don's was still there with its rooftop bar beckoning.

The Abt project that I led was part of a global USAID initiative called Health Finance and Governance (HFG) and aimed to help Vietnam develop sustainable financing for HIV/AIDS treatment and other services. This was a time of necessary transition from a program funded predominantly by international donors, primarily PEPFAR and the Global Fund, to one that would be the responsibility of the Vietnamese government to finance and operate. The HFG project worked closely with the government to prepare Vietnam's social health insurance scheme to become the primary financing mechanism for the transitioned HIV/AIDS response.

With Nancy at Don's rooftop bar by West Lake, Hanoi, in October 2017.

Having bún chả with Nancy.

There were many challenges, including the need to integrate all the donor-funded HIV treatment facilities into the public health system.

Again, we had a great group of Vietnamese staff, several of whom had worked previously on the HPI project. I believe that the HFG project made real progress. The work is not done, however, and, as I was leaving, USAID funded Abt Associates for a two-year follow-on project to help Vietnam achieve the final goal of a fully transitioned HIV/AIDS program. The leadership of that project was assumed by a new chief of party.

The HFG worked in nine provinces, so I again had the chance to travel in the country, from the Mekong Delta and Ho Chi Minh City to Haiphong, Hoa Binh, and other northern provinces. Again, Nancy and I hosted quite a few guests and did several sightseeing trips with them, including more visits to Hue and several additional DMZ tours with Mr. Vinh. I found these tours moving and thought-provoking no matter how many times I covered the ground and revisited the places I had been during my wartime tour.

It was also meaningful to watch Ken Burns and Lynn Novick's PBS documentary on the war while living in Hanoi. The film came out just as Nancy was joining me there and we binge-watched it in a week. It is very powerful in its depiction of the tragedy of the war and its consequences, both short- and long-term, for both countries.

At about this time Donald Trump took a trip to Asia. During a brief stop in Hanoi, he walked unseeingly past Vietnam's President who was at the airport to meet him. At Yokota Airbase in Japan, his first Asian landing point, Trump gave a triumphal speech in which he proclaimed of the U.S. that "We've always been on the side of freedom and peace." Clearly, Trump had not watched Burns and Novick's film. As I saw again the gallantry of the American troops in a hopelessly misguided cause, I could only reiterate the lament of so many: "what a sad, fucking waste!" Sometimes, as we watched the film, we could hear Vietnamese kids laughing and playing outside on our lane in Tay Ho and realized that they had no recollection or understanding of this. But the film's musical soundtrack, many of the classic songs of the era beautifully woven into the narrative, took me irresistibly back to those days with all their complex feelings.

Burns and Novick's film clearly showed the U.S. to have been at fault in the war. To some viewers, it also gave insufficient attention to wrongs committed by North Vietnam, the NVA, and Viet Cong. Nevertheless, the government of Vietnam apparently did not like the film. American Ambassador Ted Osius posted links to the first few episodes on his Facebook page, but they were quickly removed.

According to some, the government had two issues with the film. The first was that it showed clearly that Lê Duẩn had supplanted Hồ Chí Minh as the real power and architect of the war strategy by 1967.[2] This conflicted with the canonization of Hồ Chí Minh as *the* national hero of the entire liberation struggle. Bac (Uncle) Hồ's preserved body is on display on a bed of rose petals and visited by thousands monthly in a Soviet-built mausoleum in Hanoi's Ba Dinh Square that is modeled on Lenin's in Moscow. (These days, some Vietnamese people think Hồ's body is a fake.) The Hồ Chí Minh complex includes a large museum devoted to his life and work and the simple stilt house in which he lived and greeted children and other visitors over many years. By contrast, Lê Duẩn only has a street named after him.

A second problem for the government was that Burns' film plainly demonstrates the terrible human cost of the war to the Vietnamese—somewhere between two and four million killed and thousands permanently missing with no remains ever recovered for burial in their home villages. A large share of the Vietnamese dead were civilians, including many thousands of children. According to a Vietnamese proverb, "When tigers and elephants fight, crickets are crushed."[3]

As a teenaged girl, Lê Minh Khuê served in the Volunteer Youth Corps of the NVA and later became a war correspondent and writer of short stories. Khuê remembers the beginning of the war as a time of romanticism and naïve optimism but she quickly experienced its very real horror: "I don't think people can imagine how ferocious the war was. It makes my spine shiver whenever I think of it." Khuê spent time in Quang Tri Province, where the 3rd Marine Division operated and experienced very heavy combat casualties. Rodger Jacobs refers to the "meat grinder of the war" there, where he was wounded in Phu An, near Con Thien.[4]

It was probably even worse for the NVA. Khuê used the same descriptor as Jacobs: Quang Tri was a "meat grinder that let no one escape."[5] In a story by Tạ Duy Anh, an NVA soldier writes a letter home: "After we left Quang Tri, our battalion had only a few dozen soldiers left. The enemy was very cruel. A huge stretch of land was destroyed over and over again. Now the earth there is the color of gunpowder."[6]

The Vietnamese government apparently did not want to expose the young population to a film candidly depicting the war's terrible human and material costs. It may benefit the government politically to downplay the costs of the war, but too much blithe emphasis on the Vietnamese people's seemingly facile moving on from the war belies their real feelings and sufferings from that heavy cost. It may also subtly reinforce American stereotypes, explicitly stated by William Westmoreland in a speech to Congress in 1967, that "Orientals" in general and Vietnamese in particular, place less value on human life than we do.[7] In fact, in their private lives out of the view of foreigners or tourists, there remained for a long time significant sorrow and pain among the Vietnamese over their horrific losses of life during the war. One widow told an American visitor years after the war ended that "the sadness never leaves … our sorrow comes and goes like the river. Even at low tide there is always a trickle."[8] That trickle persists through continuing generations of Vietnamese families.

Our social life with the HFG staff in Hanoi was like that of my second tour. We had lively lunches in the office with delicious food cooked by Hương, who had worked in this capacity for HPI. We enjoyed frequent bia hơi sessions at 19C Ngoc Ha, for which our former HPI colleagues and their kids often appeared. Dr. Binh was a particularly faithful participant. Through an article in *Vietnam News* about his winning a prestigious international Olympiad competition in chemistry, Nancy found a student who was graduating from Hanoi Amsterdam, the city's best high school, and starting with a full scholarship at the Massachusetts Institute of Technology (MIT) in the fall of 2018. We offered to help him get settled in Cambridge. It was another way for us to stay in touch with Vietnam. His family invited us to dinner and gave us gifts of Vietnamese candy and Johnnie Walker Scotch before our departure from Hanoi. Nancy and I have enjoyed seeing him periodically during his time at MIT.

I made my final appearance as Santa Claus at our 2017 Christmas party, joined by Abigail and her husband Theo. The kids seemed to like

the gifts that Nancy had chosen for them. We enjoyed several group outings, including a visit to the Tam Dao bear rescue center. On my last weekend, we visited Việt Phủ Thành Chương—an art "palace" in Soc Son, near
Hanoi, established by the artist Thành Chương to display his own paintings and his extensive collection of Vietnamese sculpture and other art
going back several centuries in a beautiful complex of buildings, installa-
tions, gardens, and fountains.

After the visit to Thành Chương's palace we returned to my house
for another going away party. As a gift, the staff had had framed the new
collection of propaganda posters purchased by Nancy. "Bống," the daughter of Nguyễn Thị Hiền of our staff, presented me with a beautiful pastel
drawing she had made of a Vietnamese countryside scene.

Another sign of things coming to an end was the sad closing of Don's
Tay Ho. Nancy and I had been regular customers since its opening in 2010
and we had dinner there on the restaurant's second to last night in existence. Unfortunately, Don was unable to resolve a bitter dispute with his
Vietnamese partner and was forced to close after this evil partner hired
local motorbike truck owners to block the entrance, posted banners in
Vietnamese and English falsely charging Don with various transgres-
sions, and paid off the police so that they did nothing about this illegal

**HFG staff at Việt Phủ Thành Chương, with most of the ladies in the traditional
áo dài—September 2018.**

interference with a public business. Don's closing was a great loss to Tay Ho and all the people—both expat and Vietnamese—who loved the food, loved Don, and loved this place as almost a second home.

When everything was packed and my air and surface shipments had been collected, we had a final bia hơi session at 19C Ngoc Ha on a sunny Friday afternoon. Mr. Long again drove me to the airport where I was again seen off by members of the staff.

In September 2018, I was happy to be going home but I still felt a wistful sense of loss, particularly so because I was leaving Vietnam this time with a much stronger realization that my return trips would be few and diminishing. At some level, I realize that I must leave this chapter behind and move on to a new phase of my life. On another level, however, I know that no matter what happens, even if I'm never able to be there again in body, I will never fully leave or lose Vietnam. I remain entwined with the country: Vietnam and my friends there will always have a special place in my heart.

Epilogue

A Life of Memories, Dreams, and Doubts

And so, my Vietnam tours drew fitfully to a close. Back at the beginning, my father had wanted me to do everything he had done, and I did many of them. Whatever I did, however, never seemed to be enough for him. He always seemed to think of me as a child and never as a fully functioning and independent adult. I am afraid that to some substantial extent I adopted his judgment. This helps me to understand my besetting and sometimes immobilizing doubt over the years.

I do not claim to have made the most honorable choices about the war in Vietnam back in 1966–1967 and subsequent years. I wish that I had acted more resolutely on my opposition to it. Maybe I was not sure enough of my opposition to the war, maybe I was unable to confront my father, maybe I was just afraid. I was a part of the Sixties generation whose differences on the war were, as Myra MacPherson puts it,

> complex and volatile. For every non-goer [to Vietnam] who sometimes thinks badly of the less-than-noble way he avoided the war, there is a soldier who blames himself for having gone. For every resister who takes pride in not having gone, there is a soldier who takes pride in his service.... The same veterans who can look back ... and now take pride in their service, can also feel the war was wrong. Other veterans cannot even fathom why people their age protested. And some protesters cannot fathom why someone would have chosen to go.[1]

At the time, I went to the war and did the best I could, despite my feelings. As it turned out, I was lucky to avoid a combat role. Many others didn't go. Most of my friends got out of it, some fraudulently. So did Donald Trump, George W. Bush, and Bill Clinton. At least I didn't have to wonder, as Bruce Springsteen touchingly does in his Broadway show, "who went [and might have died] in my place?" If I had not gone to Vietnam in March 1968, my life would surely have been very different—in ways that are hard to fathom now.

Over the ensuing years, my father and I periodically and heatedly argued about the war, but we never agreed. As I grew older, I gained

233

certainty about some things, particularly how wrong the war had been. I was able to think that, were it happening today, I would have defied my father and acted against the war.

Nevertheless, my seemingly congenital and sometimes debilitating difficulty in finding certainty still bedevils me. After watching hours of an apparently compelling case presented by Adam Schiff and the other House managers in the first impeachment trial of Donald Trump, I turned the TV to the entirely parallel universe of Fox News. There, Sean Hannity and Laura Ingraham were loudly propounding Joe Biden's corruption, Ukraine's interference against Trump in the 2016 election, and the whistle-blower's (whose alleged identity had been spread all over the Internet) concoction of the whole case in cahoots with Schiff. What, I wondered, if there was some grain of truth to these conspiracy theories? What if no one really has clean hands? What if Schiff's righteous anger ("If right doesn't matter, then we're lost") obscures a dishonest campaign to use any unscrupulous means to remove Trump from office, even if that end is justifiable? During these depressing debates with myself, I recurred to Pontius Pilate's timeless proto-Post-Modernist question, "What is truth?" Indeed, sometimes, I find myself worrying that there may be no objective truth on which to stand. I hope that is not the end of the story.[2] In his Inaugural Address on January 20, 2021, President Joe Biden issued us all a charge that may offer some hope of a happier outcome: "Recent weeks and months have taught us a painful lesson. There is truth and there are lies. Lies told for power and for profit. And each of us has a duty and responsibility, as citizens, as Americans, and especially as leaders … to defend the truth and to defeat the lies."

My father moved dramatically rightward politically over the years. He seems always to have harbored a deep-seated racism, but he was originally a Stevenson Democrat and a supporter of JFK and Lyndon Johnson. He then voted for Nixon in 1968 and became an increasingly conservative Republican until his death. He came to rely on Rush Limbaugh for his news and kept a loaded shotgun in his bedroom in downtown Philadelphia in case "they" were to invade in the night.

At the end of another bitter argument with my father, probably over the war and politics, he announced that "we've come to a parting of the ways." This was not literally true. I continued a somewhat troubled relationship with him until his death. His third wife Jane tried mightily to facilitate improved relations between her husband and his children. Once, she encouraged my father and me to have an intimate man-to-man conversation about our feelings. In fact, we had a highly awkward lunch at an Italian restaurant in Greenwich Village in which nothing was resolved. Indeed, as I recall, nothing of any real substance was even said. We made small talk about sports and work and the doings of my siblings. I did try to bring the conversation to the real issues of our relationship but, somehow to a member of my father's generation of men, the very idea of a "man-to-man" talk precluded any expression of emotion or love.

I spent many years in various forms of therapy, starting with a few sessions prompted by my heavy drinking during my wartime tour in Vietnam, but beginning in earnest while I was in graduate school and continuing until I was almost 60 years old. Some of this was couples' therapy with Nancy. Much of my own work focused on my parents' divorce and my relationship with my father and how these had affected my relationship with Nancy. I was often frustrated with my last therapist because he steadfastly refused to give me "the answer" to my problems. However, his approach seems to have worked. I came to a point at which I realized that I had done the work I needed to do with him. He did not agree but allowed me to go forth on my own. With the help of this and all the therapy I did over the years, Nancy's and my marriage not only survived but grew stronger.

Sadly, on the other hand, my relationship with my father was never fully healed. At the end of a New Year's Eve dinner at our house in Watertown, during which substantial alcohol had been consumed, my father's inappropriate criticism of my sister Janet's parenting of her young sons led to a row. Janet dramatically tore up my father's Christmas check, with the result that none of us ever received another one. The argument culminated in Janet's challenging my father to tell us that he loved us—"please, just say it!" He was unable to do so, either then or ever, as far as I can recall. In the Trần family, Nguyễn Phan Quế Mai wrote in *The Mountains Sing*, "love is something that we show, not something we speak about."[3] Apparently, my father could do neither. For a long time, we had a *New Yorker* cartoon stuck to the front of our refrigerator that depicts a huge auditorium with about four people in it and a banner above the stage reading "Welcome to the Convention of Functional Families."

My father died in May 1998, just eight months after my first visit to Vietnam since the war. His fourth wife Mary Jane was annoyed that the obituary in the *New York Times* reported that "Mr. Hammett's three previous marriages ended in divorce." Strictly speaking, only the first and third had so ended, as his divorce from Ann had not been finalized before she died.

In remarks at my father's memorial service at the Racquet Club in Philadelphia, I appropriately sanitized our relationship: "Dad and I often disagreed about politics. But this was generally good-humored and designed only to stir up spirited debate, which Dad always loved." Needless to say, I did not bring up our disagreements over the war in Vietnam. Nor did I mention his incredible irresponsibility and selfishness in leaving his daughter

Nan in that traumatic situation with her mother. After visiting Dad in the hospital a few days before he died, I told Nan that I felt "furious" at him for all he had done and failed to do. But I also felt that my fury was "inappropriate" for a time so near his death. So, at his memorial service, I tried to see Dad off with some sense of love, implied forgiveness, and optimism for his spiritual future: "Goodbye, Dad. God bless you. Have fun up there."

Although his nearly lifelong heavy smoking and decades of hard drinking no doubt contributed to the multiple strokes that finally killed him, Dad did indeed have a lot of fun on earth. He could be a very charming man. He seems to have finally found the love of his life in Mary Jane, but some of his happiest times also occurred during his marriage to Jane, his third. They split their time between "The Little Jewel," a perpetually under renovation fifth-floor walkup on West 11th Street in Greenwich Village, very near the Weathermen's notorious "bomb factory," and another ongoing construction project, a brownstone on Spruce Street near Philadelphia's Rittenhouse Square.

While in New York, Dad loved hanging out with the Clancy Brothers, Pete Hamill, and others at the Lion's Head in Sheridan Square. I sometimes joined him. We also enjoyed late night visits to Marie's Crisis and sometimes to after-hours gay bars in one of which, I recall, the men's room was larger than the main part of the establishment. It was the pre–AIDS era. Arising hung-over on summer Sundays, we might bicycle around the Village and over to Little Italy for pastries and cappuccinos on Mulberry Street.

In the end, Dad was, as so many of us are, a creature of his time and his society, trapped in its assumptions and distortions. These ultimately poisoned his relationships with his children. If I had been more honest, I might have concluded my remarks at his memorial service differently, as Sylvia Plath ended a famous poem: "Daddy, daddy, you bastard, I'm through."[4] Instead, at the end, I stood when the bagpiper played "The Marines' Hymn" for him.

My father's ashes were inurned with full honors at Arlington National Cemetery on a beautiful afternoon the following October. A Marine honor platoon and marching band escorted the caisson carrying his flag-draped urn, a firing party gave a salute, the folded flag was presented to Mary Jane (and passed on to me by her children when she died), and a bugler blew "Taps." My father had been in no authentic way religious during his life. Still, Mary Jane had asked that a Protestant chaplain officiate at the Arlington ceremony. In his homily, the Navy chaplain, who happened to be Black, claimed to have "known Colonel Hammett very well." Seated in the front row, my sister Janet and I could barely keep straight faces at the thought of our racist father's alleged friendship with this Black man.

During my remarks at Dad's memorial service in Philadelphia, I had quoted Wilfred Owen's World War I poem about a British soldier killed as he slept in his trench:

> He sleeps. He sleeps less tremulous, less cold
> Than we who must awake, and waking, say Alas![5]

Many in my post–World War II generation made choices about Vietnam that fractured or strained families, struck at our consciences, and evoked profound emotions of every kind. At the open-microphone discussion of "Vietnam: The Choices We Made" at my Harvard 50th reunion, one classmate tellingly concluded that "most of us, no matter what choices we made, felt bad about them." These choices have haunted us, in dreams and awake, for the rest of our lives.

My dreams of the war do still haunt me, even as I reach my mid-seventies. I have neither reason nor right to suffer post-traumatic stress disorder. I had it easy. The horrors experienced by Ron Kovic both during and after the war are almost as foreign to me as to all those civilians who never set foot in Vietnam or any war zone. Kovic accidentally killed a Marine in his own unit during a firefight, helped to kill and maim a hut full of unarmed Vietnamese children and adults, and then was himself permanently paralyzed from the waist down in an NVA ambush. When he called for help and comfort after being evacuated to the filthy and rat-infested Bronx V.A. hospital, an aide loudly replied that "Vietnam don't mean nothin' to me.... You can take your Vietnam and shove it up your ass." Kovic became a leading activist against the war in which he was wounded and subsequent American conflicts.[6]

I never liked fireworks, thunderstorms, or other loud noises, either before or after the war. But I've never had the sort of horrific nightmares or flashbacks described by so many combat veterans like Ron Kovic or Doug Anderson[7]; or "Larry" who saw "his friends slaughtered at Khe Sanh" and laments that "there *is* no future. Only the past. Happening over and over again. It's in my ears and my nose and underneath my fingernails";[8] in many of Bruce Weigl's poems, images of the war intrude upon or commingle with scenes of home after his return. In the wake of a thunderstorm, he writes:

> Trees scraped their voices into the wind, branches
> crisscrossed the sky like barbed wire
> but you said they were only branches.

Weigl knew better:

> But still the branches are wire
> and the thunder is the pounding mortar.[9]

William Broyles has recurrently dreamt of dying with his whole platoon at the hands of smiling NVA soldiers in an ambush as they returned to Hill 10 near Danang.[10] Phil Goia's dream is of being summoned to return to Vietnam because the war isn't going well and told that some of his comrades have already gone back to help out—except that these comrades had all actually been killed in the war.[11] In Lewis Puller's dream, he was separated from his platoon and chased by NVA soldiers who are just about to catch him when he awakes, terrified and soaked in sweat.[12] The Vietnamese also had recurring dreams. In this one, described by Nguyễn Phan Quế Mai,

> my mother always returned with my father [from the war]. … Sometimes he would rush toward me on his two feet; sometimes he struggled on a single leg, leaning on a crutch. Sometimes he embraced me with his two strong arms, and at other times he had no arms at all, just two lumps of flesh protruding from his shoulders.[13]

Rodger Jacobs still dreams of "that charnal [sic] house of a helicopter ride" to Delta Med in Dong Ha after his wounding—"blood everywhere." But he also dreams, more pleasantly, of "a canteen that never ran out of cool sweet water."[14]

Tracy Kidder, my Harvard classmate and one of only a few REMFs to write a Vietnam memoir,[15] reports a dream[16] similar to one that I've frequently had. In it, I am much older but, as in the often-scrambled geographies and timelines of dreams, I am back in the Marine Corps and on my way to another tour in the Vietnam War, this time as an infantry platoon commander. Of course, when I awake, I am relieved that this is not really happening. And I am also grateful that I did, in reality, have the chance to go back to Vietnam after the war in a different way and perhaps do some good there.

Re-reading Nancy's and my Vietnam wartime letters and listening again to our audiotapes more than 50 years later unleashed in me a flood of emotions, not least of which were a strengthened love and tenderness for Nancy. Maybe I was writing this book, in part, to fall in love again.

Another of these feelings is harder to describe clearly—"wistful" is the best word that comes to mind, and I have already used it a few times in these pages. Defined as "full of yearning or desire tinged with melancholy," wistful may connote a mild mixed emotion. But my experience of wistfulness has been anything but mild. Rather, it is a powerful commingling of joy and sadness, a sense of what has been gained and what has been lost. I may have lost youth, innocence, and a conviction of immortality but I hope I have gained some wisdom and perspective and a greater capacity for faith, love, and forgiveness. Vietnam is where I first went in submission to my father and where I returned much later to declare, in some small way, my independence from him.

I continue living with my wistful memories of those earlier times during the war. Near the end of Becky Cooper's powerful personal memoir and investigation of the murder of Harvard graduate student Jane Britton in 1969—which perhaps occurred as I listened to "Who Knows Where the Time Goes" in my hooch in Quang Tri only a few months from my homecoming—she asks, rhetorically: "What would a culture look like ... that, recognizing the limitations of memory and rejecting the half-truths of reconstructions, discouraged nostalgia? What would the consequences be of a collective shedding of history?"[17]

My answer must be that such an erasure of memory and history, even with their admitted lapses of fact and truth, would be a grievous loss. As for my thoughts of those days with Nancy, Sandy Denny's gorgeous song "Moments"[18] captures them well: "These are the memories that we made so well/Lives like stories that we long to tell." The song continues: "When we're old/with not too much to say/We'll have the memories/that we made today." Like my father, I may have idealized, to some extent, a portion of my past. However, this was not, like him, to contrast it negatively with everything that followed. In my case, it was for a good cause.

I already treasure, as well, my memories of more recent and happier times in Vietnam when I, albeit influenced by my multiple lenses and "nostalgia" for the present, developed an enduring affection for the country and its people. In the long downhill slide of advancing age, I feel increasingly fortunate to have all these memories and feelings close at hand.

Author's Military History

Theodore M. Hammett completed the U.S. Marine Corps' Platoon Leaders Class (PLC) at Quantico, Virginia, during the summers of 1964 and 1966. He received a reserve commission as a Marine 2nd Lieutenant upon his graduation from Harvard College in June 1967. Following Basic School at Quantico and Supply Officers Course at Camp Lejeune, North Carolina, Hammett served a 13-month tour in Vietnam. He was the Marine supply officer for 3rd Medical Battalion, 3rd Marine Division in Phu Bai from March to August 1968 and in Quang Tri from August 1968 to April 1969. Hammett was promoted to 1st Lieutenant in September 1968.

Upon his return to the U.S., Hammett served as Supply Officer for Maintenance Battalion and Headquarters and Service Battalion, Force Troops, Fleet Marine Force Atlantic in Camp Lejeune from April 1969 to June 1970. He was released from active duty on June 12, 1970, and honorably discharged from the Marine Cops on May 12, 1972. Hammett's decorations include the Vietnam Service Medal with one star; Vietnamese Campaign Medal with 60 device; and, by virtue of his service with 3rd Marine Division during a designated period, the Combat Action Ribbon (although he saw no actual combat) and the Meritorious Unit Citation Cross of Gallantry.

Chapter Notes

Introduction

1. W.D. Ehrhart, *Passing Time: Memoir of a Vietnam Veteran Against the War*. Jefferson, N.C.: McFarland, 1986 (originally published as *Marking Time*, New York: Avon, 1986).

2. Arnold R. Isaacs, *Vietnam Shadows: The War, Its Ghosts, and Its Legacy*. Baltimore: Johns Hopkins University Press, 2000, p. 11.

3. Gerald Nicosia, *Home to War: A History of the Vietnam Veterans' Movement*. New York: Three Rivers, 2001, p. 7.

4. Sarah E. Wagner, *What Remains: Bringing America's Missing Home from the Vietnam War*. Cambridge: Harvard University Press, 2019.

5. Michael J. Allen, *Until the Last Man Comes Home: POWs, MIAs, and the Unending Vietnam War*. Chapel Hill: University of North Carolina Press, 2009, pp. 2–4.

6. Lewis B. Puller, Jr., *Fortunate Son: The Autobiography of Lewis B. Puller, Jr.* New York: Bantam, 1993; Kent Jenkins, Jr., "Vietnam Vet and Writer Lewis Puller Kills Himself," *Washington Post*, May 12, 1994.

7. Philip D. Beidler, *Late Thoughts on an Old War: The Legacy of Vietnam*. Athens: University of Georgia Press, 2007, pp. 103–04.

8. Isaacs, *Vietnam Shadows*, p. 20.

9. F. Scott and Zelda Fitzgerald, "Show Mr. and Mrs. F. to Number __" in F. Scott Fitzgerald, *The Crack-Up*, Edmund Wilson, ed. New York: New Directions, 2009, pp. 41–62. I love that my Hammett grandparents lived on Claremont Avenue in New York, where the Fitzgeralds had also lived in the early 1920s.

10. A Vietnam combat veteran and scholar of the culture of the Vietnam War "systematically destroyed" all the letters he wrote from Vietnam because he found himself to sound in them "so stupidly portentous, vapid, self-dramatizing, and callow." Beidler, *Late Thoughts on an Old War*, pp. 96–97. I am glad that I saved our letters and tapes and hope that they are not that worthless. Indeed, as a historian, I recoil at the destruction of any documentary evidence.

11. Jack McLean, *Loon: A Marine Story*. New York: Ballantine Trade, 2010.

12. Rodger Jacobs, *Stained with the Mud of Khe Sanh: A Marine's Letters from Vietnam, 1966–1967*. Jefferson, North Carolina: McFarland & Company, 2013.

13. Afghanistan veteran Erik Edstrom based his account on extensive journals he kept during his tour. Erik Edstrom, *Un-American: A Soldier's Reckoning of Our Longest War*. New York: Bloomsbury Publishing, 2020.

14. Penelope Fitzgerald, *The Knox Brothers*. Washington: Counterpoint, 2000, p. 265.

15. Elizabeth Bowen, *The House in Paris*. New York: Penguin, 1987, p. 143. She also says that "Those without memories don't know what is what." Bowen, *The Death of the Heart*. New York: Anchor, 2000, p. 99.

16. John Cheever, "The Country Husband" in *The Stories of John Cheever*. New York: Ballantine, 1980, p. 390.

17. Fitzgeralds, "Show Mr. and Mrs. F. to Number __," p. 50.

18. John Banville, *The Sea*. New York: Vintage International Edition, 2006, p. 10.

19. Viet Thanh Nguyen, *Nothing Ever*

Dies: Vietnam and the Memory of War. Cambridge: Harvard University Press, 2016.

20. Robert Atwan, "Of Memoir and Memory: We Need Better Critical Tools for Discussing the Genre." *Creative Nonfiction,* Issue 55, Spring 2015.

21. Sigmund Freud, "Screen Memories," in Gail S. Wood and Howard B. Levine, eds., *On Freud's "Screen Memories."* New York: Routledge, 2015.

22. Joshua Furst, *Revolutionaries.* New York: Penguin Random House, 2019, p. 130.

23. Paul Fussell, *The Great War and Modern Memory.* New York: Oxford University Press, 1975, pp. 311, 335.

24. Christian G. Appy, *Patriots: The Vietnam War Remembered from All Sides.* New York: Penguin, 2004, p. 536.

25. Nguyễn Phan Quế Mai, *The Mountains Sing.* Chapel Hill, NC: Algonquin, 2020, p. 263.

26. Tracy Kidder and Richard Todd, *Good Prose: The Art of Nonfiction.* New York: Random House, 2013, ch. 3.

27. Jeannie Vanasco, *The Glass Eye: A Memoir.* Portland, Oregon: Tin House, 2017, pp. 29–30. Vanasco grapples affectingly with these issues in a book that is almost as much about the crafting of her memoir as about the story she tells in it.

28. Jeannie Vanasco, *Things We Didn't Talk About When I Was a Girl: A Memoir.* Portland, Oregon: Tin House, 2019, p. 8.

29. Sarah Churchwell, "The Oracle of Our Unease." *New York Review of Books,* October 8, 2020, p. 25.

Chapter 1

1. James Carroll, *American Requiem: God, My Father, and the War that Came Between Us.* Boston: Houghton Mifflin, 1996, pp. 177, 181.

2. Henry Adams, *The Education of Henry Adams.* Boston: Sentry, 1961, p. 54.

3. John Buchan, *Pilgrim's Way: An Essay in Recollection.* Cambridge: Houghton Mifflin, 1940, p. 45.

4. Thanks to my Harvard roommate Steve Saltonstall for reminding me of this creative chant. He mentions it in his forthcoming memoir *Renegade for Justice: Defending the Defenseless in an Outlaw*

World. Lawrence, Kansas: University Press of Kansas, 2022.

5. Karl Marlantes, *Matterhorn.* New York: Atlantic Monthly, 2010; Marlantes, *What It Is Like to Go to War.* New York: Atlantic Monthly, 2011.

6. Drew Gilpin Faust, *This Republic of Suffering: Death and the American Civil War.* New York: Knopf, 2008.

7. Mai Elliott. *The Sacred Willow: Four Generations in the Life of a Vietnamese Family,* revised edition. New York: Oxford University Press, 2017, p. xxvii.

8. Isaacs, *Vietnam Shadows,* p. 39.

9. Fifty years later, Chelsea is the epicenter of Covid-19 in Massachusetts.

10. James Fallows, "What Did You Do in the Class War, Daddy?" *Washington Monthly,* October, 1975.

11. F. Scott Fitzgerald, *The Great Gatsby.* New York: Scribner, 1995, p. 7.

12. Fitzgerald, *The Great Gatsby,* p. 10.

13. Many of these groups, as I later learned from the film *Twenty Feet from Stardom,* were dominated by the rarely acknowledged Darlene Love.

14. Barack Obama and Bruce Springsteen, *Renegades: Born in the USA,* Spotify original podcast, 2021. Episode 1: "Outsiders: An Unlikely Friendship," Minute 39.

15. I overslept and almost missed the start of my first SATs in March 1962 because I had stayed up late listening on the radio to the Philadelphia Warriors' Wilt Chamberlain become the first and only NBA player to score 100 points in a game.

16. For full lyrics, see http://www.bobdylan.com/songs/murder-most-foul/.

17. Neil Sheehan, Hedrick Smith, E.W. Kenworthy, and Fox Butterfield (Gerald Gold, Allan M. Siegal and Samuel Abt, eds.), *The Pentagon Papers.* New York: Bantam, 1971.

18. David Halberstam, *The Best and the Brightest.* Greenwich, Connecticut: Fawcett Crest, 1973, ch. 19.

19. Viet Thanh Nguyen objects to both "Vietnam War" and "American War" because "Each name obscures human costs, and capital gains…" He prefers, simply, The War. *Nothing Ever Dies,* pp. 6–8.

20. The Byrds' rendition of "Mr. Tambourine Man" was great even though it was later revealed that the famous "Wrecking Crew" of session musicians, including

Larry Knechtel, Hal Blaine, Leon Russell, and Jerry Cole had played on it.

21. In Alison Ellwood's 2020 Epix documentary *Laurel Canyon*, Nash's longtime bandmate David Crosby similarly concludes that Laurel Canyon 1965–1975 represented one of the "high points" in the history of popular music.

22. For full lyrics, see https://genius.com/Barry-mcguire-eve-of-destruction-lyrics.

23. On the music of 1965 and Barry McGuire's hit song, see James T. Patterson, *The Eve of Destruction: How 1965 Transformed America*. New York: Basic, 2014, pp. 142–148, 193–194.

24. W.D. Ehrhart, "On the Eve of Destruction" in *Thank You for Your Service: Collected Poems*. Jefferson, NC: McFarland, 2019, p. 212.

25. For full lyrics, see https://genius.com/The-lovin-spoonful-do-you-believe-in-magic-lyrics.

26. Kooper's more aggressive organ was also featured with the Blues Project, whose 1966 album *Projections* included "I Can't Keep from Crying Sometimes," which I especially love. While Blind Willie Johnson is not credited on the Blues Project's album as the author of this song, it was in fact written by that enormously innovative Texas gospel and blues guitarist and vocalist. Typically, I had never heard of, much less heard, Johnson until my brother-in-law Bruce Pratt introduced me to his music in the 1990s. Thanks, Bruce.

27. For full lyrics, see http://www.bobdylan.com/songs/chimes-freedom/.

28. "Fire Rages in Four Quincy Suites; Cause of $35,000 Blaze is Unknown." *Harvard Crimson*, November 2, 1965. https://quincy.harvard.edu/fire-1965.

29. In an even more serious case a few years later, Harvard again showed no interest in pursuing, and may have actively discouraged, the investigation of the murder of Jane Britton, an archaeology graduate student, in an off-campus apartment. Although they turned out not to have been involved, several Harvard faculty members and students were potential suspects or "persons of interest" in the case. Becky Cooper, *We Keep the Dead Close: A Murder at Harvard and a Half Century of Silence*. New York: Grand Central, 2020.

30. J. William Fulbright, *The Arrogance of Power*. New York: Random House, 1966.

31. Sheehan et al., *The Pentagon Papers*.

32. Sheehan et al., *The Pentagon Papers*, pp. 242, 254.

33. Ehrhart, *Passing Time*, pp. 172–75.

34. Craig Whitlock, *The Afghanistan Papers: A Secret History of the War*. New York: Simon & Schuster, 2021.

35. Erik Edstrom and Theodore M. Hammett, "How Biden Can Transform America's Foreign Policy: Five Principles That Would End the Forever Wars and Foster Peace and Justice Around the World." *The New Republic*, March 16, 2021. https://newrepublic.com/article/161711/-biden-can-transform-americas-foreign-policy.

36. Halberstam, *The Best and the Brightest*, pp. 371–72 *et passim*.

37. Stephen L. Saltonstall, "Mack the Knife and Me," unpublished manuscript, 2020.

38. John Balaban, *Remembering Heaven's Face: A Story of Rescue in Wartime Vietnam*. Athens: University of Georgia Press, 2002.

39. Ron Carver, David Cortright, and Barbara Doherty, eds., *Waging Peace in Vietnam: U.S. Soldiers and Veterans Who Opposed the War*. New York: New Village, 2019, pp. 143–51. See also John Huyler, John Kent, Will Kirkland, Ron Mcmahan, Paul Rogers and James Skelly, "Yes, There Were Antiwar Officers." *New York Times*, February 3, 2018.

40. Tim O'Brien, "On the Rainy River" in *The Things They Carried*. Boston: Houghton Mifflin, 1990, p. 58.

41. William Broyles, Jr., *Brothers in Arms: A Journey from War to Peace*. New York: Knopf, 1986, pp. 78–80.

42. Viet Thanh Nguyen, *The Committed*. New York: Grove, 2021, p. 125.

43. For one of the most blistering of many critiques of Robert McNamara's *In Retrospect: The Tragedy and Lessons of Vietnam* (New York: New York Times Books, 1995), see Beidler, *Late Thoughts on an Old War*, pp. 139–52. Strangely, 156 Amazon reviewers give McNamara's book an average rating of 4.3/5.

44. Myra MacPherson, *Long Time Passing: Vietnam and the Haunted Generation*. Bloomington: Indiana University Press, 2001, p. 33.

45. For full lyrics, see https://genius.com/Warren-zevon-werewolves-of-london-lyrics; https://genius.com/Jackson-browne-before-the-deluge-lyrics

46. For full lyrics, see https://genius.com/Fleetwood-mac-landslide-lyrics.

47. Elizabeth Bowen, *The Heat of the Day*. New York: Anchor, 2002, p. 217.

48. Howard Jones, *My Lai: Vietnam, 1968, and the Descent into Darkness*. New York: Oxford University, 2017.

49. Ehrhart, *Passing Time.*

50. Doris Kearns, "LBJ Remembers Vietnam: 1970" in Ward Just, "Introduction" in *Reporting Vietnam: American Journalism 1959-1975*, abridged paper edition. New York: Library of America, 2000, pp. 476, 479-480.

51. Halberstam, *The Best and the Brightest*, p. 604.

52. Beidler, *Late Thoughts on an Old War*, pp. 140-43.

Chapter 2

1. C.D.B. Bryan, *Friendly Fire*. New York: Bantam, 1977, pp. 119-21.

2. Nick Turse, *Kill Anything That Moves: The Real American War in Vietnam*. New York: Picador, 2013.

3. Nico Walker, *Cherry*. New York: Knopf, 2018, p. 140. Walker's book is the Iraq War's fictional analogue to Ron Kovic's *Born on the Fourth of July* (New York: McGraw-Hill, 1976) and Lewis Puller's *Fortunate Son* (New York: Grove, 1991), among the earliest and most powerful memoirs of Vietnam warriors and veterans.

4. Walker, *Cherry*, pp. 153-154.

5. John T. Wheeler, "Khe Sanh Under Siege: February 1968: Life in the V Ring" in *Reporting Vietnam: American Journalism 1959-1975*, p. 330.

6. Puller, *Fortunate Son*, p. 164.

7. Max Hastings, *Vietnam: An Epic Tragedy, 1945-1975*. New York: Harper, 2018, p. 426.

Chapter 3

1. For full lyrics, see https://genius.com/Jefferson-airplane-today-lyrics. The "biographer" of the Airplane calls this "one of the great love songs of the era, an unabashed romantic paean devoid of both irony and gushiness." Jeff Tamarkin, *Got a Revolution! The Turbulent Flight of Jefferson Airplane*. New York: Atria, 2003, p. 117.

2. Had I been aware of it, the 13th Floor Elevators' "I Had to Tell You," which also came out in 1967, could just as easily have been our song; in its words, we would each have acknowledged echoing the other's voice and reinforcing the other's strength. I was only introduced to this great but sadly little-known band by "Albert O" on Boston's WUMB in 2019. For full lyrics, see https://genius.com/The-13th-floor-elevators-i-had-to-tell-you-lyrics.

3. Eric Nguyen, *Things We Lost to the Water*. New York: Knopf, 2021, pp. 21, 41, 55.

4. Martha Gellhorn, "The Bomber Boys" in *The Face of War*. New York: Atlantic Monthly, 2014, p. 101.

Chapter 4

1. Michael Herr, *Dispatches*. New York: Vintage International, 1991, p. 71. W.D. Ehrhart acknowledges Herr's powerful descriptions of U.S. troops' experiences but faults him for failing to call out the dishonesty and senselessness of the war as well as his glorification of combat and his denying any place or humanity to the Vietnamese people. "On Michael Herr's *Dispatches*" in Ehrhart, *In the Shadow of Vietnam: Essays, 1977-1991*. Jefferson, NC: McFarland, 1991, pp. 4-7.

2. Bruce Weigl, "The Way of Tet" in *Song of Napalm*. New York: Atlantic Monthly, 1988, pp. 5-6.

3. John A. Parrish, *12, 20 & 5: A Doctor's Year in Vietnam*. Baltimore: Penguin, 1973; Parrish, *Autopsy of War: A Personal History*. New York: St. Martin's, 2012.

4. Halberstam, *The Best and the Brightest*, p. 758.

5. MacPherson, *Long Time Passing*, p. 464.

Chapter 5

1. Weigl, "Surrounding Blues on the Way Down" in *Song of Napalm*, pp. 13-14.

2. Nguyen, *Nothing Ever Dies*, p. 119. The internal quotation is from author and screenwriter Nguyen Quang Sang, in Appy, *Patriots*, p. 216.

3. Marlantes, *What It Is Like to Go to War*, pp. 40–41.

4. Jacobs, *Stained with the Mud of Khe Sanh*, p. 80.

5. Mary McCarthy, "Hanoi—March 1968" in *Reporting Vietnam: American Journalism 1959–1975*, pp. 337–338.

6. Beidler, *Late Thoughts on an Old War*, pp. 10–11.

7. Hastings, *Vietnam*, p. 139.

8. U.S. Navy, Bureau of Naval Personnel, Chaplains Division, *The Religions of South Vietnam in Faith and Fact.* NAVPERS 15991, 1967. Rear Admiral James W. Kelly, Letter of Transmittal.

9. Hastings, *Vietnam*, p. 147.

10. Edstrom, *Un-American*, p. 97.

11. Frances Fitzgerald, *Fire in the Lake: The Vietnamese and the Americans in Vietnam.* New York: Vintage, 1972.

12. Beidler, *Late Thoughts on an Old War*, p. 146.

13. U.S. Navy, Bureau of Naval Personnel, Chaplains Division, *The Religions of South Vietnam in Faith and Fact.* III: Confucianism in Vietnam, p. 3/6.

14. Allen Glick, *Winters Coming, Winters Gone.* New York: Pinnacle, 1984, p. 194.

15. Ehrhart, *Passing Time*, pp. 155–56.

16. Ehrhart, "A Relative Thing" in *Thank You for Your Service*, pp. 20–21.

17. George Packer, *Our Man: Richard Holbrooke and the End of the American Century.* New York: Knopf, 2019, pp. 61,65.

18. Lady Borton, *After Sorrow: An American Among the Vietnamese.* New York: Kodansha America, 1996, pp. 75–78.

19. Lewis Puller also used the lyrics of this song—in particular, "I went down Virginia, seekin' shelter from the storm"—likening he and his wife's move from Philadelphia to Williamsburg, after two years in the hospital, as in part a flight from the pain of his war trauma and his already growing dependence on alcohol. Puller, *Fortunate Son*, pp. 296, 428–29. For full lyrics, see https://genius.com/Creedence-clearwater-revival-wholl-stop-the-rain-lyrics.

20. Robert Stone, *Dog Soldiers.* New York: Ballantine, 1975, p. 57. In *The Committed*, Viet Thanh Nguyen similarly reveals the war brought home to France as his drug dealing protagonist says, "I'm happy to sell the French some things. They owe us" (p. 127).

21. Christian G. Appy used this quotation from Ray Hicks in his *American Reckoning: The Vietnam War and Our National Identity.* New York: Penguin, 2016, p. xiii. I did not see Appy's use of the quotation until after I had used it myself. I guess this speaks to the seductive power of Ray Hicks' comment.

Chapter 6

1. Beidler, *Late Thoughts on an Old War*, pp. 104, 120.

2. Doug Bradley and Craig Werner, *"We Gotta Get Out of This Place": The Soundtrack of the Vietnam War.* Amherst: University of Massachusetts, 2015. For full lyrics, see https://genius.com/The-animals-we-gotta-get-outta-this-place-lyrics.

3. Ron Kovic, *Born on the Fourth of July*, 40th Anniversary Edition. New York: Akashic, 2016, pp. 31, 58.

4. Some of those who experienced and wrote about the 1920s had similar feelings. The F. Scott Fitzgerald character in Budd Schulberg's *The Disenchanted* assessed the 1920s from the vantage point of 1939: "There was something special about those days. People were wittier and they did things better... And the songs, why were our songs so much better[?]" Schulberg, *The Disenchanted.* Reprint edition, Minneapolis: University of Minnesota, 2012, pp. 52–53. Like Schulberg's portrayal, Fitzgerald himself and his Jay Gatsby not only romanticized the past but also persistently sought to recapture it: "'Can't repeat the past?' [Gatsby] cried incredulously. 'Why of course you can!'" Fitzgerald, *The Great Gatsby*, p. 116.

5. Apparently, Miley Cyrus's "Party in the U.S.A." played a similar role for the troops in Afghanistan. Edstrom, *Un-American*, p. 157.

6. Nitsuhe Abebe, "The 25 Songs that Matter Right Now." *New York Times Magazine*, March 10, 2019.

7. For full lyrics, see https://www.azlyrics.com/lyrics/peterpaulandmary/leavingonajetplane.html.

8. For full lyrics, see https://genius.com/The-troggs-love-is-all-around-lyrics.

9. Despite the trashing of "Top 40 Radio" in Bill Lichtenstein's 2020

documentary about Boston's pathbreaking FM rock station, *WBCN and the American Revolution*, I really liked WBZ. Anyway, WBCN did not launch its revolutionary format until March 15, 1968, a few days after I left for Vietnam.

10. The lyrics of this classic were always amusingly in dispute.

11. For full lyrics, see https://genius.com/Judy-collins-both-sides-now-lyrics.

12. For full lyrics, see https://genius.com/Ian-and-sylvia-early-morning-rain-lyrics.

13. For full lyrics, see https://genius.com/Ian-and-sylvia-you-were-on-my-mind-lyrics.

14. For full lyrics, see https://genius.com/Buffy-sainte-marie-universal-soldier-lyrics.

15. For full lyrics, see https://genius.com/Tom-rush-urge-for-going-lyrics.

16. For full lyrics, see https://genius.com/Tom-rush-no-regrets-lyrics.

17. For full lyrics, see http://www.bobdylan.com/songs/subterranean-homesick-blues/.

18. Before doing "Joshua Gone Barbados" on the May 23, 2021 episode of "Rockport Sundays," Rush reported a performer's "dilemma." In the song, which was written by Eric Von Schmidt, Ebenezer Joshua, leader of the government of the Caribbean island of St. Vincent, goes on vacation to Barbados ignoring the plight of striking sugar cane cutters. In fact, Joshua strongly supported the workers. While Rush concedes that the song is "badmouthing a good guy," he still thinks it's a "great song." I agree with him. For full lyrics, see https://genius.com/Tom-rush-joshua-gone-barbados-lyrics.

19. Unfortunately, several of the songs on the White Album, including "Helter-Skelter," "Piggies," "Blackbird," and arguably "Happiness is a Warm Gun" also deeply influenced Charles Manson and his "family." Vincent Bugliosi (with Curt Gentry), *Helter Skelter: The True Story of the Manson Murders*. New York: W.W. Norton, 1974.

20. For full lyrics, see https://genius.com/Judy-collins-who-knows-where-the-time-goes-lyrics. At the time, I only knew Sandy Denny for writing "Who Knows Where the Time Goes." Much later, she

became perhaps my favorite woman singer of all time.

21. We were happy to see and follow this advice from the liner notes of one of our favorites, the Paul Butterfield Blues Band's first album: "We suggest that you play this record at the highest possible volume..."

22. George Howe Colt, *The Game: Harvard, Yale, and America in 1968*. New York: Scribner, 2018, pp. 184–189.

23. Joan Didion, *The White Album*. New York: Simon and Schuster, 1979, p. 52.

24. For full lyrics, see https://genius.com/Judy-collins-i-think-its-going-to-rain-today-lyrics.

25. Sebastian Faulks, *Birdsong: A Novel of Love and War*. New York: Vintage International, 1997, p. 221.

Chapter 7

1. The attribution of this epigram is confirmed in Julian Barnes, *The Man in the Red Coat*. New York: Knopf, 2020, p. 211.

2. Walker, *Cherry*, pp. 155, 157.

Chapter 8

1. A group of Marine survivors of the FSB Russell battle maintains a website and has arranged with local authorities several tours for veterans back to the site of the remote outpost.

2. In his Foreword, W.D. Ehrhart understandably questions my eligibility for this award. There is considerable controversy on the Internet over eligibility for the Combat Action Ribbon (CAR). The official eligibility requirements call for direct involvement in combat, which I did not have. Mere service in a combat zone is not sufficient. However, my recollection is that all who served in the 3rd Marine Division, regardless of their assignments, during some period of the War that included my tour, were awarded the Combat Action Ribbon. My DD-214 discharge certificate lists the CAR and a Meritorious Unit Citation Cross of Gallantry among my decorations. The latter was also, I believe, awarded to the 3rd Marine Division for a period including my tour. I conclude that while I clearly did not meet the official criteria for individual award

of a CAR, I was in fact awarded the ribbon by virtue of my service in 3rd Marine Division.

Chapter 9

1. Ehrhart, *Passing Time*, pp. 191–92.
2. For full lyrics, see https://genius.com/The-zombies-time-of-the-season-lyrics.
3. Simon added an evocative verse about continuity amid change in his 1973 solo live version of the song. For full lyrics, see https://www.paulsimon.com/track/the-boxer-5/.
4. For full lyrics, see https://genius.com/The-5th-dimension-aquarius-let-the-sunshine-in-lyrics.
5. For full lyrics, see https://genius.com/Glen-campbell-galveston-lyrics.
6. W.D. Ehrhart, *Busted: A Vietnam Veteran in Nixon's America*, reprint edition. Jefferson, NC: McFarland, pp. 165–66.
7. Ehrhart, *Passing Time*, pp. 170–71.
8. Ehrhart, "Thank You for Your Service" in *Thank You for Your Service*, p. 263.

Chapter 10

1. For full lyrics, see https://genius.com/Creedence-clearwater-revival-bad-moon-rising-lyrics.
2. Didion, *The White Album*, pp. 41–42. Oddly, Didion never mentions the Beatles' "White Album."
3. Alison Ellwood, *Laurel Canyon*. 2-part documentary film, Epix, 2020.
4. Much later, Afghanistan combat veteran Erik Edstrom presented his accounting of the "opportunity cost" of that war—the $1.5 trillion cost of one "unnecessary" F-35 fighter jet would pay all the student debt in the United States or a private Beyoncé concert every day for 1,000 years—not to speak of the enormous human and psychic cost to him and those with whom he served. Edstrom, *Un-American*, p. 3 and part 3.
5. Taylor's affecting 2020 audio memoir *Break Shot* depicts his difficult relationship with his father and the origins of many of his songs in the disintegration of his family, his mental illness and drug addiction, and the relationships that

helped him come out the other side sober. Although I'm not a songwriter or a celebrity, and never reached heroin, I found a lot of resonance in Taylor's story.
6. Lewis Puller seriously considered contributing his Silver Star and two Purple Hearts to the cause but finally decided against it: "Though I now saw clearly that the war in which they had been earned was a wasted cause, the medals still represented the dignity and the caliber of my service and of those with whom I had served. I could no more discard them than I could repudiate my country, my Marine Corps, or my fellow veterans." Puller, *Fortunate Son*, p. 311.
7. Nicosia, *Home to War*, pp. 60–68, Chapters 5–6.
8. MacPherson, *Long Time Passing*, pp. 575–6.
9. Philip Caputo, *A Rumor of War*. New York: Ballantine, 1978, p. 213.
10. MacPherson, *Long Time Passing*, pp. 615,622.
11. Kristin Ann Hass, *Carried to the Wall: American Memory and the Vietnam Veterans Memorial*. Berkeley: University of California, 1998, pp. 2–5, 92 *et passim*.
12. Nguyen, *Nothing Ever Dies*, p. 66.

Chapter 11

1. Caputo, *A Rumor of War*, p. xvi.
2. Bao Ninh, *The Sorrow of War*. New York: Riverhead, 1996.
3. Nguyễn Phan Quế Mai, *The Mountains Sing*, p. 199.
4. W.D. Ehrhart, "Hue City Re-Visited" in Ehrhart, *In the Shadow of Vietnam*, p. 159.
5. Ehrhart, "Cheating the Reaper" in *Thank You for Your Service*, pp. 248–49.
6. The Marine command never admitted that it had been an actual siege.

Chapter 13

1. For full lyrics, see https://genius.com/Bruce-springsteen-born-in-the-usa-lyrics.
2. In his 2021 podcast with Barack Obama, Springsteen attributes the power of "Born in the U.S.A." to its resonant ability to "both be very critical of your nation and very prideful of your nation

simultaneously." *Renegades: Born in the USA*, Episode 8: "Looking Towards American Renewal," Minutes 11–12.

3. Broyles, *Brothers in Arms*, pp. 22–23.

4. Balaban, *Remembering Heaven's Face*, p. 297.

5. Borton, *After Sorrow*, p. 159.

6. American combat veterans of the War were also resilient in the face of inclement weather. Rodger Jacobs, who spent months in the rain, wind, and cold of monsoon Quang Tri Province described his postwar attitude toward rain: "when … everyone around me scurries for cover I stand outside and look up into the rain and laugh." Jacobs, *Stained with the Mud of Khe Sanh*, p. 205.

7. Marine veteran W.D. Ehrhart served at both these bases as well as in forays into the DMZ. Ehrhart, *Vietnam-Perkasie: A Combat Marine Memoir*. McFarland, 1983, chapters 30–31.

8. Appy, *Patriots*, pp. 410–11.

Chapter 14

1. Much later, I learned that this species is one of the most heavily poached birds in Indonesia, Malaysia, and Thailand because of their success in singing contests. As a result, this bird is becoming endangered. Richard C. Paddock, "Where Poachers Feed a Craze for Songbird Contests," *New York Times*, April 19, 2020, p. 19.

2. Stephen Nash, "The Empty Forests of Vietnam," *New York Times*, April 7, 2019.

Chapter 15

1. Kearns, "LBJ Remembers Vietnam: 1970" in *Reporting Vietnam: American Journalism 1959–1975*," p. 493.

2. Isaacs, *Vietnam Shadows*, p. 165; Tim O'Brien, "The Vietnam in Me," *New York Times Magazine*, October 2, 1994.

3. Appy, *Patriots*, pp. 534–35.

4. Caputo, *A Rumor of War*, pp. 125–26.

5. Wagner, *What Remains: Bringing America's Missing Home from the Vietnam War*.

6. Nguyen, *Nothing Ever Dies*, pp. 82–83. Hasings, *Vietnam*.

7. MacPherson, *Long Time Passing*, p. xxxvi.

8. Appy, *Patriots*, p. 511.

9. Caputo, *A Rumor of War*, pp. 65–89.

10. Hastings, *Vietnam*, p. 741.

11. Shashank Bengali, "Without a single Covid-19 death, Vietnam starts easing its coronavirus lockdown." *Los Angeles Times*, April 23, 2020. Accessed April 23, 2020, at https://www.latimes.com/world-nation/story/2020-04-23/vietnam-eases-coronavirus-lockdown.

12. Adam Taylor, "Vietnam offers tough lessons for U.S. on coronavirus," *Washington Post*, April 30, 2020. Accessed April 30, 2020, at https://www.washingtonpost.com/world/2020/04/30/vietnam-offers-tough-lessons-us-coronavirus/?utm_campaign=wp_todays_worldview&utm_medium=email&utm_source=newsletter&wpisrc=nl_todayworld.

13. Huong Le Thu, "Delta Variant Outbreak Challenges Vietnam's COVID-19 Response Strategy," August 11, 2021, https://www.brookings.edu/blog/order-from-chaos/2021/08/11/delta-variant-outbreak-challenges-vietnams-covid-19-response-strategy/.

14. Nguyễn Phan Quế Mai gives a pacifist spin to the legend. After defeating the Chinese with the help of a magical sword, Lê Lợi went boating on the lake and encountered the turtle who asked him to return the sword, saying "The world will only be at peace if all people let go of their weapons" (*The Mountains Sing*, pp. 122–23). Lê Lợi returned the sword to the turtle but, sadly, peace did not reign thereafter.

15. Elliott, *The Sacred Willow*, p. 367.

16. Nguyễn Ngọc Tư, "Birds in Formation" in Quan Manh Ha and Joseph Babcock, trans. and ed., *Other Moons: Vietnamese Short Stories of the American War and Its Aftermath*. New York: Columbia University Press, 2020.

17. Borton, *After Sorrow*, p. 172.

Chapter 16

1. Martha Gellhorn to Eleanor Roosevelt, January 13, 1937, in Janet Somerville, *Yours, for probably always: Martha Gellhorn's Letters of Love & War, 1930–1949*. Richmond Hill, Ontario: Firefly, 2019, p. 147.

2. Couples in which one partner is HIV-positive and the other is HIV-negative. In the vast majority of such

heterosexual Vietnamese couples, the man is the HIV-positive partner.

3. Hammett T.M., Des Jarlais D.C., Kling R...Doan N., et al. Controlling HIV epidemics among injection drug users: eight years of cross-border HIV prevention interventions in Vietnam and China. *PLoS ONE* 2012 7(8):e43141. Doi: 10.1371/journal.pone.0043141.

4. Hammett T.M., Wu Z., Duc T.T., Stephens D., Sullivan S., Liu W., Chen Y., Ngu D., Des Jarlais D.C. "Social evils" and harm reduction: the evolving policy environment for human immunodeficiency virus prevention among injection drug users in China and Vietnam. *Addiction* 2008 January; 103(1): 137–45.

Chapter 17

1. "The Pole at the Village Pagoda" in John Balaban, trans., *Ca Dao Viet Nam: Vietnamese Folk Poetry*. Port Townsend, Washington: Copper Canyon Press, 2003, p. 22.

2. For full lyrics, see https://genius.com/Tom-petty-and-the-heartbreakers-learning-to-fly-lyrics.

3. Rusby's beautiful rendition of Bob Marley's "Three Little Birds" ("Don't worry about a thing, 'cause every little thing is gonna be all right") became my song for election week 2020. I listened to it again with hopeful tears in my eyes when the race was called for Biden and Harris. For full lyrics, see https://genius.com/Bob-marley-and-the-wailers-three-little-birds-lyrics.

4. Ocean Vuong, *Night Sky with Exit Wounds*. Port Townsend, Washington: Copper Canyon, 2016, pp. 26–28.

5. Nguyễn Phan Quế Mai, trans. Bruce Weigl, *The Secret of Hoa Sen*. Rochester: BOA, 2014, p. 55.

6. Balaban, *Remembering Heaven's Face*, Chapter 18. Balaban recorded, transcribed, translated, and published many of these *Ca Dao* poetic songs.

7. "At the Exiled King's River Pavilion" in Balaban, *Ca Dao Viet Nam*, p. 67.

8. Viet Thanh Nguyen, *The Sympathizer*. New York: Grove, 2015.

9. Nguyen, *The Committed*.

10. Nguyen, *Nothing Ever Dies*, p. 283 *et passim*.

11. Andrew X. Pham, *Catfish and Mandela: A Two-Wheeled Voyage Through the Landscape and Memory of Vietnam*. New York: Picador/Farrar, 1999, p. 339.

12. Spike Lee, *Da 5 Bloods*, Netflix, 2020.

13. Ehrhart, "The Children of Hanoi" in *Thank You for Your Service*, p. 152.

14. *The Book of Common Prayer*. New York: Church Hymnal Corporation, 1979, pp. 58–59. John Cheever was an Episcopalian and self-described "liturgical churchgoer...very happy with Cranmer's 'The Book of Common Prayer.'" John Hersey, "Talk with John Cheever," *New York Times*, March 6, 1977. Cheever used that unusual adjective "inestimable" in at least two short stories, applying it to the greatness of the human race ("Goodbye, My Brother" in *The Stories of John Cheever*, p. 23) and to happiness ("The Day the Pig Fell into the Well" in *The Stories of John Cheever*, p. 264). The word also found its way into Thomas Jefferson's Declaration of Independence, applied to a people's right of representation in its legislature. While Jefferson became a Deist as an adult, he had been raised in the Anglican Church.

15. Ehrhart, "The Distance We Travel" in *Thank You for Your Service*, pp. 163–65.

16. Balaban, *Remembering Heaven's Face*, p. 192.

17. Friends of Vietnam Heritage (fvh.org) is a Hanoi-based group that sponsors a variety of events—tours, lectures, and films—on Vietnamese arts, crafts, and culture. They have also prepared a series of guidebooks on places in and around Hanoi.

18. Hass, *Carried to the Wall*, p. 88.

19. A.N. Wilson, *Incline Our Hearts*. New York: Viking, 1988, p. 172.

20. *The Book of Common Prayer*, p. 59.

Chapter 18

1. Nguyen, *Things We Lost to the Water*, pp. 111–12.

2. Tobias Wolff, "The Rough Humor of Soldiers" in *In Pharaoh's Army: Memories of the Lost War*. New York: Vintage, 1994, pp. 183–189.

3. Broyles, *Brothers in Arms*, pp. 50–51.

Chapter 21

1. Much of the material in this and the next chapter is drawn from my essay for the Harvard Class of 1967's e-book *The Choices We Made*. This is now deposited in the Harvard University Archives.
2. Puller, *Fortunate Son*, p. 437.
3. Broyles, *Brothers in Arms*, p. 267.
4. Jacobs, *Stained with the Mud of Khe Sanh*, p. 143.

Chapter 22

1. Michael Shaw, "The True Story Behind an Iconic Vietnam War Photo was Nearly Erased –Until Now." *New York Times*, February 19, 2019.
2. For full lyrics, see https://www.paulsimon.com/track/bridge-over-trou bled-water/.
3. For full lyrics, see https://genius.com/The-beatles-let-it-be-lyrics.
4. This same story is attributed to Marine Lt. David Novak by Philip Caputo ("The Unreturning Army," *Playboy*, January 1982). A somewhat similar story appears in Michael Herr's *Dispatches*, p. 77. However, Herr did not witness the event at first hand.
5. Turse, *Kill Anything That Moves*, pp. 190–91 *et passim*.
6. Nguyen, *Nothing Ever Dies*, p. 112.
7. MacPherson, *Long Time Passing*, p. 368.
8. Fitzgerald, *The Great Gatsby*, p. 189.
9. Despite Bob Dylan's putdown in "Ballad of a Thin Man" (for full lyrics, see https://www.bobdylan.com/songs/ballad-thin-man/), I continue to believe that Fitzgerald *did* know what "was happening here" and how best to describe it.
10. More broadly, according to Greil Marcus, "the book works as both a grounding and a locus point for anyone's consideration of the American subject—the deadly dance between America's promises and their betrayal." *Under the Red White and Blue: Patriotism, Disenchantment, and the Stubborn Myth of the Great Gatsby*. New Haven: Yale University, 2020.

Chapter 23

1. Stone, *Dog Soldiers*, p. 127.
2. In fact, Lê Duẩn and Lê Đức Thọ had seized power in the Vietnamese communist party in the early 1960s and had "sidelined [Hồ] at nearly all key decision-making junctures" on the war from its very beginning. Lien-Hang T. Nguyen, *Hanoi's War: An International History of the War for Peace in Vietnam*. Chapel Hill: University of North Carolina, 2012, pp. 49, 63, 101–02, 309.
3. Balaban, *Remembering Heaven's Face*, p. 68.
4. Jacobs, *Stained with the Mud of Khe Sanh*, p. 201.
5. Appy, *Patriots*, pp. 508–511.
6. Tạ Duy Anh, "The Most Beautiful Girl in the Village" in Quan Manh Ha and Joseph Babcock, trans. and ed., *Other Moons*.
7. Isaacs, *Vietnam Shadows*, p. 190.
8. Borton, *After Sorrow*, p. 120.

Epilogue

1. MacPherson, *Long Time Passing*, p. 7.
2. During the fraught period between the 2020 presidential election and the inauguration, Al Gore wrote of his hopes for the Biden administration. Among the many challenges to be overcome, Gore listed "an epistemological crisis undermining the authority of knowledge." Al Gore, "Where I Find Hope," *New York Times*, December 13, 2020.
3. Nguyễn Phan Quế Mai, *The Mountains Sing*, p. 214.
4. Sylvia Plath, "Daddy," #183 in *The Collected Poems*. New York: Harper Perennial Modern Classics, 2018, pp. 222–24.
5. "Asleep" in *The Collected Poems of Wilfred Owen*. New York: New Directions, 1965.
6. Kovic, *Born on the Fourth of July*, p. 143 *et passim*.
7. Doug Anderson, *Keep Your Head Down: Vietnam, the Sixties, and a Journey of Self-Discovery*. New York: W.W. Norton, 2010.
8. MacPherson, *Long Time Passing*, p. 243.
9. Weigl, "Song of Napalm" in *Song of Napalm*, pp. 33–35.
10. Broyles, *Brothers in Arms*, p. 274.
11. Nicosia, *Home to War*, p. 12.
12. Puller, *Fortunate Son*, p. 222–23.
13. Nguyễn Phan Quế Mai, *The Mountains Sing*, p. 70.

14. Jacobs, *Stained with the Mud of Khe Sanh,* pp. 178, 197.

15. Tracy Kidder, *My Detachment: A Memoir.* New York: Random House Trade, 2005.

16. Kidder and Todd, *Good Prose,* p. 50.

17. Cooper, *We Keep the Dead Close,* p. 349.

18. The song was written by Bryn Haworth. For full lyrics, see https://www. sandydenny.co.uk/lyrics/moments.htm. Responding to my request for permission to use these lyrics, Bryn Haworth's wife Sally Haworth wrote that this was the last song Sandy Denny recorded before she died in 1978, at the very young age of 31. A beautiful song but a sad story. Mick Houghton, *I've Always Kept a Unicorn: The Biography of Sandy Denny.* London: Faber & Faber, 2015.

Bibliography

This bibliography lists all types of works that I
consulted specifically relating to Vietnam and the War.
References to other works are given in the *Chapter Notes*.

Allen, Michael J. *Until the Last Man Comes Home: POWs, MIAs, and the Unending Vietnam War.* Chapel Hill: University of North Carolina Press, 2009.

Anderson, Doug. *Keep Your Head Down: Vietnam, the Sixties, and a Journey of Self-Discovery.* New York: W.W. Norton, 2010.

Appy, Christian G. *American Reckoning: The Vietnam War and Our National Identity.* New York: Penguin, 2016.

_____. *Patriots: The Vietnam War Remembered from All Sides.* New York: Penguin, 2004.

Baker, Mark. *Nam: The Vietnam War in the Words of the Men and Women Who Fought There.* New York: Quill/William Morrow, 1982.

Balaban, John. *After Our War.* Pittsburgh: University of Pittsburgh Press, 1974.

_____. *Remembering Heaven's Face: A Story of Rescue in Wartime Vietnam.* Athens: University of Georgia Press, 2002.

_____, trans. *Ca Dao Viet Nam: Vietnamese Folk Poetry.* Port Townsend, WA: Copper Canyon Press, 2003.

Ball, Phil. *Ghosts and Shadows: A Marine in Vietnam, 1968–1969.* Jefferson, NC: McFarland, 1998.

Beidler, Philip D. *Late Thoughts on an Old War: The Legacy of Vietnam.* Athens: University of Georgia Press, 2007.

Bilton, Michael, and Kevin Sim. *Four Hours in My Lai.* New York: Penguin, 1993.

Bissell, Tom. *The Father of All Things: A Marine, His Son, and the Legacy of Vietnam.* New York: Pantheon, 2007.

Boot, Max. *The Road Not Taken: Edward Lansdale and the American Tragedy in Vietnam.* New York: Liveright, 2018.

Borton, Lady. *After Sorrow: An American Among the Vietnamese.* New York: Kodansha America, 1996.

Bowden, Mark. *Hue: A Turning Point of the American War in Vietnam.* New York: Atlantic Monthly, 2017.

Bradley, Doug, and Craig Werner. *"We Gotta Get Out of This Place": The Soundtrack of the Vietnam War.* Amherst: University of Massachusetts, 2015.

Broyles, William, Jr. *Brothers in Arms: A Journey from War to Peace.* New York: Knopf, 1986.

Bryan, C.D.B. *Friendly Fire.* New York: Bantam, 1977.

Burns, Ken, and Lynn Novick. *The Vietnam War* (documentary film), 2017.

Butler, Robert Olen. *A Good Scent from a Strange Mountain.* New York: Grove, 2001.

Caputo, Philip. *A Rumor of War.* New York: Ballantine, 1978.

_____. "The Unreturning Army." *Playboy*, January 1982.

Carroll, James. *American Requiem: God, My Father, and the War That Came Between Us.* Boston: Houghton Mifflin, 1996.

Carver, Ron, David Cortright, and Barbara Doherty, eds. *Waging Peace in Vietnam: U.S. Soldiers and Veterans Who Opposed the War.* New York: New Village, 2019.

Casey, Michael. *Obscenities.* Pittsburgh: Carnegie Mellon University, 2002.

Chomsky, Noam. *At War with Asia: Essays on Indochina.* New York: Pantheon, 1970.

Colt, George Howe. *The Game: Harvard, Yale, and America in 1968.* New York: Scribner's, 2018.

D'Aries, Anthony. *The Language of Men: A Memoir.* Albany, NY: Hudson Whitman, 2012.

Didion, Joan. *The White Album.* New York: Simon & Schuster, 1979.

Duiker, William. *Ho Chi Minh: A Life.* New York: Hyperion, 2000.

Ehrhart, W.D. *Busted: A Vietnam Veteran in Nixon's America.* Jefferson, NC: McFarland, 2021.

_____. *Going Back: An Ex-Marine Returns to Vietnam.* Jefferson, NC: McFarland, 1987

_____. *In the Shadow of Vietnam: Essays, 1977–1991.* Jefferson, NC: McFarland, 1991.

_____. *Passing Time: Memoir of a Vietnam Veteran Against the War.* Amherst: University of Massachusetts, 1995.

_____. *Thank You for Your Service: Collected Poems.* Jefferson, NC: McFarland, 2019.

_____. *Vietnam-Perkasie: A Combat Marine Memoir.* Amherst: University of Massachusetts, 1995.

Elliott, Mai. *The Sacred Willow: Four Generations in the Life of a Vietnamese Family,* revised edition. New York: Oxford University, 2017.

Emerson, Gloria. *Winners and Losers: Battles, Retreats, Gains, Losses and Ruins from the Vietnam War.* New York: Harvest, 1978.

Fall, Bernard. *Hell in a Very Small Place: The Siege of Dien Bien Phu.* New York: Harper and Row, 1966.

_____. *Street Without Joy: The French Debacle in Vietnam.* Mechanicsburg, PA: Stackpole, 1994.

Fallows, James. "What Did You Do in the Class War, Daddy?" *Washington Monthly,* October 1975.

Fitzgerald, Frances. *Fire in the Lake: The Vietnamese and the Americans in Vietnam.* New York: Vintage, 1972.

Fulbright, J. William. *The Arrogance of Power.* New York: Random House, 1966.

Gellhorn, Martha. *The Face of War.* New York: Atlantic Monthly Press, 2014.

Glick, Allen. *Winters Coming, Winters Gone.* New York: Pinnacle, 1984.

Goscha, Christopher. *Vietnam: A New History.* New York: Basic, 2016.

Greene, Graham. *The Quiet American.* London: William Heinemann, 1955.

Gwin, Larry. *Baptism: A Vietnam Memoir.* New York: Presidio Press, 1999.

Ha, Quan Manh; Joseph Babcock, trans. and ed. *Other Moons: Vietnamese Short Stories of the American War and Its Aftermath.* New York: Columbia University Press, 2020.

Halberstam, David. *The Best and the Brightest.* Greenwich, CT: Fawcett Crest paperback, 1973.

Hammett, Theodore M. "My Father's War, and Mine." *New York Times,* June 30, 2017.

Harvard Class of 1967. *The Choices We Made.* E-book published by the class. On deposit in Harvard University Archives.

Hass, Kristin Ann. *Carried to the Wall: American Memory and the Vietnam Veterans Memorial.* Berkeley: University of California Press, 1998.

Hastings, Max. *Vietnam: An Epic Tragedy, 1945–1975.* New York: Harper, 2018.

Hayslip, Le Ly, with Jay Wurts. *When Heaven and Earth Changed Places: A Vietnamese Woman's Journey from War to Peace.* New York: Plume, 2003.

Heinemann, Larry. *Black Virgin Mountain: A Return to Vietnam.* New York: Vintage, 2006.

Herr, Michael. *Dispatches.* New York: Vintage International, 1991.

Hersh, Seymour M. "The Massacre at My Lai: A Mass Killing and Its Coverup." *New Yorker,* January 22 and 29, 1972.

Huyler, John, John Kent, Will Kirkland, Ron Mcmahan, Paul Rogers and James Skelly. "Yes, There Were Antiwar Officers." *New York Times,* February 3, 2018.

Isaacs, Arnold R. *Vietnam Shadows: The War, Its Ghosts, and Its Legacy.* Baltimore: Johns Hopkins University Press, 2000.

Jacobs, Rodger. *Stained with the Mud of Khe Sanh: A Marine's Letters from Vietnam, 1966–1967.* Jefferson, NC: McFarland, 2013.

Jenkins, Kent, Jr. "Vietnam Vet and Writer Lewis Puller Kills Himself," *Washington Post,* May 12, 1994.

Jones, Gregg. *Last Stand at Khe Sanh: The U.S. Marines' Finest Hour in Vietnam.* Boston: Da Capo, 2014.

Jones, Howard. *My Lai: Vietnam, 1968, and the Descent into Darkness.* New York: Oxford University, 2017.

Just, Ward. "Introduction." *Reporting Vietnam: American Journalism 1959–1975,* abridged paperback edition. New York: Library of America, 2000.

Karlin, Wayne. *Wandering Souls: Journeys with the Dead and the Living in Viet Nam.* New York: Nation, 2009.

Karnow, Stanley. *Vietnam: A History,* second revised and updated edition. New York: Penguin, 1997.

Khue, Le Min; Tran Bac Hoi and Dana Sachs, trans.; Wayne Karlin, ed. *The Stars, the Earth, the River—Short Fiction.* Willimantic, CT: Curbstone, 1997.

Kidder, Tracy, and Richard Todd. *Good Prose: The Art of Nonfiction.* New York: Random House, 2013.

_____. *My Detachment: A Memoir.* New York: Random House, 2005.

Kovic, Ron. *Born on the Fourth of July.* New York: McGraw-Hill, 1976.

Lamb, David. *Vietnam, Now: A Reporter Returns.* New York: Public Affairs, 2002.

Langguth, A.J. *Our Vietnam: The War, 1954–1975.* New York: Simon & Schuster, 2000.

Laurence, John. *The Cat from Hue: A Vietnam War Story.* New York: Public Affairs, 2002.

Lee, Spike. *Da 5 Bloods* (film), Netflix, 2020.

Logevall, Fredrik. *Embers of War: The Fall of an Empire and the Making of America's Vietnam.* New York: Random House, 2012.

MacPherson, Myra. *Long Time Passing: Vietnam and the Haunted Generation.* Bloomington: Indiana University Press, 2001.

Mai, Nguyễn Phan Quế; Bruce Weigl, trans. *The Secret of Hoa Sen.* Rochester, NY: BOA, 2014.

_____. *The Mountains Sing.* Chapel Hill, NC: Algonquin Books, 2020.

Marlantes, Karl. *Matterhorn.* New York: Atlantic Monthly Press, 2010.

_____. *What It Is Like to Go to War.* New York: Atlantic Monthly Press, 2011.

Mason, Bobbie Ann. *In Country.* New York: Harper and Row, 1985.

McCarthy, Mary. *Vietnam.* New York: Harcourt, Brace & World, 1967.

McLean, Jack. *Loon: A Marine Story.* New York: Ballantine, 2010.

McNamara, Robert. *In Retrospect: The Tragedy and Lessons of Vietnam. New York Times,* 1995.

Moore, Harold G., and Joseph L. Galloway. *We Were Soldiers Once...And Young: Ia Drang, The Battle that Changed the War in Vietnam.* New York: HarperPerennial, 1993.

Nguyen, Eric. *Things We Lost to the Water.* New York: Knopf, 2021.

Nguyen, Lien-Hang T. *Hanoi's War: An International History of the War for Peace in Vietnam.* Chapel Hill: University of North Carolina Press, 2012.

Nguyen, Viet Thanh. *Nothing Ever Dies: Vietnam and the Memory of War.* Cambridge: Harvard University Press, 2016.

_____. *The Committed.* New York: Grove Press, 2021.

_____. *The Sympathizer.* New York: Grove Press, 2015.

Nicosia, Gerald. *Home to War: A History of the Vietnam Veterans' Movement.* New York: Three Rivers, 2001.

Ninh, Bao. *The Sorrow of War.* New York: Riverhead, 1996.

O'Brien, Tim. *If I Die in a Combat Zone, Box Me Up and Ship Me Home.* New York: Delacorte, 1973.

_____. *The Things They Carried.* Boston: Houghton-Mifflin, 1990.

Oberdorfer, Don. *Tet!* New York: Doubleday, 1971.

Packer, George. *Our Man: Richard Holbrooke and the End of the American Century.* New York: Knopf, 2019.

Parrish, John A. *12, 20 & 5: A Doctor's Year in Vietnam.* Baltimore: Penguin, 1973.

_____. *Autopsy of War: A Personal History.* New York: St. Martin's, 2012.

Patterson, James T. *The Eve of Destruction: How 1965 Transformed America*. New York: Basic, 2014.

Pham, Andrew X. *Catfish and Mandela: A Two-Wheeled Voyage Through the Landscape and Memory of Vietnam*. New York: Picador/Farrar, 1999.

Puller, Lewis B., Jr. *Fortunate Son: The Autobiography of Lewis B. Puller, Jr.* New York: Bantam, 1993.

Saltonstall, Stephen L. "Mack the Knife and Me." Unpublished manuscript, 2020.

Santoli, Al. *Everything We Had: An Oral History of the Vietnam War by Thirty-Three American Soldiers Who Fought It*. New York: Ballantine, 1981.

Schell, Jonathan. *The Real War: The Classic Reporting on the Vietnam War*. New York: Pantheon, 1987.

Shaw, Michael. "The True Story Behind an Iconic Vietnam War Photo Was Nearly Erased – Until Now." *New York Times,* February 19, 2019.

Sheehan, Neil. *A Bright Shining Lie: John Paul Vann and America in Vietnam*. New York: Random House, 1988.

Sheehan, Neil, Hedrick Smith, E.W. Kenworthy, and Fox Butterfield; Gerald Gold, Allan M. Siegal and Samuel Abt, eds. *The Pentagon Papers*. New York: Bantam, 1971.

Shulimson, Jack, Leonard A. Blasiol, Charles R. Smith, and David A. Dawson, *U.S. Marines in Vietnam: The Defining Year 1968*. Washington: History and Museums Division, Headquarters, U.S. Marine Corps, 1997.

Smith, Charles R. *U.S. Marines in Vietnam: High Mobility and Standdown 1969*. Washington: History and Museums Division, Headquarters, U.S. Marine Corps, 1988.

Spector, Ronald H. *After Tet: The Bloodiest Year in Vietnam*. New York: Vintage, 1994.

Stone, Robert. *Dog Soldiers*. New York: Ballantine, 1975.

Turse, Nick. *Kill Anything That Moves: The Real American War in Vietnam*. New York: Picador, 2013.

Vuong, Ocean. *Night Sky with Exit Wounds*. Port Townsend, WA: Copper Canyon, 2016.

Wagner, Sarah E. *What Remains: Bringing America's Missing Home from the Vietnam War*. Cambridge: Harvard University, 2019.

Weigl, Bruce. *The Circle of Hanh: A Memoir*. New York: Grove, 2000.

_____. *Song of Napalm*. New York: Atlantic Monthly, 1988.

Wolff, Tobias. *In Pharaoh's Army: Memories of the Lost War*. New York: Vintage, 1994.

Index

Numbers in **_bold italics_** indicate pages with illustrations

259